18.62

THE GOLDEN BOOK
OF
MANAGEMENT

This is a volume in the
Arno Press collection

HISTORY OF MANAGEMENT THOUGHT

Advisory Editors
Kenneth E. Carpenter
Alfred D. Chandler

Consulting Editor
Stuart Bruchey

See last pages of this volume
for a complete list of titles

THE GOLDEN BOOK
OF
MANAGEMENT

L[yndall] Urwick

ARNO PRESS
A New York Times Company
New York • 1979

Editorial Supervision: BRIAN QUINN
Reprint Edition 1979 by Arno Press Inc.

Copyright 1956, Newman Neame Limited

Reprinted by permission of Pergamon Press Ltd.

Reprinted from a copy in the Library of the University
of Illinois

HISTORY OF MANAGEMENT THOUGHT
  AND PRACTICE
ISBN for complete set: 0-405-12306-X
See last pages of this volume for titles.

Manufactured in the United States of America

———

Library of Congress Cataloging in Publication Data

Urwick, Lyndall Fownes, 1891-
    The golden book of management.

    (History of management thought)
    Reprint of the 1956 ed. published by N. Neame, London.
    Includes bibliographies and index.
    1. Executives--Biography. I. Title. II. Series.
[HF5500.2.U79 1979]   658'.0092'2 [B]   79-7557
ISBN 0-405-12343-4

THE GOLDEN
BOOK OF
MANAGEMENT

The Golden Book of Management

A HISTORICAL RECORD OF THE LIFE AND WORK OF SEVENTY PIONEERS

Edited for the
INTERNATIONAL COMMITTEE
OF SCIENTIFIC MANAGEMENT (CIOS)
by

L. URWICK

Newman Neame Limited

LONDON

FIRST PUBLISHED IN 1956
by Newman Neame Limited
50 Fitzroy Street, London W1
*for the International Committee
of Scientific Management (CIOS)*

Printed in Great Britain
by The Millbrook Press Limited
London and Southampton
and Sir Joseph Causton and Sons Limited
London and Eastleigh

Frederick W. Taylor was once asked if he claimed any monopoly in scientific management. He replied [1]"I should say not . . . My gracious, I do not believe there is any man connected with scientific management, who has the slightest pride of authorship in connection with it. Every one of us realises that this has been the work of 100 men or more, and that the work which any one of us may have done is but a small fraction of the whole. This is a movement of large proportions, and no man counts for much of anything in it. It is a matter for evolution, of many men, each doing his proper share in the development, and I think any man would be disgusted to have it said that he had invented scientific management, or that he was even very much of a factor in scientific management. Such a statement would be an insult to the whole movement.'

---

[1] *Reply to a question from a member of the Special Committee of the House of Representatives, appointed in 1911-12 'to investigate the Taylor and other systems of shop management.' 'Testimony', page 282, in* Scientific Management *by F. W. Taylor (New York, Harper & Bros., 1947 edition).*

TABLE OF CONTENTS

FOREWORD

Within the last three quarters of a century, and principally within
the last forty years, a new branch of knowledge has claimed and won
a foremost place in the social heritage. At different times and in
different countries it has been described by various titles—Management, Scientific Management, Rationalization, the Scientific
Organization of Work, Stakhanovism and so on. Primarily it was
applied to the government of business undertakings. But from quite
an early stage it was recognized that its principles, if well founded,
must 'be equally applicable to all forms of organized human co-
operation, to the business of government in any form as well as to the
government of business.

This new department of learning, now usually called management,
was based on the proposition that the methods of thought developed
by the physical sciences, which have given to mankind so unprecedented a degree of control over material things, could and should be
applied to man himself, to the organization of his societies, small and
large, and to the political, economic and social problems to which
those societies give rise. It postulated, as one of the greatest of its
pioneers explicitly recognized, a 'mental revolution'—the substitution of inductive thinking, thinking based on facts, for the old deduc-
tive thinking, thinking based on theories or opinions, in all matters
concerning the organization of human groups.

That complete and exact knowledge is yet available in any of the
underlying sciences bearing on human behaviour, such, for instance,
as psychology, anthropology or sociology, no one can claim. In these
dynamic aspects of its field it is rather in the approach or attitude
which it employs that this new branch of knowledge differs from older
concepts. That attitude is based on the conviction that a greater
degree of exact knowledge is possible and that, already to-day, there
are truths developed by these comparatively young sciences which
could be applied with advantage to practical affairs. Beyond the point
where precision is possible problems can still be handled, as in the
comparable field of medicine, in the temper and spirit of science and
with constant reference to organized clinical experience, rather than
in the half-light of custom and of the limited data provided by individual empiricism.

Already, brief though its history has been, this new branch of
knowledge has changed profoundly men's ideas of how to conduct
business enterprises in almost every country in the world. Where it

has been applied consciously and completely to industrial and commercial undertakings it has greatly increased individual productivity and made possible dramatic economies in human effort. It holds out the best and, as many think, the only hope of a solution of those differences between capital and labour, between those who work and those who organize, which have prevented mankind hitherto from realizing anything but a fraction of the possibilities inherent in the use of power-driven machinery. Beyond the field of economic enterprises, it holds the yet undiscovered secret of how men may organize their national systems of government and the relations between nations so that the energies of each may be made available for the benefit of all and the curse of physical conflict between classes and nations may be removed for ever, releasing for new and beneficent enterprises the constructive impulses of mankind.

THE INTERNATIONAL COMMITTEE OF
SCIENTIFIC MANAGEMENT (CIOS)

The first attempt to bring together internationally persons from a number of countries with special knowledge in this field took place in 1924. The late President Masaryk in that year invited a number of representative specialists from a variety of countries to the First International Management Congress at Prague. There the decision was taken to set up permanent machinery to maintain contact between individuals throughout the world who were devoting themselves to this new branch of knowledge. At Brussels in the following year the International Committee of Scientific Management (Comité International de l'Organisation Scientifique, or CIOS) was formally established. This Committee has since organized ten triennial international congresses in various countries, with a break from 1938 to 1947, due to the second World War.

ITS DECISION TO ISSUE
'THE GOLDEN BOOK OF MANAGEMENT'

So rapid and so varied, however, have been the developments in different countries and in the various sectors of the field, that this machinery is insufficient to keep the thousands of students and workers in touch with each other's efforts. There is a danger that the contributions of many individuals who have added original and valuable ideas and discoveries to the corpus of knowledge as a whole may be lost to sight and their researches even repeated by later workers. Moreover, it is impossible even to-day to appreciate the scope and possibilities of this new body of knowledge without some acquaintance with its history and with the work of those pioneer thinkers who, now no longer living, have from many different angles and starting with many different specializations each added his fraction to the total structure.

As a contribution to the solution of this problem the International Committee of Scientific Management has decided to issue this Golden Book of Management: A Historical Record of the Life and Work of Seventy Pioneers. The proposal to issue a Golden Book having been first made by Lt Col L. Urwick, OBE, MC, MA, at the Ninth International Congress in Brussels in 1951, the International Committee later in that year secured his acceptance of the honorary international editorship of the work, and invited him to begin without delay the collection of documentary material, from all possible sources, about the individuals to be commemorated.

CONSIDERATIONS GOVERNING THE CHOICE OF NAMES

The book contains the names only of those persons who, in the opinion of the International Committee, have made original and outstanding contributions to the world body of knowledge about the subjects of management and/or administration. *It does not contain the name of any person still living.* Service to the 'management movement' in the individual's own country, or to the international management movement, was considered one of the grounds for inclusion.

The existence of published work on a management subject was a further condition. The great practising industrial managers of the world, outstanding though their immediate influence certainly was, are therefore not within the compass of the book unless they also made an intellectual contribution through published work.

The majority of the individuals included in this first volume were citizens of the United States. This apparent bias is merely a matter of chronology. Frederick W. Taylor, an American, was 'the father of scientific management'[1], although he was not the earliest of the pioneers. Already within his own lifetime his ideas began to gain recognition in every industrialized country, and in 1938 the International Committee engraved his portrait on its Gold Medal, awarded triennially for services to management. It was natural that after Taylor's death, the ideas and skills which he had initiated should find their earliest and most widespread application among nationals of his own country, a tendency both stimulated by, and a contributory cause of, the tremendous economic development of the United States in the first half of the twentieth century. National movements in the other countries of the free world have since

[1] Inscription on F. W. Taylor's tomb in Philadelphia.

flourished abundantly. But because these movements came later, their history is as yet in the making and will find its record in future volumes of this book.

The book is, moreover, in no sense a collection of competing national histories of management, but is presented as an evolving picture of an idea which is worldwide and transcends the particular nationalities of individuals. The extent to which each country has already enriched its own experience by the exchange of ideas with others will be apparent from a reading of the individual outlines contained in the book.

In countries where there was doubt as to who should be included, the choice of names was made by consultation between the Honorary International Editor and a small committee of persons of long-standing eminence in the management movement in each country. The International Committee subsequently endorsed the choices made.

It would be surprising if the choice of names commanded unanimous approval, and it is possible that exception may be taken to the inclusion or omission of certain individuals. The International Committee found it unavoidable, in order to keep the publication within practical bounds, severely to limit the number of names. But they would remind any persons who feel that names which should have been included have been omitted, that this is projected only as a first volume of the Golden Book. It is hoped that later volumes will be published at appropriate intervals. An opportunity will then be provided to consider any individuals whose names should have been included in the first volume, but who were overlooked. This first volume contains the names of all persons selected by the International Committee who died prior to 1955.

Concerning each person selected the book gives:

A portrait or photograph of the individual

The reasons, in the briefest possible form, for his inclusion

The main facts of his career

A note on his personal characteristics

The titles of his most important written works on the subject of management.

The International Committee wishes to take this opportunity of expressing its gratitude to those individuals in many countries who have contributed the work and information which have made this book possible and whose names are given in the Acknowledgments.

THE NATIONAL MEMBER ORGANIZATIONS OF THE INTERNATIONAL COMMITTEE OF SCIENTIFIC MANAGEMENT (CIOS)

Argentine	Instituto Argentino de Relaciones Industriales
Australia	Australian Institute of Management
Austria	Oesterreichisches Kuratorium für Wirtschaftlichkeit
Belgium	Comité National Belge de l'Organisation Scientifique
Brazil	Instituto de Organizaçao Racional do Trabalho
Canada	Canadian Management Council
Chile	Instituto Chileno de Administración Racional de Empresas
Denmark	Dansk Nationalkomite for Rationel Organisation
Finland	Foundation for Productivity Research
France	Comité National de l'Organisation Française
Germany	Rationalisierungs-Kuratorium der Deutschen Wirtschaft
Great Britain	British Institute of Management
Greece	Hellenic Committee of Scientific Management
Israel	Israel Institute of Productivity
Italy	Comitato Italiano di Rappresentanza Internazionale per l'Organizzazione del Lavoro
Japan	All Japan Efficiency Federation
Netherlands	Nederlands Instituut voor Efficiency
New Zealand	The New Zealand Institute of Management
Norway	Den Norske Nasjonalkomité for Rasjonell Organisasjon
Philippines	The Philippine Council of Management
South Africa	The National Development Foundation of South Africa

Spain	Instituto Nacional de Racionalizacion del Trabajo
Sweden	Svenska Nationalkommittén för Rationell Organisation
Switzerland	Comité National Suisse d'Organisation Scientifique
Turkey	The Institute for Technical Research and Development
United States	Council for International Progress in Management (USA)

GOLD MEDALLISTS OF THE INTERNATIONAL COMMITTEE OF SCIENTIFIC MANAGEMENT (CIOS)

The Gold Medal was established in 1929 and is conferred period-ically 'to reward outstanding literary or practical achievements in Scientific Management as well as outstanding services rendered to the cause of Scientific Management on the international level'.[1] It bears on the obverse the portrait of Frederick Winslow Taylor and on the reverse an inscription to the recipient in the French language.

1929	Henry Le Chatelier (France)	*Paris Congress*
1932	Karol Adamiecki (Poland)	*Amsterdam Congress*
1935	Edmond Landauer (Belgium) —posthumous award	*London Congress*
1938	Harry Arthur Hopf (United States)	*Washington Congress*
1947	Harlow S. Person (United States)	*Stockholm Congress*
1948	Masaryk Academy of Labour (Czechoslovakia)	*Transmitted by the President of CIOS to the Minister of Czechoslovakia in Stockholm*
1951	Lyndall Fownes Urwick (Great Britain)	*Brussels Congress*
1954	Lillian Moller Gilbreth (United States)	*Sao Paulo Congress*

[1] Rules and Regulations for the bestowal of Honorary Titles and Awards of CIOS, adopted by the Sub-Committee on Honorary Distinctions, Salzburg, May 7, 1952.

ACKNOWLEDGMENTS

The compilation of this book has been possible only because the Editor was privileged to draw on the willing aid of many individuals and organizations. Without this help he could not have assembled the extensive factual material given in the outlines.

The introductory sections involved judgment on the nature and importance of the contribution of each pioneer. Here the Editor has sought to base his judgments on established facts, to preserve the utmost objectivity and to secure approval in each case from persons in the respective countries qualified to comment. It has been equally his duty, however, to apply to each section, and throughout the book, a consistent interpretation of the history of management. Such an interpretation cannot be entirely free from subjective elements. For the text of the book, therefore, and for the judgments included in each introductory section in particular, he alone is responsible.

He wishes to record his deep gratitude in the first place to the following organizations:

* The American Society of Mechanical Engineers (United States), in particular Mr C. E. Davies (Secretary) and Mr Alexander Kirk;
The Department of Industrial Administration, Birmingham College of Technology (Great Britain), in particular Mr D. H. Bramley (Head of Department);

and individuals:

Mr H. B. Maynard (United States), Past President of CIOS;
Mrs Rita Hilborn Hopf (United States) until 1955 Director of the Hopf Institute of Management, Ossining, NY;
Mr Hugo de Haan, Secretary-General of CIOS;

and also, to organizations and individuals in various countries as enumerated below:

Australia

* The Australian Institute of Management (Mr Walter Scott)

Austria

* The Oesterreichisches Kuratorium für Wirtschaftlichkeit

Belgium

* The Comité National Belge de l'Organisation Scientifique (M. Robert Caussin)

* *Also aided the Editor in the selection of names from the country in question, for inclusion in the book.*

Brazil

* The Instituto de Organizacao Racional do Trabalho (Dr Moacyr E. Alvaro and Mr M. Dos Reis Araujo)

France

* The Comité National de l'Organisation Française (M. Louis Péhuet and M. L. Segonne)

Germany

* The Rationalisierungs-Kuratorium der Deutschen Wirtschaft (Dr G. Freitag)
The Verein Deutscher Eisenhüttenleute (Dr K. P. Harten)
Dr E. Bornemann

Italy

* The Comitato Italiano di Rappresentanza Internazionale per l'Organizzazione del Lavoro (Prof Ing. Luigi Palma)
Mme Francesco Mauro

Switzerland

* The Comité National Suisse de l'Organisation Scientifique (M. Jacques Chapuis)
The Institut de Psychologie Appliquée, Lausanne (M. Charles Haurez and Dr von Schnyder)
The International Association of Department Stores (Mr Derek Knee)
M. Werner Kaufmann
M. Paul Silberer

United Kingdom

The Accountant Magazine
Messrs W. & T. Avery Ltd, Birmingham
Birmingham Public Libraries, Reference Library
* The British Institute of Management (Sir Charles Renold, JP, Mr John Ryan, CBE, MC, and Mr Roland Dunkerley, JP)
The General Post Office, Library and Archives Section

* *Also aided the Editor in the selection of names from the country in question. for inclusion in the book.*

The Institute of Industrial Administration
The Institution of Mechanical Engineers (Mr R. T. Everett)
The National Institute of Industrial Psychology (Dr C. B. Frisby)
Sir Isaac Pitman & Sons Ltd (the late Mr J. Hanley)
Messrs David Rowan & Co Ltd, Glasgow (Mr Ewen H. Smith)
Messrs Rowntree & Co Ltd, York (Mr W. Wallace, CBE, and Mr Lloyd Owen)
The Royal Institute of Public Administration
Mr P. J. Allen, Dr G. H. Beaven, Miss Frances Bowie, Mr E. S. Byng, Mr J. R. Crane, Mr J. K. Eastham, Mr K. B. Elbourne, Major J. D. Gibson-Watt, Mr J. C. Gilbert, Mr Frank A. Heller, Mr Walter Hewett, Mr R. W. Isaacs, Professor J. H. Jones, Mr. F. W. Lawe, Mr P. H. Lightbody, Professor C. A. Mace, Mr H. W. Marsh, Mr H. McFarland Davis, Mrs George Elton Mayo and Mrs Patricia Elton (Mayo) Curtis, Mrs W. Nicholls, Mr C. A. Oakley, Professor T. H. Pear, Mr G. W. Perry, Professor Sir Arnold Plant, Mr Allan Plowman, Mr G. A. Robinson, Mr T. G. Rose, Miss Anne Shaw, Mrs Jean Sheldon, Dr I. M. Shenkman, Dr May Smith, Mr N. A. H. Stacey, Mrs C. (Meyenberg) Taylor, Mr J. E. Wheeler.

United States

The American Management Association, New York, NY
The Council for International Progress in Management (USA.) Inc, New York, NY
The Emerson Engineers, New York, NY (Mr Alonzo Flack)
The Edward A. Filene Good Will Fund, Inc, New York, NY (Miss Betty W. Connors and Mr Percy S. Brown)
La Salle Extension University, Chicago, Ill (Mr William Bethke)
Messrs McKinsey & Co, New York, NY (Mr Marvin Bower)
The Stevens Institute of Technology, Hoboken, NJ
The Twentieth Century Fund, New York, NY (Miss Louise Field)
Mr C. Canby Balderston, Mr J. Christian Barth, Mrs Wallace Clark, Mr Fred H. Colvin, Mr Morris L. Cooke, Mr James T. Dennison, Mr Theodore Diemer, Mrs Henrietta C. Dodd, Mr Kern Dodge, Professor Paul A. Freund, *Dr Lillian Moller Gilbreth, Miss Marion S. Halsey, Mr Paul A. Hasse, Mrs C. E. Knoeppel, Professor Herbert S. Langfeld, Professor George F. F. Lombard, Professor Myles L. Mace, Dr Raymond P. Marple, Mr Joseph K. Milliken, Miss Winifred O'Brien, Mr Allen H. Ottman, Dr Harlow S. Person,

---

* *Also aided the Editor in the selection of names from the country in question for inclusion in the book.*

xviii

Professor David B. Porter, Mr John W. Punton, Professor Edwin M. Robinson, Professor F. J. Roethlisberger, *Professor Erwin H. Schell, Mr Ordway Tead, Mrs Sanford E. Thompson, Dr L. W. Wallace, Mr John A. Willard, Mrs Edwin Williams

Members of the Editor's Staff

Miss Dorothy M. Adam (research), assisted by Miss Maureen C. Sandiford (collection of published sources) and Mrs Fay L. Russell (secretarial work).

* *Also aided the Editor in the selection of names from the country in question for inclusion in the book.*

from the portrait of James Watt Jr by Le Longe by courtesy of Major J. D. Gibson-Watt

James Watt Jr
(1769-1848)
Great Britain

and·

Matthew Robinson Boulton[1]
(1770-1842)
Great Britain

The history of modern management is often considered to begin with
the work of F. W. Taylor in the United States at the turn of the
present century. Records preserved by unusual good fortune, how-

---

[1] A portrait of Matthew Robinson Boulton is extant at Tew Park, Great Tew,
Oxfordshire, the estate which he purchased after retiring from business.
The present occupant of Tew Park is Miss Boulton, a descendant. The
editor regrets that her representative declined to allow the editor facilities
for reproducing the portrait in *The Golden Book of Management*.

ever, show interesting anticipation of scientific management in one or two countries by a century or more. In Great Britain, in particular, it could be claimed that the first illustration of scientific management in action is to be found, from 1795 onwards, in the Soho Engineering Foundry near Birmingham of Boulton, Watt & Company. It has been shown, further, that this astonishing 'early experiment in industrial organization' was the achievement not so much of the founders Matthew Boulton and James Watt themselves, pioneers in the development of the steam engine, but rather of their respective sons, Matthew Robinson Boulton and James Watt Jr.

In the Soho Foundry at that time the following management techniques were being consciously applied, on a small scale but nevertheless no less systematically than in modern concerns today:

Market research and forecasting as the basis for the establishment of a new business

Planned site location with provision for adequate communications by land and water, and for possible extension of buildings

Planned machine layout in terms of work-flow requirements

Production planning

Production process standards

Machine-operating standards

Standardization of product components

Elaborate statistical records

Advanced control records including cost accounting procedures involving the keeping of twenty-two standard books; it has been claimed that the cost and profit could be calculated on each engine manufactured, and the profit and loss on each department

A workers' training scheme

Advanced division of labour

Work study ·

Payment by results based on work study

Provision for personnel welfare, with a sickness benefit scheme administered by an elected committee of employees

An executive development scheme.

The historian of the Soho Foundry has established that 'The great development which Soho made after 1795 is . . . bound up with the names of Matthew Robinson Boulton and James Watt Jr; and it is to them that all credit must be ascribed. Combining a thorough education in the gentlemanly pursuits of the time with an early training as practical engineers in all stages of production, they brought to the task of organization an entirely new outlook'[1] . . . 'There is, in fact,

[1] Roll: *An Early Experiment in Industrial Organization,* page 165 (details of publication in Appendix II)

2

nothing in the details of the most progressive factory practice of to-day that the two sons had not anticipated. Neither Taylor, Ford, nor other modern experts devised anything in the way of plan that cannot be discovered at Soho before 1805; and the Soho system of costing is superior to that employed in very many successful concerns today. This earliest engineering factory, therefore, possessed an organization on the management side which was not excelled even by the technical skill of the craftsmen it produced.'[1]

Matthew Robinson Boulton and James Watt Jr have a very special place in the early history of management.

Curricula Vitae

Matthew Robinson Boulton

1770   Born in the Midlands.

1780-86 Privately tutored by the Rev. M. Stretch.

1786-8 Studies in Paris.

1788   Invited by his father to address the Lunar Society on events in France.

1788-9 Again in Paris.

James Watt Jr

1769 Born in Glasgow.

His early studies were in chemistry, mineralogy and natural philosophy.

Studied in Paris and be-came a sympathiser with some of the leaders of the French Revolution. The excesses of the Terror, however, caused him to leave France, and after a short stay in Italy he re-turned to England.

1790 Boulton Jr and Watt Jr appointed in joint charge of a business established some years previously by Watt Sr and devoted to the manufacture of a patented letter-copying press.

1794 Boulton, Watt & Sons formed to manufacture the complete assembly for the patented steam engine.

1796 The Soho Foundry was opened, with the management already in the hands of the junior partners. Watt Jr undertook much of the organization and administration of the foundry, and Boulton Jr undertook the commercial activities.

---

[1] Professor J. G. Smith in his Introduction to Roll, op. cit., page xv

1800 Boulton, Watt and Company formed, the sons taking over complete control. The patents of the Watt steam engine expired in this year.

1802 Banking firm established: Matthew Robinson Boulton & James Watt & Company, London.

1803 Contested competitors' patents on the grounds of infringement.

1817 Squire of the Manor, Great Tew, Oxfordshire.

1820 Elected fellow of Royal Society.

1833 Banking partnership dissolved.

1840 Retired from active interests in Boulton, Watt & Company to devote himself to his estates in Radnor and Brecon.

1842 Died aet. 72.

1848 Died aet. 79.

Personal Characteristics

From the little information which has come down to us it would seem that the natures of the fathers were reproduced in the sons. Matthew Robinson Boulton was a brilliant conversationalist with a wide circle of friends; the 'external relations' partner. James Watt Jr was the 'production' partner, concerned with the smooth running of the Foundry and something of a disciplinarian although a liberal landlord and a man of culture. The two men shared a friendship based on sound character and on sincere devotion to their respective fathers. There can be few comparable instances in the history of British industry of so sustained a family relationship in business.

Selected Publications

The only known writings of Matthew Robinson Boulton and of James Watt Jr are in the form of letters to their partners and business acquaintances. These are preserved in their original form in the historic Boulton & Watt Collection in the Reference Library of the City of Birmingham.

Watt Jr's letters are also quoted in the following publications: —
1926 *Matthew Murray: A Centenary Appreciation*

4

London: Newcomen Society, reprinted in *The Engineer*, 5th March, 1926.

1928 *Matthew Murray: Pioneer Engineer*
    132 pages. Ed. E. K. Scott. Leeds: Edwin Jowett Ltd.
Watt Jr was the author of the article on James Watt Sr in the *Encyclopaedia Britannica*, 6th ed., 1823.

By courtesy of the National Portrait Gallery, London

Robert Owen
(1771-1858)
Great Britain

The name of Robert Owen—social reformer and philanthropist—is known far beyond his own country. Robert Owen—successful industrial executive and pioneer of management—is, however, much less well-known. Yet it was in his managerial activities in the textile

5

industry that Owen was most successful in achieving the lifelong aims which he set himself.

He was one of the earliest industrialists to set aside the undiluted technical and financial criteria of success characteristic of the age and to devote himself to management as a profession. To such professional managers as Owen may one day be attributed, by historians of the Industrial Revolution, more influence on the progress of events than that for which they now receive credit.

As a successful manager, Robert Owen was one of several among his contemporaries. The place in which he stands alone in the history of management is as 'the pioneer of personnel management'. He was virtually unique in his generation, not only in appreciating the immense importance of the human factor in industry but in doing something to apply this knowledge. During the years 1800-1828 he developed, as manager of a group of textile mills in New Lanark in Scotland, what was then an unprecedented experiment. All through the period of his public activities as a propagandist and agitator for social change on a national and even on an international scale (activities which, however profound their influence on subsequent thought, currently appeared to be failures) this experiment was quietly transforming the actual lives of his New Lanark textile workers.

The transformation was gradual and characterized by two chief stages. In the first, Owen set himself to improve the factory and domestic conditions of his employees. Houses and streets were built. Workers' shops sold necessaries at cost price. The minimum working age for children was raised and daily working hours decreased. Meal facilities were provided for the mills. The surroundings in the mills were made more attractive. The paternalism of a just employer shewn in this and other respects brought about an improvement in the conduct and well-being of the New Lanark workers which was the wonder of the age.

In the second stage, Owen addressed himself to social reform in the community of which the factory was the centre; from 'a very wretched society' he created a model community. The New Lanark schools, where his educational reforms were in operation, had many visitors from home and abroad. Evening recreation centres met the problems created by the increased leisure given to the workers, and in this Owen was the forerunner, by a hundred years, of the work of Mary Follett in Boston. The 'Village of Co-operation' became the prototype of a new basis of social life and inspired imitators in communities on both sides of the Atlantic.

The claim that Owen was the pioneer of personnel management is not based on an empty attribution of philanthropic principles and practices. The first syllable of management is man. The essentials of

6

personnel management are twofold, and they both found their first clear exemplification in the work of Robert Owen. First, a personnel policy must be considered an integral part of the management of an establishment in the economic sense. 'Personnel management must pay.' The purely 'welfare' outlook on management can neither win wholehearted acceptance by employers in industry nor can it keep indefinitely the loyalty of employees. Its impact is tinged with charity, as though a factory were a proper place for 'slumming'. Owen wrote in an essay addressed to 'the superintendents of manufactories': —

'Many of you have long experienced in your manufacturing operations the advantages of substantial, well-contrived and well-executed machinery. If then, due care as to the state of your inanimate machines can produce such beneficial results, what may not be expected if you devote equal attention to your vital machines, which are far more wonderfully constructed?'

Secondly, the personnel function must not be a subordinate department of management, but must be identified with the purpose of good management itself. In our modern age we have adopted the belief that the workplace is a community and that the satisfactions which a man obtains there are an essential part of the conditions needed for harmonious social living within the democratic ideal. The community which Robert Owen built up around the workplace as the centre, the partnership which he established between employer and worker, the justice which he dispensed simultaneously with measures of welfare, entitle him to be called the pioneer of truly modern personnel management.

Curriculum Vitae

1771   Born of a middle-class family in the little market town of Newton on the Welsh border. His father was a saddler and ironmonger and the local postmaster. He was the sixth of seven children.

1778   Usher in the village school.

1781-4   Apprenticed to a retail draper in Stamford, Lincolnshire.

1784-7   Post in a drapery house in London.

1787   Employed in textile mills in Manchester.

1789-91   Became an employer, setting up with Ernest Jones his first partnership, manufacturing 'mule' type machines. After a few months Owen branched out in an independent spinning enterprise and made a financial success of it.

1791-5   Manager of a large spinning mill in Manchester. During these years he had many offers of partnership from textile manufacturers.

1795-1800 Partner in the Chorlton Twist Co., Manchester.

1800-28 Managing Director of a group of textile mills in New Lanark, Scotland.

1828-58 Retired from executive work and devoted the remainder of life to campaigning in the Press and in public speaking, for acceptance of his projects of social reform.

1858 Died on 17th November aet. 87.

Personal Characteristics

Owen was a gentle, kindly and courteous man, one whose transparent honesty of purpose and genuine love of the entire human race inspired feelings almost of adoration in those with whom he came in contact, and particularly in children. He was a man of unalterable convictions. He 'knew' himself to be right, although he was prepared to devote endless time to reasoning with those who differed from him. If he left them unconvinced, he would still persevere along his own path. If sometimes his friends thought him an autocrat and even a bore, such were his manners and his charm that he retained their respect and their affection.

Selected Publications

No summary of Owen's writings can give an adequate picture of the ground which he covered or of the diversity of the channels of which he made use. His first published papers appeared in 1812 and thereafter the literature that he produced mounted steadily to a tremendous volume, much of it repetitive or overlapping. A cross-section of his thought is the following: —

1812 *A Statement Regarding the New Lanark Establishment* Edinburgh.

1813-14 *A New View of Society.*[1]

1815 *Observations on the Effect of the Manufacturing System—* with hints for the improvement of those parts of it which are most injurious to Health and Morals. Dedicated most respectfully to the British Legislature.
20 pages. London: Hatchard.

1816 *Address to New Lanark*[1]—delivered at the opening of the Institute for the Formation of Character.

---

[1] These works are collected in a volume under the title *A New View of Society* edited by G. D. H. Cole, London, Everyman, 1927. This volume gives a representative selection of Owen's writings especially in his early and more constructive years.

8

1817   Three addresses on a *Plan to Relieve the Country from its Present Distress.*[1]

1821   *Report to the County of Lanark*[1] —a plan for relieving public distress—by giving permanent productive employment to the poor—which will diminish the expenses of production and consumption and create markets coextensive with production.

[1] See footnote on p. 8.

From a portrait in the Science Museum, South Kensington, London

Charles Babbage
(1792-1871)
Great Britain

9

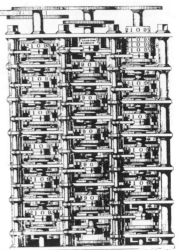

Impression from a woodcut of a small portion of Mr. Babbage's Difference Engine No. 1, the property of Government, at present deposited in the Museum at South Kensington.
It was commenced 1823.
This portion put together 1833.
The construction abandoned 1842.
This plate was printed June, 1853.
This portion was in the Exhibition of 1862.

Charles Babbage was not an industrialist or manager. He was primarily a scientist and teacher. But in connection with his mathematical studies he developed a 'calculating' or 'difference engine', and in the course of his work on this device he became very much interested in workshops and factories both in Great Britain and on the continent of Europe, and visited many of them.

His studies of their methods led him to conclusions as to their problems of management which in many respects anticipated some of the most important findings of F. W. Taylor in the United States, though Taylor was quite unacquainted with his work. These were embodied in Babbage's book *On the Economy of Machinery and Manufactures* (1832) which had, for those days, a wide circulation in Great Britain (over 10,000 copies) and was also published in the United States.

In particular Babbage pointed out the possibility of developing general principles based on scientific analysis to govern the conduct of industrial undertakings. In this matter his thought and Taylor's were closely parallel:

Charles Babbage	F. W. Taylor
'Having been induced during the last ten years to visit a considerable number of workshops and factories, both in England	'When men, whose education has given them the habit of generalizing and everywhere looking for laws, find them-

and on the Continent, for the purpose of making myself acquainted with the resources of mechanical art, I was insensibly led to apply to them those principles of generalization to which my other pursuits had naturally given rise.'
On the Economy of Machinery and Manufactures 1st Edition (London: Charles Knight, 1832).

selves confronted with a multitude of problems such as exist in every trade, and which have a great similarity one to another, it is inevitable that they should try to gather these problems into logical groups, and then search for some general laws or rules to guide them in their solution.'
The Principles of Scientific Management
(New York: Harper & Bros. 1911) and in
Scientific Management
(do. 1947 p. 103).

Other directions in which Babbage anticipated modern management practice were:

In the analysis of processes and manufacturing costs, e.g. in pinmaking.

In the use of time-study, on which he quotes with approval the observations of a French colleague, Mons. Coulomb. This is the first example of international collaboration on a management problem.

The use of printed standard information blanks for investigation.

The study of the comparative practice of business undertakings in the same field, *vide* his *Comparative View of the Various Institutions for the Assurance of Lives* (1826).

Curriculum Vitae

1792   Born on 26th December in Teignmouth, Devonshire, the son of a banker. He suffered from ill health as a child and was educated at private schools in Alpington (near Exeter) and Enfield.

1811   Student at Trinity College, Cambridge.

1812   A founder of the 'Analytical Society' which gave the impulse to a mathematical revival in England at that time.

1814   BA from Peterhouse, Cambridge (MA in 1817)

1815-27 Lived in London, devoting himself to scientific activities.

1827-8 Travelled in continental Europe, studying foreign workshops and factories.

1828-39 Lucasian Professor of Mathematics (the chair of Isaac Newton) at Cambridge.

1832   Stood unsuccessfully for Parliament on liberal principles.
and 1834
1871   Died on 18th October aet. 79.

He was a Fellow of the Royal Society at the age of 24; Gold Medallist of the Astronomical Society; prominent in the foundation of the British Association and the Statistical Society; and a member of scientific bodies in all parts of the world, including the Paris Academy of Moral Sciences and the Royal Irish and American Academies.

Personal Characteristics

Babbage's autobiographical *Passages from the Life of a Philosopher* show him to have been a wit and a humorist, although fundamentally a man disappointed by the failure to attain full recognition for the fruits of his life-work. The Dictionary of National Biography[1] has a vivid passage: —

'In his latter years Babbage came before the public chiefly as the implacable foe of organ grinders. He considered that one-fourth of his entire working power had been destroyed by audible nuisances, to which his highly strung nerves rendered him peculiarly sensitive. In the decay of other faculties his interest and memory never failed for the operations of the extensive workshops attached to his house. There what might be called the wreckage of a brilliant and strenuous career lay scattered, and thence, after his death . . . . some fragmentary portions of the marvellous engine, destined to have indefinitely quickened the application of science to every department of human life, were collected and removed to the South Kensington Museum.'

Selected Publications

BOOKS

1816 Translation of Part I of *An Elementary Treatise on the Differential and Integral Calculus of La Croix*
      728 pages. Cambridge; Printed by J. F. Smith for J. Deighton & Sons.

1826 *A Comparative View of the Various Institutions for the Assurance of Lives*
      London: J. Maurman, Ludgate Street. German Transn. Weimar 1827.

1830 *Reflections on the Decline of Science in England and on Some of its Causes*
      London: B. Fellowes, Ludgate Street.

---

[1] Article on Babbage (details of publication in Appendix II).

1831 *Specimen of Logarithmic Tables* printed with different coloured inks and on variously coloured papers, 21 Vols, London.
'The object of this work, of which one single copy only was printed, is to ascertain by experiment the tints of the paper and colours of the inks least fatiguing to the eye. One hundred and fifty-one variously coloured papers were chosen and the same two pages of my stereotype Table of Logarithms were printed upon them in inks of the following colours: light blue, dark blue, light green, dark green, olive, yellow, light red, dark red, purple and black. Each of these twenty volumes contains papers of the same colour, numbered in the same order, and there are two volumes printed with the same kind of ink. The twenty-first volume contains metallic printing in gold, silver and copper, upon vellum and on variously-coloured papers.'

1832 *On the Economy of Machinery and Manufactures*
420 pages. 1st Edn. London: Charles Knight, Pall Mall East. There were numerous English editions and American reprints and translations into German, French, Italian, Spanish, etc.

1837 *The Ninth Bridgewater Treatise*
266 pages. London: J. Murray.

1848 *Thoughts on the Principles of Taxation, with Reference to a Property Tax and its Exceptions*
24 pages. London: J. Murray. 2nd Edn. 1851. 3rd Edn. 1852. Italian Transn. Turin 1851.

1851 *The Exposition of 1851; or, Views of the Industry, the Science and the Government of England*
London: John Murray. 2nd Edn. 1851.

1864 *Passages from the Life of a Philosopher*
London: Longmans Green.

ARTICLES

Over 70 printed Papers, Pamphlets, etc. on mathematical, scientific and philosophic subjects, including: —

1822 'The Application of Machinery to the Calculation of Mathematical Tables'
Memoirs of the Astronomical Society, Vol. I, p. 309.

1822 'Observations on the Application of Machinery to the Calculation of Mathematical Tables'
Memoirs of the Astronomical Society, Vol. I, p. 311.

1826 'On a Method of Expressing by Signs the Action of Machinery'
Transactions of the Philosophical Society, Vol. II, p. 218.

1829 'Essay on the General Principles which Regulate the Application of Machinery'
Metropolitan Encyclopaedia.

Ernest Solvay
(1838-1922)
Belgium

Ernest Solvay was a great Belgian industrialist. Starting from modest origins, he built up a fortune and a business with world-wide connexions for the manufacture of alkalis, based on a new and economical process which he himself had brought to perfection. Solvay was a man who could perceive the broad trends in the industrial development of his day. He was a leader in progressive management in his own numerous factories, instituting the 8-hour day (1907), holidays with double pay (1913), and other liberal measures of personnel policy such as a profit-sharing scheme and medical and social assistance for employees. His great personal fortune was used to endow a series of foundations which established in Belgium the Institute of Social Sciences and of Sociology, strengthened the Workers' Educational Institute, and also several institutes in the domain of the physical sciences.

He was a pioneer of 'productivity'. Between 1947 and 1954 this word became in Europe generally the current popular synonym for management. The European Productivity Agency was established in 1953 as part of the machinery for realising the Marshall Plan and many Western European countries set up 'Productivity Centres'. Managers and workers alike were exhorted by those controlling their political destinies to become more 'productivity-minded'.

Compatriots of Ernest Solvay must have learned of the 'new religion' with a certain reserve, for in his writings of half a century before is to be found an astonishingly modern exposition of the need for productivity. He had said, the improvement of human well-being depends on the achievement of an ever greater volume of production of goods and services along with a decrease in the effort required. This can be made possible by the progressive installation of more and better machinery. It is to the interest of the worker equally with that of the manager to adopt the 'productivist' state of mind.

If the need for 'productivity' is universally accepted today, it was not so clearly apparent at the time Solvay enunciated his theories. They were in many respects original. Economists had for many years before stressed the importance of *production* in the total well-being of a nation. The ideal of *productivity* or more production for the same effort was being developed by F. W. Taylor in America in terms of a single industrial unit. But from Solvay came the idea of productivity in terms of a nation as a whole, and in this he was certainly a pioneer of later thought.

When Solvay went on to use his 'productivist' theories as the basis for a far-reaching plan of social reform, where the state would own shares in every factory and would regulate each man's fortune in terms of his productivity, he failed to win general support. Modern productivity theories differ from the 'productivism' he advanced in restricting themselves to the economic sphere and in propounding no general solutions for political and social problems. Solvay's essential contribution, however, remains an interesting one and it may be noted that the country of which he was a citizen is among the most highly productive in the world.

It is interesting to quote here from one of the last public addresses given by Henry Le Chatelier at a great scientific congress at the Sorbonne in 1935. Having reviewed the most recent advances in science and technology he concluded: —

'That is the past; we must now think of the future. I have always cherished the memory of a conversation I once had with the great Belgian engineer, Solvay. "Today," he said to me, "Science and Technology have reached their peak; in this field there is nothing more to be looked for. The young engineers who follow us should have other and quite different preoccupations. Their duty is to study the human factor of which we know virtually nothing. Yet

15

it is of capital importance in industry and will become continually more and more so." He did not wish to suggest, you will understand, that there will be no further technical progress, but merely that such progress would be achieved by methods already established. On the other hand, in dealing with the moral and social problems of industry, we have no method, we have not yet developed an established procedure, we do not know how to direct our enquiries. In this field too, we should apply scientific method. But the problem is a complex one . . . In short the study of the many different aspects of the human factor in industry demands special methods.'

Curriculum Vitae

1838   Born on 16th April at Rebecq, Brabant. Educated at the College of Malonne. Illness prevented him from pursuing regular studies and he was largely self-educated. He began his career in a technical post at a gas plant in Brussels. While still holding this post he carried on the research which led to his development of the ammonia process for alkali manufacture.

1865   Solvay & Cie founded. After a difficult initial period this family business gradually attained a position of international standing in the manufacture of alkalis by the Solvay process.

1892-1900   Senator in the Belgian Parliament.

1893-1913   Founded and endowed in Belgium the Institute of Physiology, the Institute of Social Sciences, the School of Sociology, and the School of Commerce, and made large donations to the Workers' Educational Institute. Also founded the International Physical Institute and the International Chemical Institute.

1914   Created the Comité National de Secours et d'Alimentation, on the outbreak of the war.

1918   King Albert of the Belgians, the day of his return to Brussels, paid tribute to Solvay as the creator of the National Committee.

1922   Died on 26th May aet. 84, at Ixelles.
He held the Liebnitz Medal for distinction in Science.

Personal Characteristics

Though Ernest Solvay gained the fruits of worldly success, he remained an idealist for whom money-making was incidental to the search for near-perfection in every activity, whether it was the processing of the materials of industry or the solution of the problems of society.

Selected Publications

1897 *Etude sur le Progrès Economique et la Morale Sociale*
Annales de l'Institut des Sciences Sociales, tome III, pp. 401-415. Bruxelles.

1898 *Le Productivisme Social*
Annales de l'Institut des Sciences Sociales, tome IV, pp. 411-437. Bruxelles.

1900 *Etudes Sociales. Notes sur le Productivisme et le Comptabilisme*
172 pages. Bruxelles: Lamertin.

1901 *Lettres Relatives à la Fondation de l'Institut de Sociologie* adressées le 12 Fevrier 1901 à MM. les Bourgmestre et Echevins de la ville de Bruxelles et à M. Charles Graux, Administrateur-Inspecteur de l'Université Libre de Bruxelles.

1910 *Industrie et Science (Biogénie et Sociologie)* Discours prononcé à l'Occasion du XXV anniversaire de la Societé Belge des Ingénieurs et Industriels, le 30 Octobre 1910.

1910 *Questions d'Energetique Sociale* Notes et publications de M. Ernest Solvay (1894-1910).
229 pages. Bruxelles: Institut de Sociologie Solvay.

17

Oberlin Smith
(1840-1926)
United States

With Oberlin Smith, the scene changes to the United States, to the germs of thought that were to bear fruit in the great contributions to management in that country. These fruits appeared first in the work of F. W. Taylor. One of Taylor's acknowledged precursors was, however, Oberlin Smith, whose original contribution to management was his system of mnemonic symbols for machine parts.

Oberlin Smith was the successful founder, and president for 63 years, of the Ferracute Machine Company which manufactured dies and presses, and it was in his own company that his system of order numbers was first applied. An engineer and inventor of note, he was one of the original members of The American Society of Mechanical Engineers (ASME). A number of his papers contributed in the eighties had a management angle. Many of them were original in presentation and in the force and humour with which he advanced his views. He was the ninth President of the Society in 1890. As an engineer who was also an employer and a man of wide intellectual interests, he shared with H. R. Towne the credit for insisting that the scope of engineering was much wider than a narrow professional and purely technical view of the subject would suggest. Between them they prepared the Society to offer to the nascent study of management that platform and that support which have been of such inestimable value in the development of the American business tradition.

F. W. Taylor based his own system of symbols for machine parts chiefly on the system devised by Smith. In *Shop Management* (1903) Taylor stated: —

'Among the many improvements for which the originators will

18

probably never receive the credit which they deserve the following may be mentioned ... The mnemonic system of order numbers invented by Mr. Oberlin Smith ...'[1]

Oberlin Smith's paper 'The nomenclature of Machine Details' was presented at the second regular meeting of The American Society of Mechanical Engineers in 1881. The requisites for a good system of names and symbols were, he said:

'1. *Isolation* of each from all the others that did, do, or may exist in the same establishment.

2. *Suggestiveness* of what machine, what part of it, and if possible, the use of the said part—conforming, of course, to established conventional names, as far as practicable.

3. *Brevity,* combined with simplicity.'

The principles here set out (and by 'suggestiveness' Smith meant mnemonic) had considerable influence on all the later systems devised to meet the problem of nomenclature.

Taylor also credited to Oberlin Smith the basis of his routing scheme. Smith had made detailed drawings about 1875-6 for his Bridgeton works which contained the essential elements of classification, symbolizing, and routing and described the operations and sub-operations to be performed on each piece and in the assembling of the machines to which the pieces belonged. The system then developed was not applied in full, only because the work at the time involved little repetition of processes.

Smith's paper on order numbers established one of the earliest international links in management. In 1889 Emile Garcke and J. M. Fells published their *Factory Accounts,* one of the earliest management books to appear in Great Britain: in it they reprinted Oberlin Smith's paper in full. It was also reprinted in a number of American publications, notably in C. Bertrand Thompson's *Scientific Management* (1914).

Curriculum Vitae

1840   Born on 22nd March in Cincinnati, Ohio. Attended the State schools; during vacations he worked on farms and also learned carpentry. He continued at the West Jersey Academy and received his technical training at the Philadelphia Polytechnic Institute.

1863-1926 Founder-president of a concern established in Bridgeton N.J. for the manufacture of improved dies and presses which he had invented.

[1] *Shop Management,* page 201 (New York: Harper & Bros., 1911 Edn.)

1877	The business was incorporated as the Ferracute Machine Co. and has for many years taken a leading part in the commercial development of the die-working of metals.
1901	New Jersey Commissioner to the Pan-American Exposition in Buffalo.
1926	Died on 19th July aet. 86, in Bridgeton, N.J.

Personal Characteristics

In Oberlin Smith may perhaps be singled out the vivacity with which he pursued his many intellectual interests. He was particularly given to astronomical discussions. Mrs Smith tells of bringing such a debate, which Mr Smith was enjoying with a house guest, to an end at one a.m. on a Sunday morning. To her surprise and amusement at six-thirty later the same morning she heard the resumption of the heated discussion. Mr Smith had got into bed with his guest and the two were hard at it once more![1]

Selected Publications

ARTICLES

1881 'Experimental Mechanics'
New York: Trans. ASME, Vol. 2, pp. 55-69.

1881 'Nomenclature of Machine Details'
New York: Trans. ASME, Vol. 2, pp. 358-369. Reproduced in *Scientific Management* by C. B. Thompson, Harvard, 1914.

1882 'The Systematic Preservation of Drawings'
New York: Trans. ASME.

1886 'Inventory Valuation of Machinery Plant'
New York: Trans. ASME, Vol. 7, pp. 433-439.

1887 'Intrinsic Value of Special Tools'
New York: Trans. ASME, Vol. 8, pp. 258-268.

1890 'The Graphical Analysis of Reciprocating Motions'
New York: Trans. ASME, Vol. 11, pp. 260-270.

1900 'Modern Machine Shop Economies'
New York: Cassier's Magazine, Vol. 27, pp. 295-299.

1911 'Impressions regarding Foreign Shop Methods'
Cleveland: Iron Trade Review, Vol. 48, pp. 826-828.

1911 'Naming and Symbolising'
New York: Trans. ASME.

[1] Anecdote from obituary in *Journal* of ASME.

Henri Fayol
(1841-1925)
France

Henri Fayol was the most distinguished figure which Europe contributed to the management movement up to the end of the first half of the present century. His very deep scientific training and interest, both as engineer and geologist, were brought to bear on thirty years of practical experience as chief executive of a great French mining and metallurgical combine—Commentry - Fourchambault - Decazeville ('Comambault'). When he took charge this undertaking was on the verge of bankruptcy. When he retired its financial position was impregnable, it had made a contribution of the greatest value to the national effort in the first World War, and it had an administrative, technical and scientific staff famous throughout France.

Fayol always maintained that his amazing practical success was due, not primarily to personal qualities (though it is clear from the testimony of his contemporaries and the high honour in which he was

21

held that he possessed these in abundance), but to the application of certain simple principles which could be taught and learned. These constituted his 'Theory of Administration'. This isolation and analysis of administration as a separate function was his unique and original addition to the body of management theory. It paved the way for the evolution of the whole modern approach to problems of higher management by way of functional analysis. It exercised and still continues to exercise a profound influence on all efforts to clarify and to organize thinking as to the qualities required for, the nature of, and the correct analysis of 'top management'. It was and is supported and sustained by the great prestige both of his scientific work and of his achievements as a practical administrator.

After his retirement, at the age of 77 in 1918, he devoted the remaining seven years of his life to spreading an understanding of his theory and pointing out its application to fields other than business — military, naval and governmental. For he maintained strongly that any theory of administration which is valid cannot be limited to business. It must be equally applicable to all forms of organized human co-operation.

While at first inclined to be unsympathetic about F. W. Taylor's work, he quickly perceived that it was essentially complementary to his own field of study. Taylor had merely started at one end of the industrial hierarchy, the lathe-worker at his bench, while he had started at the other, the chief executive at his desk. Both were applying the same scientific principles. At the opening of the Second International Management Congress at Brussels in 1925 he declared publicly how false he found the views of those who tried to discover conflict between his principles of administration and Taylor's.

This speech opened the way for his two eminent compatriots, Henry Le Chatelier and Charles de Fréminville to propose a unification between the 'Centre d'Etudes Administratives' which he had founded and the 'Conférence de l'Organisation Française' which they had established to introduce Taylor's ideas to France. The two bodies were accordingly united in the 'Comité National de l'Organisation Française'. The rapidity and friendliness with which this unification of effort took place were in themselves an instance of intellectual integrity and generosity taking priority over possible organizational rivalry, which should long remain an example to the management movement.

With the foundation in 1925 of the 'CNOF', France became the first country in the world to be furnished with an institution equipped, both by the intentions of its founders and by the work already done, to promote the study and application of scientific methods to business and other institutions *regarded as a whole*.

Curriculum Vitae

1841   Born of a French bourgeois family.

1856-8 Attended the Lycée at Lyons.

1858-60 Attended the School of Mines, St. Etienne.

1860   Appointed Engineer of the Commentry pits of the S.A. Commentry-Fourchambault.

1866   Appointed Manager of the Commentry pits.

1872   Appointed General Manager of the Commentry, Montircq and Berry group of mines.

1888   Appointed Managing Director of Commentry-Fourchambault.

1891   Purchase of the Bressac Mines.

1892   Absorbed the mines and works of Decazeville.

1900   Purchase of the Joudreville mines in the Eastern French coalfield.

1918   Retired as Chief Executive of 'Comambault' but remained a Director.

1925   Dinner of Honour in Paris given by Old Students' Association of the School of Mines, St Etienne to celebrate the 65th anniversary of his graduation. He died in this year aet. 84.

Henri Fayol was awarded the Delesse Prize of the Academy of Sciences, the Gold Medal of the Societé d'Encouragement pour l'Industrie Nationale, and the Gold Medal and the Medal of Honour of the Societé de l'Industrie Minérale. He was appointed Chevalier of the Legion of Honour in 1888, Officier in 1913, and Commander of the Order of the Crown of Roumania in 1925.

Personal Characteristics

One who met him in the last year of his life has described him as 'still young—upright, smiling, with a penetrating and direct glance. M. Fayol meets you as a friend. His natural air of authority, his kindness, his youthfulness of spirit, which makes him interested in everything, enabling him to be a past master in the art of being a grandfather (and even a great-grandfather), are both impressive and, at the same time, most attractive.'

Selected Publications

BOOKS

1916 *Administration Industrielle et Générale—Prévoyance, Organisation, Commandement, Coordination, Contrôle,* Bulletin de

la Societé de l'Industrie Minérale.
Republished in book form, Paris: Dunod, 1925. First English translation, *General and Industrial Administration* by J. A. Conbrough, Geneva, International Management Institute, 1929. Second English translation, *General and Industrial Management* by Constance Storrs, London, Pitman, 1949, with a foreword by L. Urwick.

1921 *L'Incapacité Administrative de l'Etat—Les Postes et Télégraphes,* Revue Politique et Parlementaire, March. Republished in book form, Paris: Dunod, 1921.

1927 *L'Eveil de l'Esprit Public*
Paris: Dunod—a volume edited by Fayol but published after his death. It contains:—
Importance de la Fonction Administrative dans le Gouvernement des Affaires
L'Enseignement de l'Administration dans les Ecoles Techniques Supérieures
La Réforme Administrative des Services Publics (v. above) and *L'Administration Positive dans l'Industrie,* a short paper by Fayol published in *Technique Moderne,* February 1918.

ARTICLES

1900 Paper on 'Administration' to the Congrès des Mines et de la Métallurgie.

1908 Discourse on the 'General Principles of Administration' to the Jubilee Congress of the Société de l'Industrie Minérale.

1917 'L'Enseignement de l'Administration dans les Ecoles Techniques Supérieures', Bulletin de la Société des Ingénieurs Civils de France.

1918 'Importance de la Fonction Administrative dans le Gouvernement des Affaires', Bulletin of the Société d'Encouragement pour l'Industrie Nationale.
'La Réforme Administrative des Services Publics', Revue du Commerce et de l'Industrie.

1919 'L'Industrialisation de l'Etat', Bulletin de la Société de l'Industrie Minérale.

1921 'La Réforme Administrative des Postes et Télégraphes.' Pamphlet.

1923 'La Doctrine Administrative dans l'Etat', Second International Congress of Administrative Science, Brussels, 1923. English translation, 'The Administrative Theory in the State', by Sarah Greer in *Papers on the Science of Administration,* ed. by Luther Gulick and L. Urwick, New York, Columbia University Press, 1937.

24

Henry Robinson Towne
(1844-1924)
United States

The most significant contribution to management of Henry Robinson Towne, President of the Yale & Towne Manufacturing Company, was the leading part which he played in persuading his fellow engineers to extend the traditional scope of their professional interest to include management subjects. At the time of his famous paper to The American Society of Mechanical Engineers (ASME) in 1886 — 'The Engineer as an Economist' — such a conception was revolutionary. Not until 1907 did the Society recognise the subject of management engineering, and up to 1915 a large and influential section of the membership continued vehemently to deny that there could be a science of management or, if there could, that it was any concern of an engineering society. Towne's paper of 1886 was essentially a plea for the recognition and development of such a science. He said:

'The matter of shop management is of equal importance with that of engineering . . .'

'The management of works is unorganized, is almost without literature, has no organ or medium for the interchange of experience, and is without association or organization of any kind . . .'

'The remedy must not be looked for from those who are "business men" or clerks or accountants only; it should come from those whose training and experience has given them an understanding of both sides (the mechanical and the clerical) of the important questions involved. *It should originate from engineers!'*

As President of ASME in 1889-90 and as a leading member of its councils around this period, Towne's influence was constantly exercised to provide through the Society a platform and a professional environment where those interested in management could meet and encourage one another. This influence, and his strong support for the work of F. W. Taylor, were crucial in the growth of interest in management within the Society.

Towne was also a pioneer in the elaboration of an important management technique. In 1889 he presented to ASME the results of the 'gain-sharing' system operating in his own works. This was a modified form of profit-sharing on a group basis, the gains being awarded to departments on the basis of relative efficiency. An attempt at improvement on the traditional piece-rate system, it was the first of a number of pioneering experiments in wage payment schemes, in the United States and elsewhere, as a means of stimulating output. Though Towne's scheme was soon to be superseded by Taylor's more scientific system, it did much to encourage other experiments, not least those of Taylor.

Curriculum Vitae

1844   Born on 28th August in Philadelphia. He came of old English stock, being the direct descendant in the ninth generation from William Towne, who emigrated from Yarmouth, England in 1640 and settled in Salem, Mass. His father was a respected citizen of Philadelphia and connected with several machinery manufacturing industries. He was educated at private schools and the University of Pennsylvania, and also completed a course at the Sorbonne in Paris.

1861-5 He gained his practical shop training in the Port Richmond Iron Works, both in the shop and the drafting rooms, leading on to work in charge of erection of machinery in the navy yards of Boston, Portsmouth and Philadelphia.

1866-7 Studied engineering in Europe, accompanying a notable

26

American engineer, Robert Briggs. One of the fruits of that association was an important investigation into the transmission of power by belting, of which the results appeared in a paper by Briggs and Towne, in the *Journal of the Franklin Institute,* 1868.

1867-8 Engineer with William Sellers & Co., Philadelphia.

1868 Contacts between Towne and Linus Yale Jr led to the formation of the Yale Lock Co., which in 1883 became the Yale and Towne Manufacturing Co., Stamford, Conn. The sudden death in 1868 of Yale at the outset of the new enterprise put Towne in sole control and he remained President until 1916, after which he was Chairman of the Board.

1882 Joined The American Society of Mechanical Engineers, founded two years previously. In 1884-6 he was Vice-President, and in 1889 President.

1889 Led the delegation to the Paris Universal Exposition of the four American engineering societies.

1905 The Taylor system was initiated into Yale & Towne Manufacturing Co. under the supervision of Carl Barth.

1924 Died on 15th October aet. 80.

Towne found time to take part in widely diverse activities. He was a president of the Merchant's Association of New York; a president of the Morris Plan Company of New York; a director of the Federal Reserve Bank of New York, of the Industrial Finance Corporation, the American Dredging Co., and the Lincoln Safe Deposit Co. He was also Treasurer of the National Tariff Commission Association.

He was made an Honorary Member of The American Society of Mechanical Engineers in 1921.

Personal Characteristics

Towne combined, almost to an unique degree, technical engineering ability with executive capacity and economic vision. He became president of the Yale & Towne Manufacturing Company at the age of twenty-four. From then until his retirement the company *was* Henry R. Towne. As a great executive, he naturally possessed the art of surrounding himself with able associates. But he himself was always the leader, the moving spirit of that famous organization. He was also a man of wide culture and had assimilated in his youth the humane traditions of the Old World. He never appeared to better advantage than as leader of the American engineering delegation to England and France in 1889. In England the professional, social and official events called for the exercise of most tactful dignity. In France, there was required in addition a command of the language

27

to be appreciated only by those who recall his graceful and fluent response in French to the welcome extended at the reception tendered by M. Gustave Eiffel, as president of the Societé des Ingenieurs Civils de France, upon the occasion of the luncheon given on the platform of the great tower on the Champ de Mars.

Selected Publications

ARTICLES

1886 'The Engineer as an Economist'
New York: Trans. ASME, Vol. 7, pp. 428-432.
1889 'Gainsharing'
New York: Trans. ASME, Vol. 10, pp. 600-626.
1906 'Our Present Weights and Measures and the Metric System'
New York: Trans. ASME, Vol. 28, pp. 845-925.
1912 'Axioms Concerning Manufacturing Costs'
New York: Trans. ASME, Vol. 34, pp. 1111-1129.
1912 'General Principles of Organization applied to an Individual Manufacturing Establishment'
New York: Trans. Efficiency Society. Vol. 1, pp. 77-83.
1915 'Frederick Winslow Taylor: A Sketch of his Life'
New York: *Engineering Magazine*, Vol. 49, pp. 161-163.
1916 'Tribute to F. W. Taylor at Annual Meeting'
New York: *Journal* of ASME, Vol. 38, pp. 53-54.

Captain Henry Metcalfe
(1847-1917)
United States

In the concluding paragraphs of his *Shop Management* (1903) F. W.
Taylor wrote: —
'Unfortunately there is no school of management. There is no
single establishment where a relatively large part of the details of
management can be seen, which represent the best of their kinds.
The finest developments are for the most part isolated, and in
many cases almost buried with the mass of rubbish which sur-
rounds them. Among the many improvements for which the originators will probably never receive the credit which they deserve
. . . may be mentioned . . . the card system of shop returns invented and introduced as a complete system by Captain Henry
Metcalfe, USA, in the government shops of the Frankford Arsenal.

(This) represents . . . a distinct advance in the art of management. The writer appreciates the difficulty of this undertaking as he was at the time engaged in the slow evolution of a similar system in the Midvale Steel Works which, however, was the result of a gradual development instead of a complete, well thought out invention as was that of Captain Metcalfe.'[1]

Metcalfe's book, *The Cost of Manufactures and The Administration of Workshops, Public and Private* (1885) recorded, in fact, the first example of a complete system of shop returns based on the unit principle—'The independence of a representative unit of record is the basis of the system I propose.' That the author's general attitude corresponded with that subsequently propounded by F. W. Taylor appears in the following sentences:

'It may be stated as a general principle that while Art seeks to produce certain effects, Science is principally concerned with investigating the causes of those effects. Thus, independently of the intrinsic importance of the art selected for illustration, there always seems room for a corresponding science, collecting and classifying the records of the past so that the future operations of the art may be more effective. The administration of arsenals and other workshops is in great measure an art, and depends upon the application to a great variety of cases of certain principles which, taken together, make up what may be called the science of administration.'

In the book Metcalfe also reproduced in full (pp. 110-118) Oberlin Smith's paper of 1881: 'Nomenclature of Machine Details'.

These sentences combine with the early date of his experiments (before 1885) to entitle Captain Metcalfe to a place in this book.

Curriculum Vitae

1847 Born in New York on 29th October. He was descended from a Yorkshire family represented among the early colonists of Virginia. His maternal great-grandfather John Colles came to the U.S. in 1771 with his kinsman Christopher Colles, the famous engineer who conceived the Erie Canal.

1868 Graduated from West Point and assigned to the Ordnance Department.

1873 Recorder of the Small-Arms Board which adopted the Springfield Breech-Loading Rifle. Patented his cartridge-block or detachable magazine. This was made of wood and was subsequently replaced by a metal clip, but was the origin of the prin-

---

[1] *Shop Management*, page 202 (New York: Harper and Brothers, 1911 edition).

30

ciple of magazine loading. It was used in the Russo-Turkish War under the name of the *Metkafomba*.

1876 Superintended the erection of the U.S. Government Building at the Centennial Exhibition.

Appointed Director of Inspection of small-arms and ammunition made in New England for Turkey in the Russo-Turkish War. Awarded the Order of the Osmanic by the Turkish Government.

Later he served as Superintendent successively of the Frankford Arsenal, the Benicia Arsenal, the Watervliet Arsenal, and as Instructor in Ordnance and Gunnery at West Point.

1893 Retired aet. 46, to Cold Spring on the Hudson where he occupied himself with public affairs, becoming head of the Water Commission and President of the School Board.

1917 Died on 17th August aet. 70, at Cooperstown, N.Y.

Personal Characteristics

Captain Metcalfe has been described by his contemporaries as 'an able executive with a mind of his own, loyal, sincere and with an all-encompassing desire for thoroughness. He was intuitive and had a keen sense of humour'.

Publications

BOOK

1885 *The Cost of Manufactures and the Administration of Workshops, Public and Private*
New York: John Wiley & Sons.

ARTICLE

1886 'The Shop Order System of Accounts'
New York: Trans. ASME, Vol. 7, pp. 440-488.

Henry-Louis Le Chatelier
(1850-1936)
France

Although Henry Le Chatelier ranks as a pioneer of scientific management, he was not an industrialist or directly connected with industry. His distinguished career was primarily in industrial chemistry and metallurgy, a field in which he came to hold a world-wide reputation.

His particular importance for scientific management is that he devoted the whole influence of his great scientific reputation to introducing the teachings of F. W. Taylor into France and French-speaking Europe. Though he was close on fifty years old when he first came into contact with Taylor's work, he appreciated immediately its significance. He soon became Taylor's friend. In 1904 he had founded the famous *Revue de Métallurgie*, and in this journal in 1909 he began to publish extracts from Taylor's work and to teach how his principles could be applied to industry. This forceful and persistent elucidation secured widespread acceptance of Taylor's philosophy and methods and did much to prevent the misapplication which handicapped their introduction in other countries.

In 1920 Le Chatelier formed the French Conference on Scientific Management (Conférence de l'Organisation Française). A successful first French Management Congress was held in Paris in 1923. In 1926 this Conference was united with Fayol's Centre d'Etudes Administratives to form the Comité National de l'Organisation Française, which has remained ever since the chief management organization in France.

'When Le Chatelier summarized his views concerning scientific management, he concluded that "the Taylor system is nothing else but the application of the principles of organization and the scientific method to tasks of every description". He firmly believed that there was no dividing line between pure and applied science; to him the scholarly approach was the only sound method of attack to be employed in the solution of new problems. Upon thousands of his students he impressed the validity of this credo, and sent them out, year after year, into the laboratories and the industrial world, fortified with knowledge that was to prove an inestimable asset in the work they were called upon to do.'[1]

In the closing years of his life this great scientist became more and more preoccupied with the human and moral problems posed by a mechanized economy. His last public utterance was devoted to the effects of technological advance on the moral fabric of our society.

Curriculum Vitae

1850	Born on 8th October. His father was one of the early builders of the French railway system.
	He was educated at the Collège Rollin, the Ecole Polytechnique, and the Ecole des Mines, Paris.
1878	Appointed to the Chair of General Chemistry at the Ecole des Mines.
1888	Professor of Mineral Chemistry, Collège de France.
1897-1907	Professor of General Chemistry, Collège de France.
1907	Inspector-General of Mines.
1907-1925	Professor of General Chemistry at the Sorbonne.
1914-18	Commissioned by the Minister of Armaments to work in armaments-producing factories.
1924	Presided over the Second French Management Congress,

[1] Harry Arthur Hopf: *The Scholar in Management*, page 36 (Ossining, N.Y., Hopf Institute of Management, 1940).

and led the French delegation to the First International Management Congress at Prague in the same year.

1936   Died aet. 86. In the following year a memorial conference held in his honour was presided over by the President of the French Republic.

He was awarded the Gold Medal of the International Committee for Scientific Management at the Fourth International Congress held in Paris in 1929. He was an Honorary Member of the Comité National de l'Organisation Française, the Taylor Society (now the Society for the Advancement of Management) and The American Society of Mechanical Engineers; a member of the French Academy of Sciences; President of the Mineralogical Society, of the Society for Encouragement of National Industry, and of the Society of Physics; Honorary President of the 1935 International Congress of Mining, Metallurgy and Applied Geology; a Foreign Member of the Netherlands Society of Sciences and of the Berlin Academy of Sciences; and a Commander of the Legion of Honour. He was awarded the Prix Jerome Ponti (1892) and the Prix La Caze (Academy of Sciences) (1895).

Personal Characteristics

It has been said of him that: 'his scientific and moral integrity were absolute; he was as modest in character as he was eminent in capacity, as disinterested in personal advantage he was prodigal in invention, a man whose moral qualities do him even more honour than his intellectual gifts'.[1]

Selected Publications

BOOKS

Le Chatelier's published work in the physical sciences was voluminous; much of it is in the *Revue de Métallurgie* which he founded in 1904. Of his eleven books only three were concerned with aspects of management:

1925 *Science and Industry*
  Paris: Library of Scientific Philosophy, Ed. Flammarion.
1934 *Taylorism*
  Paris: Dunod.
1936 *Method in the Experimental Sciences*
  Paris: Dunod — in effect a new edition of *Science and Industry*, but with the examples drawn from his own work considerably changed.

[1] M. L. Guillet: Article in the Memorial Volume *Henry Le Chatelier*.

The bibliography of articles, lectures and so on printed in the Memorial Volume covers 15 pages. Those on management subjects of special interest are: —

1915 'The Principles of Organization'
Nature, 4th December, p. 359.

1915 Preface to French translation of *Scientific Management in the Home* by Christine Frederick. *Revue de Métallurgie* XII pp. 348-350. Republished as a brochure in 1918 with a Preface and Conclusion. Paris: Dunod.

1919 'Our Enquiry into the Taylor System (Replies)'
Information Ouvrière et Sociale II No. 57.

1920 'Advice to Students of the National Colleges wishing to familiarize themselves with the Methods of Scientific Management in Industry'
15 pages. Paris: Société des Amis de l'Ecole Polytechnique.

1926 'Common Sense in Management'
Revue Economique Internationale. Brussels: June.

1928 'The Development of Leaders'
Bulletin of the Société Industrielle de Mulhouse, pp. 214-236.

1929 'The Taylor System'
Ancre.

1930 'Science—the Third Quality of the Executive'
Lecture on the Tenth Anniversary of X-Information.
25th March. *X-Information* (Association des Anciens Elèves de l'Ecole Polytechnique, Paris).

1930 'Rationalization and the Economic Crisis'
Mon Bureau Republished as a pamphlet 'Rationalization and Unemployment'. Librairie Française de Documentation Commerciale et Industrielle. 47 pages.

1930 'Industry, Science and Organisation in the Twentieth Century'
Three lectures given at the Ecole Sociale d'Action Familiale de Moulin-Vert.
88 pages. Paris: Dunod.

1931 'The Problem of Industrial Employment'
Mon Bureau September.

1934 'The Forty-Hour Week'
X-Information 25th June (Association des Anciens Elèves de l'Ecole Polytechnique, Paris).

James Rowan
(1851-1906)
Great Britain

One of the problems facing the historian of management is the comparatively minor part played by the representatives of British industry in the development of management thought at the beginning of the twentieth century. As the first of the industrialized countries Great Britain supplied a number of the people who traced the first outlines of the philosophy subsequently developed by Taylor, Gantt and the Gilbreths. Charles Babbage, Boulton and Watt, and Robert Owen all contributed important elements to the total picture. But from 1900 till after the close of the first World War Great Britain added little to the general interest in the subject which had been developing rapidly in the United States of America. Even at the latter date her original contributions were rather to the fields of industrial psychology and labour management than to industrial management in general.

James Rowan was, however, an exception. Partner in a business of marine engine manufacturers in Glasgow, Scotland, he made himself fully informed on developments in management in other parts of Great Britain and in America. One of the elements out of which scientific management was built up was the increasing interest, partly the result of disillusionment with some earlier experiments in profit-sharing, displayed by practical engineers in incentives. Examples of this interest in the United States were H. R. Towne's 'Gain-Sharing' (1889), F. A. Halsey's 'The Premium Plan of Paying for Labor' (1891), F. W. Taylor's 'A Piece Rate System' (1895), and H. L. Gantt's 'A Bonus System of Rewarding Labor' (1901), all papers read to The American Society of Mechanical Engineers.

Rowan considered all these systems, but did not find them 'suitable for the purposes of marine-engine manufacture'. In a paper written in 1901 entitled 'A Premium System of Remunerating Labour', he referred to 'Mr. Fred W. Taylor's Paper on the Premium System, published in *Cassier's Magazine* of October 1897' and to 'the objections to the ordinary piece-work system which were so well expressed by Mr. Slater Lewis in the *Engineering Magazine*' (Vol. 18, 1899-1900, p. 203). He was impressed by the tendency of workers on piece-rates to fix an arbitrary standard of output beyond which they would not put forward further effort for fear of rate-cutting.

Rowan's own scheme, applied in his own works in 1898, was simple. It consisted of a fixed time allowance on each job at an hourly rate for the job. A job data book was built up from which future hourly rates could be determined. The premium paid to the worker was calculated by adding to the hourly wage the same percentage as that by which he had reduced the time allowed for the job. This scheme worked well in practice. In Rowan's own works the original standard times were improved on by an average of 20% in the first year to 37% in the fourth year. The scheme is still being used in Glasgow at the present day, and has been applied with beneficial effects in many other engineering works in Great Britain.

An incentive scheme, especially when unsupported by time study and methods analysis, is only a fragment of scientific management as a whole, and its results can represent only a fraction of the problem facing every manager. Rowan himself realised this, and his interest in management went much further. It may be ascribed to his influence that at the International Engineering Congress in Glasgow in 1901, papers on management subjects by British authors were for the first time presented at a function organized by the Institution of Mechanical Engineers. The three papers were:

'A Premium System of Remunerating Labour' by Rowan himself.
'Some Factors Affecting The Economical Manufacture of Marine Engines' by William Thomson.
'Workshop Methods: Some Efficiency Factors in an Engineering Business' by William Weir and J. R. Richmond.

There is no doubt that Rowan's work gave a great stimulus to the use of premium bonus in British engineering works. In 1902 *The Engineer* published a series of articles, reprinted in pamphlet form and running into several subsequent editions, supporting this method of remuneration. In the same year a national agreement regulating its application was signed at Carlisle by the Engineering Employers' Federation and the Amalgamated Society of Engineers. In 1903 a publisher thought it worthwhile to issue Bonus Tables for calculating wages on the Bonus or Premium Systems.[1]

It is equally clear that what attracted many employers about Rowan's plan was its avoidance of an awkward issue with labour over rate-setting. Rowan's scheme was a memorable precedent which was to be followed by a reaction in Great Britain, towards a more narrowly technical view of the functions of the engineer. It was to be a quarter of a century before the Institution of Mechanical Engineers again took up the serious study of management problems.

Curriculum Vitae

1854   Born on 18th March in Glasgow. Educated at Glasgow Academy and Glasgow University.
1870-1875   Served apprenticeship with David Rowan, Engineer, (Marine Machinery), with further experience in the yards of the Fairfield Shipbuilding and Engineering Co. Ltd.
1880   Assistant Manager, David Rowan.
1885   Made Partner; the name of the firm was changed to David Rowan & Son.
1888   Assumed complete control.

1 Henry A. Golding: London, Charles Griffin & Co., 1903.

1898   Introduced the premium bonus system which bears his
his name, soon after the close of the great engineering
dispute of 1897-8.
1906   Died on 19th November aet. 55 in Glasgow.
He served as President of the North-West Engineering Trades Employers' Association, and as Vice-President of the Institution of Engineers and Shipbuilders in Scotland.
He was a member of The American Society of Mechanical Engineers, and of the Institutions of Naval Architects, Civil Engineers and Mechanical Engineers.

Personal Characteristics

James Rowan was a man of a genial and generous nature, popular with friends and fellow employers. He was reputed for his immense energy and enthusiasm in putting his new schemes into operation.

Selected Publications

1901 'A Premium System of Remunerating Labour'
Paper to The Mechanical Section of the International Engineering Congress, Glasgow. Proceedings of the Congress. London: Institution of Mechanical Engineers.
1903 'A Premium System Applied to Engineering Works'
Paper to Institution of Mechanical Engineers, London.

James Mapes Dodge
(1852-1915)
United States

James Mapes Dodge was the first American industrialist to introduce
the Taylor methods of shop management as a complete system into
his concern. When this event occurred it was a signal triumph for

scientific management, for the Link-Belt Company was a concern of great standing in the American engineering industry of the time. The Company had pioneered in the manufacture of the link belt chain and had important manufacturing centres in Philadelphia, Chicago and Indianapolis. Dodge had been President of one part of the concern since 1892.

He had first become interested in Taylor in connection with the latter's discovery of high-speed tool steel. Always a leader in introducing new developments, Dodge decided to tool up with high-speed steel the Link-Belt Philadelphia plant (which was situated very near the Midvale plant where Taylor had worked from 1878 to 1890). Over a single week-end the line shaft speed was doubled in the entire plant, so that all machine tools with the exception of the grinders were operating on the Monday morning at twice the speed they had been running on the Friday night. The rapidity of the change brought many new difficulties. Finally Taylor's associate, Barth, was called in to reorganize the management of the tool room, a task which he accomplished successfully.

Dodge was finally converted to Taylor's management methods generally by Taylor's paper 'Shop Management' in 1903. Soon after, Taylor was invited to apply his system completely in the Link-Belt Co. By that time Dodge was himself an eminent man in American industry, being already a past President of The American Society of Mechanical Engineers (ASME). It was greatly to the advantage of both men that he now became the first executive to accept Taylor's system as a whole, a stout champion of Taylor's general cause, and also one of Taylor's warmest personal friends.

'It took over two years,' said Dodge, 'for our organization to surrender fully, and so change our mental attitude that we became really receptive. I mean by this that I found no difficulty at all in having the heads of various departments agree that the introduction of the Taylor system would be most desirable, but in each case it was for everybody else in the establishment but entirely unnecessary for him.'

The Link-Belt Philadelphia plant was, in the later years of Taylor's life, one of the show-pieces round which he conducted the many visitors who came to see his system in operation. Dodge was, with H. R. Towne, one of those responsible for Taylor's election as President of ASME in 1906. Subsequently he was among the most open of Taylor's supporters, particularly during the hearings of the Eastern Rates Case in 1910 and the Committee of Congress enquiry in 1911-12. The eminence of the Link-Belt Company in America, today truly a giant in its field, is more than sufficient testimony to the success of the methods instituted by Dodge under Taylor's guidance.

Curriculum Vitae

1852   Born on 3rd June at Waverly, N.Y. His father was a prominent member of the Bar in New York City, and his mother a gifted writer of books, stories and poems.

He was educated at Newark Academy, Cornell University, and Rutger's College.

His first practical experience was gained at the Morgan Iron Works, New York City.

1873-6   Successively journeyman, foreman, and superintendent of construction, in the shipbuilding works of John Roach & Sons at Chester, Penna.

1876-8   Partnership with E. T. Copeland for the manufacture of mining machinery in New York City.

1868   Partnership with William D. Ewart and his associates in Chicago for the technical and commercial development of Ewart's invention of the link belt chain. He became superintendent of the Indianapolis Malleable Iron Works, where the chain was put into production.

1884   Returned to the East and established in Philadelphia the firm of Burr & Dodge as representatives of the Ewart Manufacturing Co. of Indianapolis.

1888   The Link-Belt Engineering Company was formed as a corporation to consolidate business operations in Philadelphia and New York.

1892 onwards   President and active manager of the Link-Belt Engineering Company and the Dodge Coal Storage Co. (afterwards called the J. M. Dodge Co.).

1906 onwards   Chairman of the Board of the Link-Belt Co., which in that year merged the Link-Belt Engineering Co. of Philadelphia, the Link-Belt Machinery Co. of Chicago, and the Ewart Manufacturing Co. of Indianapolis.

1915   Died on 4th December aet. 63, in Philadelphia.

He received the honorary degree of Doctor of Science from Stevens Institute of Technology (1913); was President of The American Society of Mechanical Engineers (1902-3); Vice-President of the Franklin Institute (1903-5); and a founder and first President of The Society to promote the Science of Management.

He was an engineering inventor of eminence. A Report published by the U.S. Patent Office early in the century shows that at that time he, together with George Westinghouse, had been granted more patents by the U.S. Government than any other two men in the country.

He was awarded the Elliott Cresson Gold Medal in 1904 by the

Franklin Institute of Pennsylvania, for his invention of the Dodge system of conveying coal in and out of storage.

Personal Characteristics

The following description of Dodge appears in the memorial volume of the Newcomen Society: —
'With all his impressive qualities as a gifted mechanician, a forceful executive, and thoughtfully considerate employer, James Mapes Dodge combined yet another characteristic, that of a genial liveliness which distinguished him at once in every circle of society. His humorous pleasantries were ever fresh and seemingly inexhaustible. His drollery was never failing, his ready wit ever combined with penetrating wisdom, and his animated countenance was expressive of both. As a story teller he was simply inimitable, and was a constant source of merriment and glee. Mark Twain once said that "Jim" Dodge was "the greatest story teller in America".'

Selected Publications

1903 'The Money Value of a Technical Training'
New York: Trans. ASME.
1906 'History of the Introduction of a System of Shop Management'
New York: Trans. ASME. Reprinted in *Scientific Management* by C. B. Thompson, Harvard, 1914.
1911 'The Spirit in which Scientific Management Should be Approached'
Reprinted in *Scientific Management* by C. B. Thompson, Harvard, 1914.
1912 'The Present State of the Art of Industrial Management'
Report of a Committee of ASME.
1913 'Industrial Management'
New York: *Industrial Engineering and Engineering Digest.*

Joseph Slater Lewis
(1852-1901)
Great Britain

Joseph Slater Lewis played only a small part in the story of the pioneers of British management. But he won his place by virtue of a single book: *The Commercial Organization of Factories* (1896). The book was the earliest comprehensive analysis published in Great Britain of the fundamentals of industrial administration with special reference to the control function. It appeared at a time when control in industry was mostly a matter of rule-of-thumb; there had been scant progress since 1869 when the British journal *The Engineer* described the engineers' attitude to commerce and administration: 'Right within twenty per cent of the actual cost is regarded as a very good estimate, and one reflecting much credit on the Engineer and all concerned ... There is no good treatise on the subject.'[1] It is interesting to read Slater Lewis's statement of the purpose of his book:

'It is beyond question ... that the largest and most successful industrial undertakings are those where minuteness of detail and perfection of organization have received paramount consideration: a fact which should, in itself, especially in these days of world-wide competition, make the commercial organization of factories a matter of the first importance in every country with any manufacturing pretensions.'

and again:

'This book is intended as a practical handbook for the use of manufacturers who wish to adopt modern methods of organization. It is written throughout from the point of view of an organizer and manager, rather than from that of a professional accountant, and the author hopes that this feature will commend it to those who have to bear the responsibility of conducting large engineering and manufacturing undertakings.'

The book is intensely interesting in detail. It reviews the whole field of production and cost-control, providing the first known example in Britain of monthly profit and loss accounts; sets out the progress of work through the factory in a single chart, the first 'flow chart' of its kind; makes use of graphic methods for management objects; elaborates a systematic theory of organization, presenting the first organization chart to be found in British business literature; and enlarges upon the dynamic aspects of organization and of management in describing how the manager must set the tone of the organization by his own leadership. This last comparatively small section of a voluminously documented work shows that even in detail Lewis was reaching out towards a general principle, namely, that management is to be regarded as a distinct profession that can be taught and learned.

The Commercial Organization of Factories is a truly remarkable book. Its arrangement and production set standards which have seldom since been equalled in the literature, and were in themselves an example of the art of management. It was anything but typical of its time. It was too 'modern', exhibiting a conception of work-shop management and production control, set in a framework of general business management, comparable with that to be found in the best

---

[1] *The Engineer*, leading article entitled 'The Estimates of Consulting Engineers', page 166, issue of 3rd September, 1869.

text-books of later generations. It was published simultaneously in London and New York, and was hailed by the Institution of Electrical Engineers in Britain as 'a monument to its author and a boon to all who desire to organize their manufacture on sound commercial lines'.[1] The Institution of Mechanical Engineers in Britain also recognized the merits of what it described[2] as 'the standard book' on the subject it covered. That it did not win a popular reputation is due to the very fact that it was a textbook of *management,* and not, as might appear, from its title, one of costing, estimating and workshop procedures which were the subjects of contemporary emphasis. It is interesting to note that at the moment when the United States, under the influence of Taylor and his associates, was about to take a long step forward in the art of management, Slater Lewis was accepted as an English colleague in the forefront of the American movement. He contributed a number of articles to leading American journals in the management field.

Curriculum Vitae

1852   Born in Helsby, Cheshire.
He went through a preliminary private education and then spent some years at the Mechanics' Institution at Manchester.

1868-72 Apprenticed to a land agent in Norwich.

1872-9 In the coal trade.

1879   Set up in Helsby as an electrical engineer on his own account.

1880   Visited United States to dispose of the rights of his patent self-binding insulator.

1881-9   Managing director of a small company manufacturing the insulator and other electrical products.

1889   Consulting and service work as an electrical engineer in Birmingham.

1892   General Manager, W. T. Goolden & Co. Ltd., London, electrical engineers.

1895   Head of dynamo and electrical engineering dept., Salford Rolling Mills, Manchester.

1900   Director of British Electrical Engineering Co. Ltd.

1901   Died in July aet. 49.

He was a member of the three Engineering Institutions (Civil, Mechanical and Electrical), and a Fellow of the Royal Society of Edinburgh.

[1] Memoir, 1901.
[2] Memoir on J. Slater Lewis, Proceedings, December 1901, page 1286.

Personal Characteristics

Little is known of Slater Lewis's personality. The somewhat precise tone of the technical chapters of his book is lightened by his evident interest in the human problems of morale and leadership, and many phrases show him to have been keenly alive to what Oliver Sheldon called thirty years later 'the philosophy of management'.

Selected Publications

BOOK

1896   *The Commercial Organization of Factories*
        London and New York: Spon Books.

ARTICLES

Joseph Slater Lewis contributed a number of articles to leading American journals in the management field, e.g.

1899-1900 'Works Management for the Maximum of Production'
          New York: *Engineering Magazine,* Vols. 18 and 19.
1901   'The Mechanical and Commercial Limits of Specialization'
          New York: *Engineering Magazine.* Vol. 20.

Hans Renold
(1852-1943)
Great Britain

It has been said in the preceding sketch that Slater Lewis's book, *The Commercial Organization of Factories,* was too 'modern' in the Britain of 1896. It remained too modern for a considerable time, for in Britain the new conception of management developed slowly. Not until the years of the first World War and after did signs appear that a British 'scientific management' was taking root which assimilated the American contribution and was yet peculiarly British in character. A pioneering practical experiment in British scientific management was, however, being carried out prior to the war of 1914 by at least one engineering firm—Hans Renold Ltd.

In 1913 Hans Renold, by birth a Swiss, described the management practices of his own Lancashire firm which had been developed in

48

the years since its foundation in 1879, in an address to the Manchester Association of Engineers entitled 'Engineering Workshop Organization'. The salient achievements of the firm in management, as presented in this paper, were: an enlightened staff recruitment policy; an organization structure based on functional specialization and recorded on charts published with the paper; the existence of written standard management instructions and practices prepared and administered by functional departments; and an interlocking committee system acting as a consultative mechanism among the management staff. The Renold system of carefully conceived monthly cost control returns was particularly interesting: these returns covered not only financial matters but also manufacturing activities and stocks. The system had been developed by Renold with the aid of the costing expert A. H. Church and became the foundation of modern scientific costing in Great Britain.

Renold was probably the first British industrialist to appreciate the work of F. W. Taylor and to adapt it to British management practice. He was certainly the only industrialist prior to the first World War who experimented deliberately and comprehensively with Taylor's methods. In his paper of 1913 he adopted the simple standpoint of defining scientific management as 'neither more nor less than commonsense tabulated and applied with fact and reason when facing the everyday problems as they arise'. He went on to expound the achievements of Taylor and took care to distinguish between sound principles and their unsound application.

In another part of his paper Hans Renold showed great understanding of the true nature of management. ' . . . there is no denying that the working of an efficient system requires men of tact and power to lead . . . More often than not, when difficulties arose it was because the common respect which every man, especially superiors, owes to his fellow workers was wanting, and therefore the necessary tact for a successful management could not exist.' Renold had grasped not only the mechanics of management but its dynamics. It is only now, several decades later, that this line of thought is finding widespread acceptance.

In the remarkable organization that he created—a generation ahead of its time and an outstanding illustration of British scientific management in practice—the place of Hans Renold as a pioneer can be measured.

Curriculum Vitae

1852   Born at Aarau, Switzerland.
             Educated in the district and county schools; during vaca-

tions he worked as apprentice in mechanics' shops.

1870	Technical training at the Polytechnic School, Zurich.
1873	Came to England and worked with machine export firms.
1879	Bought a small business in Salford, Lancashire, and began, on his own account, the manufacture of roller chains.
1903	Formation of Hans Renold Ltd.
1916-1918	A member of the Manchester Armaments Output Committee.
1928	Resigned aet. 76, from Chairmanship of Hans Renold Ltd. but continued in office as a Director.
1943	Died aet. 91, at Grange-Over-Sands, Lancashire.

He received the degree of D.Sc. (honoris causa) from Manchester University in 1940.

Personal Characteristics

A few days after Hans Renold's death his son, addressing the staff and workers, tried to explain the secret of his achievement. 'I think that the keynote of his whole life was a passion for good work. He enjoyed money when it came, but commercial success was of quite secondary interest. What drove him on was the joy of creation—of doing something just as well as he knew how. "Good enough" was a sentiment that was quite unknown to him. It might well have been written of him, "Whatsoever thy hand findeth to do, do it with thy might". His relations with other people were based on this same deep instinct . . . That also was at the root of his relations with his employees . . . His respect went out to the good workman. He collected good workmen around him, and the mutual respect between good workmen knows no social distinctions.'[1]

Publication

1913 'Engineering Workshop Organization'
Paper to Manchester Association of Engineers.

---

[1] C. G. (later Sir Charles) Renold: Hans Renold, a Memorial Address, privately printed, 1943.

Harrington Emerson
(1853-1931)
United States

The highlight of Harrington Emerson's career and, perhaps, his most important contribution to the development of management was his statement made during the hearings of the Inter-State Commerce Commission in 1910-1911 when the shippers on the Eastern seaboard opposed an application by the railroad companies to raise rates. He gave evidence on oath that the railroads could save 'a million dollars a day' on their operating costs. This claim hit the headlines. In twenty-four hours 'Scientific Management', hitherto an obscure technology practised by a few unknown engineers, became national news across America. This sudden publicity had important consequences, not all of them desirable. The attention of business men throughout the nation was attracted to Scientific Management. But the publicity probably stimulated the opposition from certain sections of organized labour which seriously handicapped its subsequent development.

Emerson was an engineer whose thought had developed independently along the lines of Scientific Management and who had used analogous methods to reorganize the workshops of the Santa Fe Railroad. There he had devised a system for integrating shop procedures which had most successful results in terms of cost savings. When called by L. D. Brandeis as a principal witness for the shippers in the 'Eastern Rates Case', he was the only one who testified with first-hand experience of the particular industry in dispute, namely railroad transport. He thus spoke with authority when he said flatly in court that if the American railroads improved their management as had been done in Santa Fe, the total savings would total more than a million dollars a day.

Both before and after this episode, Harrington Emerson was one of the limited number of genuinely qualified persons who practised the profession of 'efficiency engineer', a term of which he himself was the originator. He was a populariser of Scientific Management in his active consultancy work, in his prolific writings on different aspects of 'efficiency', and in his education of a vast following of business men in his methods. He expounded the concepts of standard times, of standard costs and preventable wastes, and indicated how scientific method could be applied to many different activities, even to potato growing, where he stressed the importance of the psychological factors which could influence people to increase output. He was also the first man to call attention to the lessons which business management could learn from military experience. Part of his education was in Germany and in his writings he drew freely on the examples of brilliant army staff organization provided by the campaigns of 1866 and 1870. Later in his career Emerson became particularly interested in the selection and training of employees—an aspect of Scientific Management which had not hitherto been greatly developed. In his writings on this subject he was concerned to justify Scientific Management to the working man, emphasizing its value in finding the place for which the individual is best fitted.

His was a particularly original contribution to the early development of Scientific Management for though he was in close touch with

the Taylor group he was not part of it and his additions to the body
of principles of management were independent.

Curriculum Vitae

1853   Born on 2nd August, in Trenton, New Jersey. His father was
        a professor of English Literature at the University of Troy,
        N.Y. He was educated in England, France, Germany, Italy
        and Greece.
1876   Head of the Modern Language Dept., University of Neb-
        raska.
1882   Left the University to engage in banking and real estate
        operations in Milford and Ulysses, Nebraska.
1885-91 Special economic and engineering research work for the
        Burlington Railroad.
1895-99 United States representative of a British syndicate investing
        in America: investigated finances and operations of many
        industrial plants and mines in Mexico, the United States
        and Canada.
1899-01 Manager of a glass manufacturing company.
1901-07 Professional consulting management engineer.
1904-07 Carried out the reorganization of the Atchison, Topeka and
        Santa Fe Railroad; introduced a bonus plan, standard costs,
        accounting by tabulating machines, planned maintenance
        for equipment and rolling stock.
1907-23 President of The Emerson Company, efficiency engineers,
        New York.
1910-11 One of the principal witnesses in the Eastern Rates Case.
1911   Member of Civilian Expert Board on Industrial Manage-
        ment of the U.S. Navy Yards (with Gantt and Day), to in-
        vestigate the functions and conditions of the yards.
1921   Appointed member of the Hoover Committee for the Elimi-
        nation of Waste in Industry, and assigned to cover the coal
        and railroad industries.
1929   Attended the International Management Congress in Paris.
1931   Died on 2nd September aet 78, in New York City.

Personal Characteristics

Harrington Emerson was not only the man of action implied by the
description 'efficiency engineer' but also an intellectual and a scholar.
He is especially remembered for a personality which gave him considerable power to influence those with whom he came in contact,
whether it were business leaders in industry or younger men seeking
to learn his own profession.

Selected Publications

BOOKS

1900 *Efficiency as a Basis for Operation and Wages*
New York: Engineering Magazine Co.
1912 *The Twelve Principles of Efficiency*
New York: Engineering Magazine Co.
1913 *The Scientific Selection of Employees*
New York: The Emerson Co.
1921 *Course in Personal Efficiency*

ARTICLES

1904 'A Rational Basis for Wages'
New York: Trans. ASME.
1904 'Tool Room Practice in a Railroad Repair Shop'
New York: *Engineering Magazine.*
1905 'Shop Betterment and the Individual Effort Method of Profit-Sharing'
New York: *Engineering Magazine.*
1907 'Methods of Exact Measurement applied to Individual and Shop Efficiency at the Topeka Shops of the Santa Fe'
New York: Emerson Co.
1908 'The Efficiency Method of Determining Costs to Eliminate all Waste from Foundry Operations'
Cleveland, Ohio: *Iron Trade Review.*
1908 'The Modern Theory of Cost Accounting'
New York: *Engineering Magazine.*
1908 'Preventable Wastes and Losses on Railroads'
New York: *Railway Age Gazette.*
1911 'Standards of Efficiency in Shop Operation'
New York: *Iron Age*, Vol. 87.
1912 'Comparative Study of Wage and Bonus Systems'
New York: The Emerson Co.
1912 'Cost and Efficiency Records'
New York.
1912 'Practising Efficiency and Knowing Costs'
New York: The Emerson Co.
1915 'Personality in Organization'
New York: Efficiency Soc. *Journal.*

The Michelin Brothers
André Michelin: 1853-1931
Edouard Michelin: 1859-1940
France

If Scientific Management was introduced into France and continental Europe by the Frenchmen Fayol, Le Chatelier and de Fréminville, all of whom appear in this book, it was popularized by the Michelin Brothers. As a result of the series of booklets entitled *Prospérité* which André and Edouard Michelin published in the period 1928-1936, the ideas of Taylor came to be common knowledge in France.

Because the partnership of the Michelin brothers was lifelong, their work is described here as a single achievement. Everyone knows the jolly Michelin tyreman 'Bibendum' and the Michelin road maps, but fewer know the extent of the Michelin contribution to modern management. The early success of the brothers was due to their development of the detachable pneumatic bicycle tyre and their invention of car tyres, which gained for their concern the lead in world developments in tyre manufacture.

By the turn of the century they were, in their own business, applying methods very near to the principles of scientific management, although the work of Taylor was as yet unknown to them. In 1912, Edouard Michelin first read of Taylor's work in Le Chatelier's *Revue de Metallurgie*. In a matter of a few weeks he had established contact with Taylor. In 1913, André Michelin first met Taylor at a dinner given for Taylor in Paris by Le Chatelier. André relates that on leaving the restaurant he hurried at once to buy two stop-watches, one of which he sent off that very evening to his brother at the factory in Clermont-Ferrand; such was the effect of Taylor's 'timid exposition' of his methods on that occasion.

After 1918 the brothers set themselves to make known Taylor's work throughout France in the interest of national prosperity. The 'Taylor-Michelin Committee' was created in 1921 in collaboration with Le Chatelier. During ten years 860 students from the engineering and technical colleges were sent on training courses. Le Chatelier wrote a booklet for their use: *Advice to Students of the National Colleges Wishing to Familiarize Themselves with the Methods of Scientific Management in Industry*. The Committee published informative articles in the Press, showed documentary and propaganda films, organized conferences and lectures and above all reached a very wide public through the *Prosperité* booklets, supplied free of charge by Michelin & Cie.

After 1931 the brothers continued to apply Scientific Management in their own business, and Edouard's periodical notes to his staff, which have been collected in a booklet, make an interesting comparison with the notes by which Fayol used to record the administrative mistakes he observed and the remedies he applied. Their public activities decreased from this time onwards, but it was for the good reason that Scientific Management was becoming more widely understood.

Curriculum Vitae

André: Educated at the Ecole des Arts et Manufactures and the Ecole des Beaux Arts (architecture).
Edouard: Educated at the Ecole des Beaux Arts (painting).
The brothers both abandoned their chosen careers to save the family business (rubber products) from bankruptcy. Edouard settled in Clermont-Ferrand to manage the factory. André lived in Paris and conducted the external relations of the business.
1891 Patent lodged by Michelin & Cie for a detachable rubber tyre.
1895 First motor vehicles on pneumatic tyres entered by Michelin & Cie in Paris-Bordeaux race.

1899 A motor vehicle equipped with Michelin tyres was first to reach 100 kilometres per hour.
1909 Michelin & Cie financed the building of 3,000 workers' houses.
1911 The Michelin Prize was won for the first aircraft to fly from Paris and land on the Puy de Dôme in Southern France.
1914 The Michelin factory manufactured aircraft.
1916 Family allowances for Michelin employees and their widows.
1929 First pneumatic tyre created for railway carriages by Michelin.
1931 Death of André aet. 78.
1938 First tyre of metallic rubber fabric created by Michelin.
1940 Death of Edouard, aet, 81.
André was an Honorary President of the Aero-Club de France, a Chevalier of the Legion of Honour, and an Officer of the Academy. The last years of Edouard were overcast by the tragic deaths of his two sons, Edouard in an aircraft accident (1932) and Pierre in an automobile accident (1937).

Personal Characteristics

The brothers were complementary personalities and dissimilar in many ways. André was the 'public relations' man. He lived in Paris and made the social contacts required. Edouard remained in Clermont and managed the factory, and was a quiet-spoken man of peremptory manner.

They were however both noteworthy for their clarity of mind, practical good sense, rapidity of thought and passionate love of work. Both were painstakingly accurate in detail. Their tremendous faith in the future was accompanied by genuine humility regarding their own achievements. Above all, the *Prosperité* booklets are redolent of the Michelin brothers' sense of fun.

Selected Publications

1928-36 *Prospérité*. Editions Michelin, Clermont-Ferrand. A three-monthly review devoted to scientific management. The subjects were of three kinds:
Popular numbers:
    Sam et François
    Le Succès
    Cela Vaut-il la Peine de s'Occuper de la Méthode Taylor?
    1927. 2nd ed. 1930.
    Ce que Taylor dit de sa Méthode
    Sa Majesté le Client

Sur le Tas ou Conseils pour débuter dans la Méthode Taylor
L'Automobile Source de Richesse—L'Auto contre la Crise
Technical numbers:
Pourquoi et comment Chronométrer?
Comment nous avons Taylorisé nos Ateliers de Mécanique
d'Entretien
La Préparation du Travail
Suggestions
Un Exemple de Travail Continu, ou la Construction de nos
Maisons Ouvrières
Deux Exemples d'Application de la Méthode Taylor chez
Michelin
La Construction de Maisons Ouvrières en Série chez
Michelin
La Méthode Taylor dans l'Etude d'une Machine
Le Chronographe
Remarques sur la Formation Professionnelle
Miscellaneous numbers (chiefly on social subjects):
Une Dépense qui Paye: un Service Médical
Oeuvres Sociales de Michelin & Cie
Une expérience de Natalité
Allocations et Rentes pour Familles Nombreuses
Comment Alimenter vos Bébés
L'Autobus de Lempdes
Une Expérience d'Education Physique

By courtesy of The Viking Press, New York

Louis Dembitz Brandeis
(1856-1941)
United States

Louis D. Brandeis made his total contribution to management in less than two years. He was a famous lawyer who ultimately became an associate justice of the United States Supreme Court, and his contribution to management, important though it was, is but a small segment of his total achievement in his own sphere. This contribution was, however, to bring the Taylor system of industrial management to the forefront of public interest during the hearings of a single legal case.

The story cannot be better told than in F. W. Taylor's own words. Taylor wrote to a friend in January 1911:

'A very extraordinary thing has happened through a Boston lawyer named Louis D. Brandeis . . .

Brandeis has for many years devoted a considerable part of his time to serving in the capacity of, as he calls it, "the people's lawyer". He has taken a great variety of cases, notably brought about the ten-hour law for women in Oregon and then in Illinois, and all public work of this sort he has done for nothing.

When the Eastern railroads asked the Interstate Commerce Commission for an increase in the freight rates, Brandeis took up the case of the shippers to prevent this arbitrary increase in rates, and adopted a very ingenious and what I think will prove to be a successful course in at least modifying the increase in freight rates which the railroads asked for. He went before the Interstate Commission in Washington, claiming that the practical management of the railroads was completely out of date and inefficient, and that they could save, through efficient management, far more than they could accomplish through an increase of freight rates; manifestly to the great benefit of both themselves and the whole country.

In proving his case, he brought before the Interstate Commerce Commission the various managers and owners of the companies which are running under our type of management—Mr. Dodge, of the Link-Belt; Hathaway, of the Tabor; Towne, of the Yale and Towne Co., and a lot of others; and he was so successful in setting forth the merits of scientific management that he has awakened the whole country, and the interest now taken in scientific management is almost comparable to that which was aroused in the conservation of our natural resources by Roosevelt.'

Taylor's view of the importance of the incident was correct. Although the case argued by Brandeis was rejected by the Commission as being insufficient proof, the decision nevertheless went against the railroads and it is believed that the Commission was influenced by Brandeis more than it cared to acknowledge. At any rate, Brandeis had brought the Taylor system to a place in the sun, and Taylor received visits and letters from hundreds of people as a result of the hearings. The American Society of Mechanical Engineers has pointed out that although the hearings caused an uproar, 'Brandeis's masterly analysis of the principles of scientific management in his brief was scarcely noticed'.[1]

In another respect Brandeis is to be remembered in the history of management. In October 1910 he called together a small group of engineers in the apartment of H. L. Gantt in New York to choose the most suitable designation for the new philosophy of management which they were to expound and defend at the forthcoming hearings. A number of titles were suggested, including 'Taylor system', 'functional management', 'shop management', 'efficiency'. Finally the group decided unanimously to adopt the term 'Scientific Management' for the purpose of the hearings. Thus for good or ill, was the term coined which has most constantly been used to describe the 'mental revolution' which Taylor postulated for our times.

Documents left by Taylor show that the question of railroad costs continued to interest Brandeis and himself for several years. The stubborn opposition of the railroad managements, however, decided him to dissuade Brandeis from contemplating further action in this sphere.

Curriculum Vitae

1856	Born, Louisville, Ky., 13th November.
1874-75	Student, Annen-Realschule, Dresden.
1875-78	Harvard Law School, subsequently admitted to the St. Louis Bar.
1879-97	Lawyer, Warren & Brandeis, Boston.
1889	Admitted to the Bar of the United States Supreme Court.
1897-1916	Senior, Brandeis, Dunbar & Nutter, Boston.
1897-1911	'People's Attorney' for Public Franchise League and Massachusetts State Board of Trade.
1907-13	Unpaid Counsel for William B. Lawrence in New Haven merger controversies.
1907-14	Unpaid Counsel for the State in defending hours of labour and minimum wage statutes of Oregon, Illinois, Ohio, and California.
1910-11	Unpaid Counsel for Commercial Organisations in Interstate Commerce Commission Railroad Rate Case.
1910-16	Unpaid Chairman, Arbitration Board, New York Garment Workmen's strike, and under subsequent protocols.
1911-15	Worker and adviser in Progressive Politics.
1912	Joined Zionist Movement.

[1] American Society of Mechanical Engineers: *History of Scientific Management in America* (details of publication in Appendix II).

1913-14	Special Interstate Commerce Commission Counsel in Five Per Cent Rate Case.
1916	Confirmed by Senate as Associate Justice, United States Supreme Court.
1939	Retired 13th February.
1941	Died aet. 85 in Washington, D.C., on 5th October.

Personal Characteristics

Brandeis was a brilliant public figure. Through his law partnership he attained financial independence by the age of thirty, and frugal living and conservative investment made him later a wealthy man. He used this independence to take up enthusiastic public service without payment, finding an absorbing outside interest in the causes which interested him.

He had a lifelong opposition to 'bigness' and the many crusades of which he was the storm centre were directed chiefly against monopolies and trusts. But most of the progressive social reform projects of his day claimed his services at one time or another and he gave these services generously. His unifying passion was to preserve individual freedom. The special importance of his conjunction of active law practice with unpaid public service was that, unlike many apostles of reform, he was thoroughly immersed in the realities of business and finance, and brought to bear on public issues the zeal for facts and the highly trained analytical faculty characteristic of a lawyer. This discipline procured for his idealistic liberalism an impressive influence on affairs.

Selected Publications

BOOKS

1911 *Scientific Management and the Railroads*
92 pages. New York: Engineering Magazine Co.
1914 *Business—A Profession*
327 pages. Boston: Small, Maynard & Co.
1918 *Case Against Night Work for Women*
With J. C. Goldmark. 452 pages. New York: National Consumer's League.

ARTICLES

1910 'Can The Principles of Scientific Management be Applied To Railway Operation?'
New York: *Engineering News*, Vol. 64, pp. 600-601.

1910 'Evidence in Matter of Proposed Advances in Freight Rates'. Brief submitted to the Interstate Commerce Commission. Senate Document 725, 61st Congress, 3rd Session, Vol. 8 (Scientific Management), pp. 4752-4845.
1911 'The New Conception of Industrial Efficiency' New York, *Journal of Accountancy*, Vol. 12, May, pp. 35-43.
1911 'An Aid to Railroad Efficiency' New York: *Engineering Magazine*, October. Reprinted in *Business—A Profession* (see above).
1911 'Organized Labor and Efficiency' New York: *Survey*, April 22, Vol. 26, pp. 148-151.
1912 'Efficiency in Your Home and in Your Business' New York: *American*, December 10.
1912 Foreword (2 pages) to *Primer of Scientific Management* by F. B. and L. M. Gilbreth. New York: D. Van Nostrand Co.
1915 'Efficiency Systems and Labor' New York: *Harper's Weekly*, Aug.15, Vol. 59, p. 154.

Charles de la Poix de Fréminville
(1856-1936)
France

Charles de Fréminville was the collaborator of Henry Le Chatelier in bringing scientific management to France. An engineer in railways and then in the motor industry, and interested from his early career in management, de Fréminville was from 1907 onwards in close touch with Le Chatelier. It was not till he made Taylor's acquaintaince in 1912, however, that de Fréminville became an enthusiastic exponent of Taylor's methods. In 1913 he began to write for Le Chatelier in the *Revue de Metallurgie* and to launch a campaign in addresses to economic and industrial organizations. These activities are regarded by Frenchmen as the turning point of the French management movement. It was de Fréminville's special achievement faithfully to interpret Taylor's doctrines and yet to adapt them to French industry and to the French temperament.

In 1920 his efforts, jointly with Le Chatelier, were materially responsible for the creation of the Conférence de l'Organisation Francaise, of which de Fréminville became President in 1924, and which was united in 1926 with Fayol's Centre d'Etudes Administratives. When Fayol announced, during the opening session of the Second International Management Congress in Brussels in 1925, his belief in the unity between his own work and that of Taylor, it fell to de Fréminville to grasp the hand thus warmly extended as a symbol of the fusion of two complementary lines in the evolution of management thought. De Fréminville's capable presidency, from 1926 to 1932, ensured that the activities of the new Comité National de l'Organisation Française were many and fruitful.

His election to the Presidency of CIOS in 1929 was the culminating international tribute to his work.

Curriculum Vitae

1856	Born at Lorient, descendant of a family long distinguished in France. Graduated from Ecole Centrale as Engineer of Arts and Manufactures.
1878	Engineer in the Equipment Section, Paris-Orléans Railway.
1885 & 1887	Visited the United States to study developments in electric transport.
1899	Technical Director, subsequently Assistant Managing Director, Panhard & Levassor Motor Co.
1914-18	Consulting engineer in military factories and naval yards; reorganized, among others, Penhoet Naval Construction Co. and Schneider Co.
1919	Member of French Government Economic Mission to U.S.A.
1927-33	Member of Council, International Management Institute, Geneva.
1929	President of the Fourth International Management Congress, Paris, and of CIOS.
1936	Died in June, aet. 80, after a short illness.

He was a holder of the Cross of the Legion of Honour (1929); President of the Society of Civil Engineers (1934); an Honorary Vice-President of The American Society of Mechanical Engineers (1913); and Member of the Taylor Society (United States).

Personal Characteristics

His simplicity, kindliness and generosity of spirit were at the service of all and sundry who showed the least interest in the subject of which he was a master. At international meetings, not always distinguished for their freedom from national intrigues, his integrity of purpose, his sole preoccupation with the advancement of scientific method, was a beacon shrouded only by a most disarming modesty. As a chairman in his own rightful domain—the meetings of the National Committee in Paris—he would welcome the embarrassed stranger from another country with the same combination of warmth and dignity which made the atmosphere of his private apartment. And even the massacre of his beloved language which sometimes followed was shriven and shrouded in the courtesy with which he would give a clear and stimulating lead to the discussion. In particular, many young men owed their progress in the art of management to the guidance that de Fréminville gave to their first steps. A compatriot has called him not only a great engineer, but an honest man in the sense which this expression enjoyed in the century of Louis XIV. He was a man of culture, and his leisure moments were devoted to the arts—to sculpture in particular, and to the art he considered most important of all—that of living.

Selected Publications

BOOK
1918 *The Fundamental Principles of the Taylor Methods*
Paris: A. Maréchal.

ARTICLES, ADDRESSES, ETC.
From among the many important contributions made by de Fréminville, the following will serve as an indication of the scope of his writings: —
1914   'Le Système Taylor' (The Taylor System)
        Bulletin de la Société d'Encouragement pour l'Industrie Nationale, March.
1915   'Introduction to: 'Le Facteur Humain dans l'Organisation du Travail' (The Human Factor in Scientific Management)
        A French translation by Perrot and de Fréminville of a work by James Hartness, a former president of the American Society of Mechanical Engineers.
1917   'L'utilisation des Mutilés pour l'Organisation du Travail' (The Employment of Disabled Persons in Scientific Management)

Revue de Métallurgie, July-August.

1918   'Quelques Apercus sur le Système Taylor' (Some Impressions of the Taylor System)
Edition de l'Association Industrielle, Commerciale et Agricole de Lyon et de la Région.

1919-20 'Cinq Conférences sur l'Organisation du Travail' (Five Lectures on Scientific Management)
Paris: Ecole des Hautes Etudes Commerciales (Stage de l'Intendance).

1920   'The Appreciation of H. L. Gantt in France'
Paper at the Gantt Memorial Conference of the American Society of Mechanical Engineers.

1920   'The Manager's Responsibility for Production'
Philadelphia: *Proceedings* of the Academy of Political and Social Science, June.

1920   Preface to 'Sur La Pratique de l'Organisation des Ateliers Modernes' (On the Practice of Management in Modern Factories) by Caillant and Warin.

1921   'Analyse et Préparation du Travail dans les Ateliers' (Analysis and Preparation of Work in Factories)
Conférence aux élèves de l'Enseignement Technique Feminin). Paris: *Mon Bureau,* 15th July.

1923   'L'Organisation Méthodique du Travail dans la Papeterie en Amérique' (The Methodical Organization of Work in the Paper Industry in America)
Chimie et Industrie, July.

1925   'Henry Ford and His Methods'

1926   'Evolution de l'Organisation Scientifique du Travail' (Evolution of Scientific Management)
Paper given to the International Management Congress, Brussels, 1925. *Revue de Metallurgie,* April and May.

1926   'L'Organisation Méthodique du Travail et la Place faite à l'Ouvrier Habile dans l'Atelier Moderne'
(Systematic Management and the Place open to the Competent Worker in the Modern Factory)

1927   'The Evolution of Scientific Management'
Paper to the Third International Congress, Rome.

1929   'Recent Changes in Economic Affairs in the United States'

1934   'Discours de prise de Présidence de la Société des Ingenieurs Civils de 12 Janvier 1934'
Inaugural Speech on assuming the Presidency of the Society of Civil Engineers
(Paris: *Fascicule Bimensuel des Ingénieurs Civils,* No. 1, January).

67

Frederick Arthur Halsey
(1856-1935)
United States

Frederick A. Halsey originated in American industry the first successful incentive system of wage payments to improve upon the ordinary piece rate system. The question how to increase the output of labour was of great interest to engineers at the close of the last century. Before Halsey presented his paper to The American Society of Mechanical Engineers in 1891 three wage payments systems were known, all of which had important defects. Day rates had the defect of not being based on the incentive principle. Ordinary piece rates failed because they were constantly associated by the worker with rate-cutting by the employer, as soon as the worker had achieved any substantial rise in his output. Lastly, the gain-sharing plan presented by H. R. Towne to the Society in 1889 was deficient, as Halsey showed, in that the increased output, no doubt due to the efforts of the better workers, provided rewards without distinction between good workers and bad.

Halsey's 'premium plan of paying for labor' was an original contribution to management from many points of view. His avowed aim was to eliminate rate-cutting, with all that it implied in antagonism between worker and employer. The plan consisted in a guaranteed daily or hourly rate for fixed quantity of work, agreed with the worker on the basis of his customary performance in the past, and then a premium payment, for any additional work, of about one-half to one-third of the sum the employer would have paid for this work under the daily or hourly rate. Under this scheme the worker's earnings would not be excessive even if he doubled his output, and hence the employer, who would gain the most from the additional output, would be dissuaded from cutting the rate.

The premium plan had a very great influence not only in the United States but also in Great Britain where it was, together with Taylor's piece-rate system, the model for many incentive schemes. The Halsey premium plan was introduced for example into Taylor, Taylor & Hobson, Ltd., lens and optical instrument makers of Leicester, England, in 1900. James Rowan's premium system of 1901 was undoubtedly based upon Halsey's premium plan. In the United States Halsey influenced Taylor's work on incentives, and although the premium plan was overshadowed by Taylor's piece-rate system, it continued to be used in cases where its advantages remained evident. In 1911 at the Watertown Arsenal, for instance, one of Taylor's followers installed a variant of the Halsey plan because it was considered a better incentive than the piece-rate system for mainly non-repetitive types of work.

The important limitation of Halsey's premium plan, a limitation found in all schemes prior to the piece-rate system of Taylor, was that it took the customary output of workers as the basis of calculation. Taylor's new contribution was to show how the scientific measurement of work could do much more to increase and improve management output than could any methods of payment, however they might be manipulated. The application of both these plans in subsequent years, however, showed that there were good points in each.

Though Taylor's desire to improve the workers' earnings was as genuine as Halsey's, his systematic planning of every movement of every worker in the shop made high output depend more on the planning department than on the initiative and constructive co-operation of the individual worker. Halsey's plan depended more on the latter element. Suggestion schemes came more frequently into existence under Halsey's plan than under Taylor's; and the improved methods tending continuously to emerge from this form of positive alliance with the man on the job have been the basis of some of the most successful examples of modern management. Taylor's was the system of the greatest significance for the future of management. But some have said that Halsey knew men better than Taylor.

Curriculum Vitae

1856 Born on 12th July at Unadilla, N.Y., a descendant of Thomas Halsey who came from England to Lynn, Massachusetts, with his wife Phoebe in 1637 and was one of the founders of Southampton, Long Island, New York. The Golden Parsonage, Great Gaddesden, Hertfordshire, in which Thomas Halsey grew up, is still the home of the Halsey family in England.

1878 Bachelor of Mechanical Engineering, Cornell University. Elected a member of Sigma Xi.

1878-80 Worked in various machine shops.

1880-90 Draftsman in the Rand Drill Company, later by merger the Ingersoll-Rand Company of New York. He soon became Chief Engineer of the Company, in which capacity he designed for it numerous straightlir air compressors and invented the Slugger rock drill.

1890-04 Engineer and General Manager, Canadian Rand Drill Co. Ltd., Sherbrooke, Quebec.

1894 Associate Editor, 'American Machinist' New York. Editor from 1907, and later Editor Emeritus.

1911 Retired from editorship owing to ill-health.

1911-14 Associate professor in mechanical engineering, Columbia University, New York.

1911-35 Author of various books and papers.

1916 Commissioner of the American Institute of Weights and Measures, a body which he had established as one means of successfully defeating the movement to introduce the metric system into the United States.

1935 Died on 20th October aet. 79, in New York City.

In 1923 he was awarded the first Gold Medal to be conferred by The American Society of Mechanical Engineers, for his paper of 1891 on the Premium Plan. The citation stated that the adoption of the methods there proposed had had a profound effect towards harmonizing the relations of worker and employer.

Personal Characteristics

Halsey was a forceful personality. That he was also a generous man was made apparent in his reaction to Taylor's criticisms of his Premium Plan. At the reading of Taylor's paper 'A Piece Rate System' in 1895, where Taylor's comments on 'Messrs. Towne and Halsey's Plans' must have been painful hearing for him, Halsey rose at once to say:

'If Mr. Taylor can determine the maximum output of the miscellaneous pieces of work comprised in the everyday operation of the average machine shop, he has accomplished a great work, and the present paper should be followed at once by another giving the fullest details of his method.'

It was yet long before Halsey could accept that maximum output could be determined, but when he finally did so he generously acknowledged Taylor's achievement.

He showed in his own working relations that he was a leader of men. He is remembered particularly as a chief who never allowed his own clear-cut views to intrude on the maximum freedom of action accorded to every individual working under him.

Selected Publications

1891 'The Premium Plan of Paying for Labor'
Trans. ASME.
1897 'Some Special Forms of Computers'
Trans. ASME.
1899 'Administration of the Premium Plan'
American Machinist.
1899 'Experience with the Premium Plan of Paying Labor'
American Machinist.
1899 'The Use of the Slide Rule'
1900 'Economics of the Premium Plan'
American Machinist.
1902 'Origin of the Premium Plan: A Personal Statement'
American Machinist.
1903 'The Metric System'
Trans. ASME.
1904 'The Metric Fallacy' (rewritten 1919)
1909 'From Piece Work to the Premium Plan'
American Machinist.
1913 'Halsey's Handbook for Machine Designers and Draftsmen'
1914 'Methods of Machine Shop Work'
1917 'Metric System in Export Trade'
1918 'Weights and Measures of Latin America'

Frederick Winslow Taylor
(1856-1915)
United States

Frederick Winslow Taylor's tomb at Germantown outside Philadelphia bears the simple phrase 'The Father of Scientific Management'. It is a title which has been accepted not only by his compatriots but by management movements the world over. His writings have been translated into a score of languages. Since 1938, the gold medal of the International Committee for Scientific Management has borne his portrait. In 1918, Lenin wrote in *Pravda* with reference to Russian industry, 'We should immediately introduce piece-work and try it out in practice. We should try out every scientific and progressive suggestion of the Taylor system'. The very ubiquity of his influence has led at times to misunderstanding of his work. But the historian, after careful examination of the evidence, can only conclude that the emergence in the 20th century of a science of business management, directed towards enhancing the economic and social contribution of business to the democratic way of life, was an achievement which owed more to Taylor than to any other single man.

That Taylor benefited from the work of some earlier pioneers, he was the first to acknowledge, and this will be evident to readers of this book. When he began his career efforts had already been made, on both sides of the Atlantic, towards drawing together the work of the two principal technical professions concerned with the management of a factory—engineering and accountancy. Interest had developed in various labour incentive schemes. Several devices for better managerial control of production processes had been worked out. The subject of cost-accounting was being actively discussed. From these slender beginnings, however, F. W. Taylor developed, at first almost single-handed and by thinking the problem through from its basic element—the process carried out by a single worker at a particular time—a whole new attitude to the art of managing business enterprises. This attitude he himself described as 'a mental revolution'. From it the philosophy of the best and most modern management in the 20th century has taken its inspiration.

At the time Taylor began his work, business management as a discrete and identifiable activity had attracted little attention. It was usually regarded as incidental to, and flowing from knowledge-of-acquaintance-with, a particular branch of manufacturing, the technical know-how of making sausages or steel or shirts. Men called on to conduct the aggregates of capital, plant, equipment, materials and human beings by which these articles were made 'picked up' their management skill by experience and 'trial and error'. They overlooked the fact that in this particular context the learner's errors are other people's trials. The idea that a man needed any training or formal instruction to become a competent manager had not occurred to anyone.

It was through the gradual elaboration of techniques for analysing and measuring elementary processes that Taylor progressed towards a new philosophy of management. His earliest concern, as a gang-

73

boss at the Midvale Steel Works, Philadelphia, was to end the practice of 'soldiering' or restriction of output by the workers for whom he was responsible. From his own practical experience as a lathe operator he knew that much higher outputs were possible without unreasonable effort. He decided that the difficulty was due to ignorance on both sides. Management demanded and the men were ready to give 'a fair day's work' for 'a fair day's pay'. But neither side had a clear idea what, quantitatively, constituted 'a fair day's work'. Both were relying on vague impressions and traditions which led to constant disputes.

He reached a solution of this problem through the exact and detailed measurement, which yielded 'standard' times, of the movements used on every process, and by reorganization of tasks and of the system of payment in the light of these data. Inevitably such work led to many other developments in planning, in the flow of materials and jobs, in tool supply and so on, designed to make it possible for each worker to achieve 'standard' or better at all times. Taylor thus arrived at the two principles which he believed to be the essence of his philosophy of management—'scientific management' as it came to be called. These principles were:

'both sides (management and men) must take their eyes off the division of the surplus as the all-important matter, and together turn their attention towards increasing the size of the surplus.'

and

'both sides must recognize as essential the substitution of exact scientific investigation and knowledge for the old individual judgment or opinion, either of the workman or the boss, in all matters relating to the work done in the establishment.'[1]

In short, if men are to co-operate together effectively, and every business is essentially a system of human co-operation, all concerned must have, (i) a common purpose (ii) a common method. Taylor devised many new techniques as the instruments of his work. His inventive genius and fertility of ideas were such that he could have achieved eminence on this count alone. Forty technical patents stand to his credit, including the revolutionary discovery of high-speed steel. He was equally productive of new management methods and devices. Many, if not the majority, of the methods characterized as 'modern' today can be traced to ideas initiated by him and his followers close on half a century ago. Though they have been refined and developed almost out of recognition, the germ can usually be found in Taylor's writing and practice. In 1902 he decided, however,

1 Testimony before the Special Committee of the U.S. House of Representatives, 1912. Published in *Scientific Management* by F. W. Taylor. New York: Harper and Brothers, 1947 edition.

that he 'no longer could afford to work for money'.[1] He devoted the rest of his life to advocating, not particular techniques, but the new principles which he believed were his real contribution to the world.

As is the case with most innovators he was much misunderstood. Many who called themselves his 'disciples' imitated his methods, while remaining blind to the principles behind them and indifferent to the sense of social responsibility essential to their successful application. Thus his ideas became the target of the most bitter opposition both from big business and from the trade unions.

Nor was the written statement of his philosophy complete. The activity of management is partly a matter of mechanics, of creating and controlling a structure, and partly one of dynamics, of inspiring and energizing the group of people who work within this framework. Because Taylor was preoccupied with the first and indispensable preliminary task, clarifying the mechanics, some critics accused him of lacking an appreciation of or any constructive approach to the dynamics. It is true that some of his devices, such as functional foremanship as he described it, may not stand the test of time. His own life and writings, however, provide ample evidence of the integrity and essential rightness of his personal attitude towards those who worked with him and of his concept of the obligations of management to society as a whole. There was never a strike in any plant where he personally was operating. It was in accord with his whole outlook that his immediate followers, particularly Gantt and Gilbreth, made a larger contribution to the dynamics of management. One of his major preoccupations towards the end of his life was the fear that those who came after would mistake the methods he had developed for the spirit which had made them possible. And in that spirit, that philosophy, his passion for the well-being of his fellow men was the outstanding element. His outburst in 1912 when stung by hostile criticism from a Committee of Congress epitomizes his contribution to a new democratic philosophy of fundamental importance for our century:

'Scientific Management is not an efficiency device, nor is it any bunch or group of efficiency devices; it is not a new system of figuring costs; it is not holding a stop-watch on a man, and writing things down about him; it is not time study; it is not motion study; it is not the printing and ruling and unloading of a ton or two of blanks by a set of men saying "Here's your system, go to it"; it is not divided foremanship, or functional foremanship; it is not any of the devices which the average man calls to mind when Scientific Management is spoken of. Now, in its essence, Scientific Manage-

[1] Copley: *Frederick W. Taylor*, vol. i, Foreword, p. xviii.

ment involves a complete mental revolution on the part of the working man engaged in any industry, and it involves an equally complete revolution on the part of those on the management's side —the foreman, the superintendent, the owner, the board of directors, and without this complete mental revolution on both sides Scientific Management does not exist . . .'[1]

and, replying to the question, whether the management principles he had developed could not be abused:

'I have never said that Scientific Management could be used for bad (ends). It is possible to use the mechanism of Scientific Management for bad (ends) but not Scientific Management itself. It ceases to be Scientific Management the moment it is used for bad (ends)'.[1]

By 'bad' (ends) he meant, as his whole life-work testified, purposes which were selfish or sectional, harmful to the well-being of a democratic society or of any important segment of such a society. He started his working life as a labourer on the shop-floor at Midvale and he was constant to the end to what he believed to be the ultimate interests of simple men.

Curriculum Vitae

1856   Born on 20th March in Philadelphia.

1872-4   Phillips Exeter Academy.
He received an excellent general education which included European travel and attendance at French and German schools. He intended to study law and qualified for Harvard, but temporary eye trouble decided him to turn to engineering.

1875-8   Apprenticed in the Enterprise Hydraulic Works, a small machine shop in Philadelphia, to the trades of pattern maker and machinist.

1878-90   Joined Midvale Steel Works, Philadelphia, as a machine-shop labourer. He became successively shop-clerk, machinist, gang boss, foreman, maintenance foreman, head of the drawing office and chief engineer. In 1883 he obtained a degree in Engineering, by evening study, from the Stevens Institute of Technology, New Jersey.

1890-93   General manager, Manufacturing Investment Co., manufacturers of paper fibre.

1893-98   Consulting engineer in management. Among his clients were William Deering & Co., Northern Electrical Manufac-

---

1 Copley: *op. cit.*

turing Co., Lorain Steel Co., and Simonds Rolling Machine Co. At this time he mastered accounting by private study.

1898-01 Bethlehem Steel Co., Bethlehem, Pennsylvania. During this period he and White made the discoveries leading to the development of high-speed tool steel, first demonstrated at the 1900 Paris Exposition.

1901-15 Retired from working for payment. From now until his death he devoted his energies, as unpaid consultant, lecturer, etc., to furthering acceptance of Scientific Management in the United States and abroad.

1910 Brandeis' handling of the 'Eastern Rates Case' attracted nation-wide attention to Scientific Management.

1911 Congressional Committee of Enquiry appointed, as a result of a strike at the Watertown Arsenal to investigate 'the Taylor and other systems of shop management'. The use of time-study and the payment of premium bonuses was banned on all government work.

1915 Died on 21st March aet. 59, in Philadelphia.

He was a President of The American Society of Mechanical Engineers (1906) and was made honorary Sc.D. of the University of Pennsylvania (1906), and honorary Ll.D. of Hobart College (1912). He received an award (1900) from the Exposition Internationale Universelle, Paris, and, jointly with White, the Elliott Cresson Medal of the Franklin Institute of Pennsylvania (1902) for his work on high-speed cutting tools.

Personal Characteristics

Taylor was a blend of opposing impulses: his genius was 'sparked' by internal conflict. His father was of an exceptionally gentle and retiring disposition. His mother was a woman of the liveliest intellectual curiosity and strong personality: from her side of the family he probably inherited his taste for mechanical invention. Both were Quaker in background and nonconformist and independent in principle.

From this common feature came the strongest element in his character, his intense sense of duty and of social obligation. He neither smoked nor drank, regarding even tea and coffee as stimulants to be avoided. He has been described as possessing 'a whale of a New England conscience'. He liked to say that it was more worthwhile in life to make a pleasure of duty than a duty of pleasure.

He might have had a brilliant career purely as an inventor. But he would have regarded it as self-indulgence. Whenever he had invented a useful device or perfected a new idea, his social conscience stepped

77

in and insisted that he must persuade his contemporaries to adopt it. He once described his interest in inventing things as 'something of a temptation'. He was exceptionally quick-minded and his patience, infinite in technical research, was not inexhaustible in human relations. Nor was he, for all his zeal, perfectly equipped as a propagandist: he often found difficulty in expressing himself in writing. He was primarily an engineer.

Yet for all his personal austerity he was full of human sympathy and fun. On his record at Midvale he was an outstanding practical executive. Despite his early struggle with his men, his complete integrity won their respect and his intense enthusiasm swept them along. One of his colleagues said of him 'he would have filled up a corpse with enthusiasm, if only the corpse could hear'.

It was tragic that the evening of his days should have been shadowed by the loss of personal friends and the misunderstanding of his work. That that work should be identified with a type of management designed to oppress the workers does a grave injustice to his memory. He was as democratic in temper as he was dedicated in spirit: from dawn to dusk his intensely hard-working life was devoted to their service.

Selected Publications

The best known of Taylor's writings were in the form of papers given to The American Society of Mechanical Engineers, many of them subsequently reproduced in book form.

1886 *The Relative Value of Water-gas and Gas from the Siemens Producer for Melting in the Open-hearth Furnace*
Trans. ASME, Vol. 7, pp. 669-679.

1893 *Notes on Belting*
Trans. ASME, Vol. 15, pp. 204-259.

1895 *A Piece-Rate System*
Trans. ASME, Vol. 16, pp. 856-903 (Reproduced, e.g. by *The Engineering Magazine*, Vol. 10.)

1903 *Shop Management*
Trans. ASME, Vol. 24, pp. 1337-1480. Reproduced in book form. New York: Harper & Bros., 1910.

1905 *Concrete, Plain and Reinforced* (with S. E. Thompson)
New York: Wiley & Sons.

1906 *On The Art of Cutting Metals*
Trans. ASME, Vol. 28, pp. 31-350. Later published as a book.

1906 *A Comparison of University and Industrial Discipline and Method*
Article in *The Stevens Indicator*, Vol. 24, pp. 37-46, 1907.

1909 *Why Manufacturers Dislike College Graduates*
Article in *The Sibley Journal of Engineering,* Vol. 24, reproducing a paper to the Society for the Promotion of Engineering
Education.
1910 Contribution to the Joint Meeting of ASME and the Institution of Mechanical Engineers, Birmingham, July, reproduced
in extenso in the Proceedings of the Institution, and in summary form in *Engineering* (London) 5th August.
1911 'The Gospel of Efficiency'
Articles in *The American Magazine,* Vols. 71-72. (Reproduced
in three articles in *World's Work*—London edition—May,
June, July.)
1911 *Principles and Methods of Scientific Management*
New York: Harper & Bros. Also in *The American Journal of
Accountancy,* Vol. 12, 1911. (Subsequent editions and translations.)
1912 *Concrete Costs* (with S. E. Thompson)
New York: Wiley & Sons.

Carl Georg Lange Barth
(1860-1939)
United States

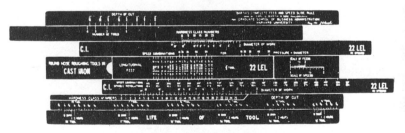

A Barth Slide Rule

'Barth was one of the two greatest management engineers that the United States has produced.'[1] These words, written by another pioneer of management, may surprise the many people to whom the name of F. W. Taylor is familiar but the name of Barth unknown.

[1] Dr. H. S. Person: *Advanced Management* (New York), vol. iv, No. 5, Section 1. 1939.

Barth was in fact the earliest, ablest, and closest associate of Taylor. The first contribution he brought to Taylor's work was his exceptional ability for engineering mathematics.

'When Barth became Taylor's assistant at the Bethlehem Steel Co. in 1899, the latter was in possession of a vast accumulation of experimental data relating to machine operations which no one had been able to analyze successfully. Taylor had submitted the data to several university professors of mathematics who had been unsuccessful in getting anything of value out of them. Taylor submitted them to Barth who soon developed the famous formula of twelve variables described in Taylor's *Shop Management*. On the basis of this formula he then developed the Barth slide-rule.'[1]

The slide-rule enabled the person preparing the instruction card for the machine operator easily to utilise the formula, in the set-up of a machine, for the best performance of any operation within the capacity of the machine. After this achievement Barth became Taylor's right hand man. The new slide-rule, which Barth claimed as an important advance in the art of slide-rule construction in general, proved to be the solution to most of Taylor's metal-cutting problems. Indeed, many of the standardized tools on which Taylor's system depended were the fruit of Barth's personal ingenuity. 'If they became known as Taylor tools, they were so only in the sense that Taylor had inspired and directed the course of the experiments. If he avoided singling out Barth for special attention, it was for the good of the movement just as he subordinated his own part. But he came to recognize that this operated to do Barth not a little injustice.'[2]

Barth was of value to Taylor not only as a mathematician. He rendered much service in Taylor's other researches into time study, fatigue study, and so on, and in Taylor's work of introducing Scientific Management into manufacturing concerns. He was adept at devising practical procedures by which the Taylor principles could be implemented. In 1903, when progressive managers like James Mapes Dodge were impatient to use the new high-speed tool steel, Barth was appointed on Taylor's suggestion to supervise the application of the new methods in the Link-Belt Philadelphia plant. This was the first of many assignments which Barth undertook to install the Taylor methods either in part or as a complete system of management. In the early days Taylor was the outside consultant charging no fee, and Barth was what was later termed the 'system man' responsible for the actual installation. Barth soon became a consultant in

[1] Dr. H. S. Person: *Advanced Management* (New York), vol. iv, No. 5, Section 1. 1939.
[2] F. B. Copley: *Frederick W. Taylor* (details of publication in Appendix II), vol. ii, page 253.

his own right. His slide-rules were often the means of bringing about conversions to Taylor's methods. Taylor frequently introduced Barth as 'the man who solves impossible problems'. In his testimony before the Special House Committee he said:

'Mr. Barth here has been perhaps the most efficient man of all the men who have been connected with scientific management in devising new methods for turning out work fast. I can remember a number of—one or two—instances in which almost overnight he devised a method for turning out almost twenty times as much as had been turned out before with no greater effort to the workman.'

Barth continued, up to the time of Taylor's death in 1915, to work with Taylor in the plants which were the models of the new system. When the Harvard School of Business Administration was inaugurated in 1908, it was Barth who convinced the Dean that the School should accept the Taylor System as the standard of modern management.

The words of Dr. Person may appropriately close this outline: 'Taylor had the vision . . . But he did not like to handle the details. Here he needed able associates. Barth was the ablest among them . . . It appears fair to say that the association of these two types of genius made each more creative than he might otherwise have been.'

Curriculum Vitae

1860	Born on 28th February in Christiana, Norway.
	He received a high school education and then entered the Horten Technical School, run under the auspices of the Navy Department.
1877-81	Apprenticed in the Navy Yard, also acting in the last two years as a part-time, then a whole-time instructor in mathematics at the Horten School.
1881	Emigrated in April to the United States.
1881-95	Draughtsman with William Sellers & Co., Philadelphia, machine tool manufacturers, ultimately rising to chief designer.
1895-7	Chief draughtsman, Rankin & Fritch Foundry & Machine Co., St. Louis, and later designer of special machinery in the St. Louis Water Department.
1897	Instructor in mathematics and mechanical drawing at International Correspondence Schools, Scranton, Penna.
1898-9	Instructor in mathematics and manual training, Ethical Culture School, New York.
1899	Machine-shop engineer and special assistant to F. W.

Taylor at the Bethlehem Steel Co., Bethlehem, Penna.

1901   Left Bethlehem to work again with William Sellers & Co., Philadelphia.

1903   Consulting engineer in private practice, often collaborating
onwards   with Taylor in the earlier years in plants such as the Tabor Mfg. Co., Philadelphia, The Link-Belt Co., Philadelphia, and also working independently, for instance in the Yale & Towne Mfg. Co., Stamford, Conn.

1911-16   Lecturer on Scientific Management, Harvard University, also 1919-22.

1912   Carl G. Barth & Son, founded in Philadelphia as a firm of consulting engineers. Most of the firm's work was to train clients' personnel in the techniques of the Taylor system.

1914-16   Lecturer on Scientific Management, University of Chicago.

1923-39   Semi-retirement, always being available for consultation when called on. He devoted much of his time to higher mathematics.

1939   Died on 28th October aet. 79, in Philadelphia.

He was made an honorary member of the Taylor Society (1920), the only other honorary members being Taylor and Le Chatelier. He was a life member of The American Society of Mechanical Engineers.

Personal Characteristics

Carl Barth was short and slender, with a severe, professorial look. He was easily excitable and haughty of manner, although absence of smiles was compensated by a look of great animation. 'Some of the biggest business men this country has produced have had the lesson taught them that Carl Barth courts no one. When in his younger and more frisky days he would walk into a shop to report on what could be done to reorganize it on a Taylor basis, he had no hesitation in letting it appear how forcibly he was struck by the contrast between it and what he was used to. It was as if he had said "My God! so this is what you call a machine shop!" Hearing of this Fred Taylor would beseech him not always to find that everything was wrong—would beseech him to have a little tact. Whereupon Carl Barth would experience all the emotions of a pot called black by a kettle. What Homeric laughter would pass all down the line of the Taylor following at the bare mention of the word tact! And the spectacle of Fred Taylor and Carl Barth locking horns over this issue—that surely was the limit.'[1]

[1] Copley: *op. cit.* vol. ii, p. 27.

Selected Publications

BOOK

1919-20   *Supplement to F. W. Taylor's 'On the Art of Cutting Metals'*
12 articles published in *Industrial Management* in 12
monthly issues between September 1919 and November
1920. These articles constitute the equivalent of a complete
book on the development of the Complete Feed and Speed
Slide Rule.

ARTICLES

1903   'Slide Rules for the Machine Shop as Part of the Taylor
System of Management'
New York: Trans. ASME, Vol. 25.

1912   'Betterment of Machine Tool Operations by Scientific Metal
Cutting'
New York *Engineering Magazine*, Vol.42.

1916   Standardization of Machine Tools'
New York: Trans. ASME, December.

1918   'The Income Tax, An Engineer's Analysis with Sugges-
tions'
Philadelphia Chapter of ASME. Journal of the Engineers
Club of Philadelphia, June-July.

1919   'Labor Turnover, A Mathematical Discussion'
Bulletin of the Taylor Society, Vol. V, No. 2.

1922   'The Improved Belt Slide Rule'
Management Engineering, June.

1924   'A Suggestion for a Premium System'
Management and Administration, July, Vol. 8, No. 1.

1925   'A New Graphical Solution for Time Allowances in Task
Setting'
Management and Administration, Vol. 9, No. 2.

1926   'The Barth Standard Wage Scale'
Manufacturing Industries, Vol. 11, No. 5.

Edward Albert Filene
(1860-1937)
United States

Edward Albert Filene was the founder of the Twentieth Century Fund and the architect of the International Management Institute. He was also a pioneer of retail management.

He began the practice of management from the bottom in a small retail business in Boston. Basing his policy on principles first stated in the 19th century by the Frenchman Boucicaut (the 'father of the department store'), Filene developed his business, through efficient organization and a series of dramatic innovations in sales methods, into one of the first great American department stores on the modern pattern. These principles were in effect, 'small profits and quick returns' and 'the customer is always right'. He wrote authoritative books and articles on the principles of retail management. In them he affirmed that the long-term aims of business coincide with those of social progress. 'The merchant's true function, he said, is not making money at the expense of the customer, but satisfying genuine wants adequately.' Thus a 'social' policy was also good business, and he made a fortune to prove it. His book *The Model Stock Plan* (1930) probably had a greater impact on retail management than any other book written on the subject of distribution.

Filene used his fortune, among innumerable other business and public activities, to endow the Twentieth Century Fund, a research institution conducting its own studies in economic and social problems. Many of the Fund's studies have a close bearing on management both in the United States and in other countries of the world. The Fund aims at rigorous and impartial fact-finding, carried out by intelligent researchers, and presented in book form and in pithy news items which are publicized to keep the American people aware of the facts of their economy. Its pioneering work along the lines laid down by Filene has made it famous. Some others of the many organizations he helped to create did not observe his principles and have been less enduring. Of one of the latter he said 'They assemble their own opinions instead of facts to solve business problems. I was forced to the conclusion that neither the ends of business nor the ends of democracy can be served by such a policy.'

Filene, through the Fund, took the decisive initiative in creating the International Management Institute, which operated from 1927 to 1933. The Institute's creation came as a new achievement of the international management movement shortly after the successes of the first international conferences. For the first time the movement was now represented in a permanent body with its own international secretariat. Financed jointly by the Twentieth Century Fund and the International Labour Office and located in Geneva, the Institute acted as an international clearing-house for the exchange of information on better methods of management. It published a monthly bulletin in three languages, held a number of technical conferences, issued many reports on special subjects, assisted in the re-organization of a number of international bodies, and perhaps most important of all, helped to bring into personal contact individuals in many countries who shared a common interest in the technique of business organization.

The Institute was the only body to be entrusted with international research and communication on management problems either before or since the six years of its existence. It fell victim to Hitler's rise to power in Germany and the depression of the early 1930s which cut by two-fifths the purchasing power of the dollar in terms of Swiss francs. The conjunction of these two events destroyed, for the time being, Filene's interest in Europe, but not before the Institute had justified his idea by much useful pioneering work in management.

Curriculum Vitae

1860 Born on 3rd September in Salem, Mass. His father had emigrated from German-held Poland to settle in New England, and had started several retail stores.

He had a public and high school education, and planned to attend Harvard, but his father's failing health obliged him to enter the family business (1879) with his brother Lincoln Filene. Throughout his career he was President of William Filene's Sons Co., though from 1928 onwards he had no active part in the operating of the store.

1909 Organized the credit union movement of the United States.
1919 Founded the Twentieth Century Fund.
1921 Founded the Credit Union National Extension Bureau, directing the mutual association of credit unions throughout the United States.
1933 Chairman, Massachusetts State Recovery Board.
1935 Founded the Consumer Distribution Corporation.
1936 Founded the Good Will Fund Inc. (now the Edward A. Filene Good Will Fund Inc.).
1937 Died on 26th September aet. 77 in Paris, France.

He was an LL.D. of Lehigh University (1931), Rollins College (1932) and Tulane University (1935).

He was an Officer of the Legion of Honour (France); Cavaliere, Order of the Crown (Italy); Commander of the Order of the White Lion (Czechoslovakia); and was awarded the Austrian Gold Cross of Merit. He was active in very many political, social, and economic societies, including the Society for the Advancement of Management. Not the least of his international services was his invention of the simultaneous translation device (the Filene-Finlay Simultaneous Translator) subsequently used at the Nüremberg war criminal trials and now used at every international gathering of importance.

Personal Characteristics

'Ten years after his death men whose judgment is equally good and whose opportunities of observing Edward A. Filene were equally adequate still disagree flatly about what manner of man he was. He was a paradox in a dozen ways . . . He prided himself on a marked indifference to the ordinary charities, yet he gave away his entire fortune. He contended that selfishness is the basic motive of human activity and stripped himself to improve the lot of mankind. He was a large employer and in many respects an autocratic one who fought consistently for the right of wage earners. He could be startlingly mean in small matters and as startlingly generous when thousands or millions were involved . . .

87

There was the big man who built up an obscure women's speciality shop into the greatest store of its kind in the world, who played a large part in establishing the United States Chamber of Commerce and the International Chamber of Commerce, who apprehended—comprehended is rather too strong a word—the trend of modern economics long before his contemporaries, who understood mass distribution before Ford understood mass production, who grasped the principles of the New Deal before Roosevelt did, who set up two great foundations and became the Counselor of statesmen and potentates all around the earth.

That man deserved the respectful consideration of mankind and got it.'[1]

But though he was basically thoughtful and generous he was not a happy man. He never married. He quarrelled readily with friends and associates and drove those who worked for him. This personal isolation deprived him, in the opinion of those who knew him well, of some of the sympathy and understanding that his work merited.

Selected Publications

1924 *The Way Out*
139 pages. New York: Doubleday, Page & Co.

1925 *More Profits from Merchandizing*
159 pages. Chicago: A. W. Shaw & Co.

1930 *The Model Stock Plan*
253 pages. New York: McGraw-Hill.

1932 *Successful Living in this Machine Age*
274 pages. New York: Simon Schuster.

1934 *The Consumer's Dollar* (pamphlet)
29 pages. New York:, The John Day Co.

1935 *Morals in Business* (booklet reprint of lecture)
45 pages. Committee on the Barbara Weinstock Lectures, University of California.

1937 *Next Steps Forward in Retailing*
(with collaboration of Werner K. Gabler & Percy S. Brown)
309 pages. New York: Harper.

1939 *Speaking of Change* (selection of speeches & articles)
Tennessee: Kingsport Press, Kingsport. (For associates of Edward A. Filene—material selected during Filene's lifetime but published after his death.)

---

[1] Extracts from Johnson: *Liberal's Progress*, pages 1-35 (details of publication in Appendix II).

Henry Laurence Gantt
(1861-1919)
United States

Henry Laurence Gantt was one of the earliest pioneers in the Scientific Management group in the United States to direct his major interest to the human being in industry. 'In all problems of management,' he wrote, 'the human element is the most important one.' In its first years the movement had had a different emphasis. Taylor, although his ultimate objective had undoubtedly been to improve the lot of the working man, had sought the solution of industrial problems through the analysis of processes, the planning of work and organization; for individual motivation he had relied largely on financial incentives. His was an essential first step. But Gantt's methods, applied when 'Taylorism' was under a cloud owing to labour opposition, were undoubtedly a further step. He has been called the forerunner of modern industrial democracy and his work is only today being fully recognized. To many familiar with modern management methods he is known only by the one particular chart that bears his name—though he evolved many charts. Yet his contributions of detail—the bonus plan, the charts, the methods of production control—were, as with Taylor, but tools, the methods through which he expressed his central philosophy.

For many years a close associate of Taylor's, Gantt made his first original contribution to management with his 'task and bonus' system of wages, the results of which were presented in a paper to The American Society of Mechanical Engineers in 1901. This system was working successfully at the Midvale Steel Co. earlier than Taylor's differential piece-rate system, and it won acceptance long afterwards because it was simple, generally applicable, and less severe than Taylor's on failure to attain standard. Its advantage was to assure to the worker a definite reward for finishing a task in the time allotted and an extra reward if he could do still better. The system had the same essential basis as that of Taylor, namely, that of a scientifically measured task.

His next contribution was to evolve graphic charts for production control. The 'daily balance chart', the forerunner of the later but better-known 'Gantt Chart', was designed to give a picture of the results of the day's work by noon of the following day and thus to facilitate continuous pre-planning of production. From the daily balance chart he went on to graphic cost control and idle expense charts. The final evolution, the bar-chart which bears his name, made the important change of planning production programmes in terms of *time* instead of in quantities. Nothing could be simpler than the Gantt Chart, yet nothing could at the time have been more revolutionary.

In his later years, his influence in bringing American industry, and particularly the American engineering profession, to accept the new concepts of management was enhanced by his success in insisting that the training of workmen should become a responsibility of management. In 1908 he was putting forward views not generally accepted until the end of the First World War. By then he was already thinking further ahead, to 'democracy in industry' and the humanizing of the science of management. In his later writings he rose to philosophical stature in his proposals for equality of opportunity in industry, and for the identification of the interest of employers and employed on the basis of scientifically ascertained facts.

He was, of all the leading pioneers of management, possibly the most sensitive to the importance of acceptable leadership as the primary element in the success of any business undertaking. He was called 'an apostle of industrial peace'.[1] His famous Yale lecture in 1915 bears the title 'Industrial Leadership'. It is one long plea for the wider recognition of the human factor in management and of the fact that the financial incentive is only one among many of 'the motives which influence men'. In common with Harrington Emerson, he suggested that business should not restrict its 'case studies' to its own limited experience of this particular problem. It might with advantage draw on the much longer records of military and governmental organizations which had been handling large numbers of employees for many more centuries than the few decades in which business enterprises had been dealing with 'big battalions'.

In 1929 it was decided by The American Society of Mechanical Engineers and the Institute of Management (later the American Management Association) to establish a Henry Laurence Gantt Gold Medal, to be awarded 'for distinguished achievement in industrial management as a service to the community'. The first award went posthumously to Gantt himself—'For his humanizing influence upon industrial management and for invention of the Gantt Chart'.

Curriculum Vitae

1861   Born on 18th May on a plantation in Maryland. His family were prosperous farmers, but their fortunes were dissipated in the Civil War while Gantt was still in early childhood, and his early years were marked by some privation.
            He was educated at the McDonagh School, and John Hopkins College (Degree of A.B. 1880).

1880-83   Teacher of natural sciences and mechanics at McDonagh School.

1884-6   Worked as a draughtsman with a firm of ironfounders and qualified at Stevens Institute (1884) as a mechanical engineer.

1887-93   Midvale Steel Co., Philadelphia; from Assistant in the Engineering Department he became Assistant to the Chief Engineer (F. W. Taylor) and then Superintendent of the Casting Department.

[1] By Fred J. Miller, Past President of The American Society of Mechanical Engineers, at the first ceremony of award of the Gantt Medal in 1929.

1893-1901	Held a succession of technical executive posts, save for one year (1894-5) as a consultant in Philadelphia. Most of the time he was in close contact with Taylor, for instance in consulting work at the Bethlehem Steel Co.
1902-19	Consultant. In 1917 he relinquished private activity to accept a Government assignment in the Frankford Arsenal, and later one in the building of ships for the Emergency Fleet Corporation.
1919	Died on 23rd November aet. 58, at his Pine Island Farm, New York.

He was a Vice-President of The American Society of Mechanical Engineers (1914-15) and received the Distinguished Service Medal for his assistance in the war effort.

Personal Characteristics

Gantt was the temperamental opposite of Taylor, although they were close associates for many years. 'Taylor was thoroughgoing. Gantt did not wish to go any further than you were willing to have him. Taylor was profound, revolutionary; Gantt adaptable, opportunist ... At Bethlehem, as elsewhere, Gantt's ready ability to make the best of whatever situation arose was of great service in supplementing Taylor's bulldog ability.'[1] We are told that he won Taylor's confidence by promptly solving a mathematical problem which had baffled Taylor, 'Gantt reaching his solution by emphasizing the coincidences and minimizing the differences, and so tracing out a law, a method highly characteristic of his fluent, adaptable nature'.[2]

In his later years he attained the stature of a leader and thinker in industry. The many tributes paid to him at the memorial meeting of The American Society of Mechanical Engineers made clear that his high ideals for harmony within the industrial community were the reflection of genuine gifts of leadership, and of the ability to enlist the enthusiasm of others in a worthwhile endeavour. The greatest tribute to his memory is the number of leaders in management in the next generation who ascribed their inspiration to his example and teaching.

Selected Publications

BOOKS
1910 *Work, Wages and Profits*
312 pages. New York: Engineering Magazine Co.

[1] Copley: *Frederick W. Taylor*, vol. ii, page 23.
[2] *ibid*, vol. i page 252.

1916 *Industrial Leadership*
128 pages. Yale University Press, New Haven, Conn.
1919 *Organizing for Work*
Harcourt, Brace and Howe.

PAPERS

Gantt read twelve papers to The American Society of Mechanical Engineers, two early ones on technical subjects and the rest on aspects of management. Among the most important are: —

1902 'A Bonus System of Rewarding Labor', Trans. ASME, Vol. 23, pp. 341-372.

1903 'A Graphical Daily Balance in Manufacture', Trans. ASME, Vol. 24, pp. 1322-1336.

1908 'Training Workmen in Habits of Industry and Co-operation', Trans. ASME, Vol. 30, pp. 1037-1063.

1915 'The Relations between Production and Costs', Trans. ASME, Vol. 37, pp. 109-128.

1918 'Efficiency and Democracy', Trans. ASME, Vol. 40, pp. 799-808.

ARTICLES, ADDRESSES AND REPORTS

Gantt was a prolific writer and an active speaker. Most of his early writings were on technical problems, but from about 1902 onwards he produced an almost continuous flow of publications and pronouncements on the various aspects of management in which he was currently interested as his principles and methods developed. Over 150 titles are listed in the official biography by Alford.

Paul Sollier
(1861-1933)
Belgium

With Sollier of Belgium the contribution of psychology to the management of industry appears for the first time in this book. In continental Europe, the pioneering years were the 1920's when academic psychologists first began to look beyond their clinics to explore the practical application of psychology to problems of the human being at work in the factory. From the application of physiology on the one hand, and psychology on the other, grew in continental Europe the science of 'psychotechnics', or in Anglo-Saxon terms, industrial or occupational psychology.

Paul Sollier was the pioneer of psychotechnics in Belgium. He was by training a psychiatrist, and was for many years Professor of Pathology at the Belgian Institute for Advanced Studies in Brussels. He gradually however became interested in the practical application of psychology in industry, and in 1923 he founded the 'Section d'Ergologie' at the Institute. This developed into the 'Ecole Belge d'Ergologie' which, with its associated laboratory, became the centre of research into industrial psychology in Belgium and a model for other countries. Sollier greatly developed the activities of the school in the ten years which followed and which ended with his death. He instituted numerous new courses, undertook research projects, secured the collaboration of Belgian industry in his field of studies and laboratory experiments, and himself invented several mechanical research devices. From this work originated the Belgian contribution to vocational guidance and selection, operator training, merit rating, rehabilitation of disabled workers, and the other techniques of industrial psychology which have today so profoundly modified the understanding of people in many countries of the 'human factor' in industry.

He was a prolific writer, first in the French *Journal de Psychologie* (1925 onwards) and then in two specialized journals which he was largely instrumental in founding: the *Revue de la Science du Travail* (1929 onwards) and the *Bulletin Ergologique* of the Belgian Committee for Scientific Management (CNBOS) (1931 onwards). Today the titles of his articles seem to us familiar, often outmoded, subjects for research. But at the time their novelty was great, for these journals did much to disseminate and develop knowledge of a scientific nature about the human factor in industrial work.

Sollier summarized his life-work in his book *La Psychotechnique* (1933), finished after his death by his colleague and successor, Professor José Drabs. The Association Internationale de la Psychotechnique is today a flourishing and active institution in which participate the organizations of applied psychology of most of the countries of the free world. The name of Sollier should not be forgotten as one who did much to make psychotechnics an accepted branch of management studies.

Curriculum Vitae

1861   Born in France, of French nationality.
1890   Doctor of Medicine, Paris. Subsequently Interne of the Paris Hospitals, Director of the Sanatorium of Boulogne-sur-Seine, France, and Professor of Hygiene in the Paris Schools of Nursing.
1897   Professor of Pathology, Institut des Hautes Etudes de Belgique (Belgian Institute for Advanced Studies), Brussels.
1915-19 Director of Centre Neurologique Militaire, Lyons, France.
1924   Having the previous year created the Section d'Ergologie, he now created the Laboratory for Industrial Psycho-Physiology at the Belgian Institute for Advanced Studies.
1925   The Section d'Ergologie became the Ecole d'Ergologie annexed to the Institute, and the Laboratory undertook the research work of the School.
1933   Died aet. 72.

He was a Laureate of the Belgian Academy of Sciences (Lallemand Prize, 1920), Commander of the Legion of Honour, of the Order of Leopold, and of the Order of Orange of Nassau: Knight of Christ of Portugal: and Knight of Saint-Anne of Russia.

Personal Characteristics

Sollier is remembered as having been physically robust and as possessing, in addition to his more serious qualities, great charm.

Selected Publications

BOOKS

1933 Sollier and Drabs: *La Psychotechnique (Psychotechnics: Introduction to a Technique for Studying the Human Factor in Work)*
Brussels: Editions du Comité Central Industriel de Belgique. Paris: Alcan.

ARTICLES

Sollier published more than 150 articles, of which from 1926 to 1933 the greater part were on psycho-physiological subjects related to the study of the human factor in industry and published in the new journals devoted to psychotechnics: *Revue de la Science du Travail* (1929 onwards) and *Bulletin Ergologique du Comité National Belge de l'Organisation Scientifique* (1931 onwards).
The following are some of the titles:
'Automatization in work'
'Experiment in functional classification of looms for the purpose of vocational guidance'
'Fatigue and energy expenditure'
'Medicine of industry and the factory'
'Practical study of attention'
'The prediction of accurate motor performance'
'Pre-selection of morse telegraphists'
'Problem of aptitudes'
'Psychotechnical research on filing clerks'
'Rational choice of typists and stenographers'
'Reaction time to stop signals'
'Scientific choice of chauffeurs'
'Technical aptitude and apprenticeship'
'Technique of vocational guidance'

Hugo Münsterberg
(1863-1916)
United States

Hugo Münsterberg was the father of industrial psychology—the first man to propose that the new knowledge which inductive psychology was developing in universities and experimental laboratories could be put to use to further the objectives of industry. He was also the first to define the scope and method of this new applied science.

Not only was Münsterberg the foremost among theoretical psychologists of his time, but he had also early in his career been initiating the use of psychology for practical purposes—education and crime-detection for example. From about 1910 he and his students began experimental research into its application to industry, trying out their tests in many large industrial plants. The outcome was Münsterberg's pioneering book *Psychology and Industrial Efficiency* in 1913, preceded by a German text in 1912. Münsterberg distinguished two significant social movements in America, to both of which psychology could make a contribution: 'the effort to furnish to pupils leaving school guidance in their choice of a vocation, and the ... movement toward scientific management in commerce and industry'.[1] After paying a perceptive tribute to the work of F. W. Taylor, and stressing that applied psychology is concerned with means, not ends, Münsterberg put forward in this book his programme for the contribution of the psychologist to industry:

'We select three chief purposes of business life, purposes which are important in commerce and industry and every economic endeavour. We ask how we can find the men whose mental qualities make them best fitted for the work which they have to do; secondly, under what psychological conditions we can secure the greatest and most satisfactory output of work from every man; and finally how we can produce most completely the influences on human minds which are desired in the interests of business. In other words, we ask how to find the best possible work, and how to secure the best possible effects.'[2]

He supported this systematic formulation of the aims of the new science by giving the results of his experiments under each of the three heads. One of these experiments, his tests for the selection of street-car drivers, was entirely novel. It marked the beginning of vocational guidance on scientific lines in industry.

The book stimulated the development of the new science not only in Germany and the United States, but elsewhere also. Great numbers of business men came to consult Münsterberg at Harvard. In the First World War, his influence was immeasurably extended when nearly every combatant nation used psychology to select and train its armed forces. The United States, on entering the war in 1917, developed and applied army tests for two million men—an unprecedented experiment in the use of psychology. In great measure owing to Münsterberg's work, industrial psychology was, by the end of the war, firmly established as one of the most important aspects of the science of management.

Curriculum Vitae

1863   Born on 1st June in Danzig, Germany, of Jewish parentage. His father was a lumber merchant.
1872   Gymnasium of Danzig.

[1] H. Münsterberg: *Psychology and Industrial Efficiency*, page 39.
[2] *ibid*, page 24.

1882	University of Geneva (one semester), then University of Leipzig studying medicine and psychology.
1885	Ph.D. in psychology, University of Leipzig, under Wundt.
1887	Doctor of Medicine, University of Heidelberg.
1887-92	Lecturer, then assistant professor, in philosophy at University of Freiburg, teaching psychology privately in his spare time.
1892-5	At the age of 29 he went to Harvard University at the invitation of William James to take charge of the psychological laboratory as professor of experimental psychology.
1895-7	Resumed teaching at Freiburg.
1897	Returned permanently to Harvard as professor of psychology.
1903	Largely through his efforts, the cornerstone was laid of Emerson Hall at Harvard University, the third floor of which was used as a laboratory specially equipped for experimental psychology.
1910	Exchange professor from Harvard to University of Berlin, where he helped to create the Deutsch-America Institute.
1912	Attended the meeting of German experimental psychologists in Berlin.
1916	Died on 16th December aet. 53, at Harvard.

He received the honorary degrees of A.M. from Harvard in 1901, LL.D. from Washington University, St. Louis, in 1904, and Litt.D. from Lafayette College in 1907.

He was a President of the American Psychological Association in 1898 and of the American Philosophical Association in 1908; was a Fellow of the American Academy of Arts and Sciences and a member of the Washington Academy of Sciences; organizer and Vice-President of the International Congress of Arts and Sciences at St. Louis (1904); Vice-President of the International Philosophical Congress at Heidelberg.

Personal Characteristics

Hugo Münsterberg was in every sense an outstanding figure. It has been said that from the outset of his brilliant career he was 'a storm-centre, the object of both vehement attacks and unstinted praise'.[1] His Jewish parentage (although he became a Christian) and the personal antagonisms he aroused blocked his career in Germany, and although he achieved greatness in his adopted country, the United States, he never relinquished his German nationality and continued to hope for acceptance in his Fatherland.

[1] Quoted in Roback: *History of American Psychology*, page 200.

99

He was a great publicist and sought to influence affairs. His books and articles written in popular style and his many public activities brought psychology to the attention of the world at large and greatly advanced its acceptance by practical men in industry. It was no mean achievement for one who was also recognized as a foremost authority on the theory of the subject. His ingenuity in suggesting new fields for experiment was extraordinary. As he became more and more a public personage, he had less time to give his students. ' . . . students were too awed by his extra-curricular activities to bother him; for surely they would not be expected to intrude when he was closeted with the Argentine ambassador, or was serving as host to a German prince, or giving an interview to a metropolitan editor, or advising the head of a detective bureau, or entertaining a wealthy brewer, who might be enlisted as a patron of a projected museum.'[1]

Perhaps because he did not achieve a real bond with his students, he left no disciples and his reputation did not endure as long as it deserved, being marred towards the close of his life by his political activities in Germany and the United States. Yet he was 'of a kindly spirit, hospitable, generous, appreciative of others. His mental energy seemed limitless, his industry tireless, his optimism unquenchable'.[2] Above all, his contemporaries recognized in him a giant of originality and his students have testified to his influence upon them: 'In his seminary, he was at his best, and there we got the meat of our work. Never did any loose conclusion or faulty method get by him . . . We were all drawn to Harvard by the same force—it was *the* centre for psychology at the time . . . He radiated scientific impulses, and profoundly altered the course of American psychology . . .'.[3]

Selected Publications

Münsterberg wrote in all more than twenty volumes, besides a prodigious number of articles in periodicals. Only those publications relating to the applications of psychology to industry are noted here.

1910 *American Problems—From the Point of View of a Psychologist*
New York: Moffatt, Yard and Company.
(Contains chapters on 'The Choice of a Vocation' and 'The Market and Psychology.)

---

[1] Roback: *op. cit.*, page 204.
[2] 'Minute on the Life and Services of Professor Hugo Münsterberg', *Harvard University Gazette*, reporting a meeting of the Faculty of Arts and Sciences on 16th January,1917.
[3] K. Dunlap: *History of Psychology in Autobiography*, vol. ii page 42. Quoted in Roback: *op. cit.*, page 199. It should be mentioned that the magnetic attraction at Harvard at this time was not only Münsterberg but also his senior colleague William James.

1912 *Psychologie und Wirtschaftsleben*
Leipzig: J. A. Barth. Republished with modifications as:
1913 *Psychology and Industrial Efficiency*
320 pages. Boston: Houghton, Mifflin Co.; London: Constable & Co.
1914 *Grundzuge der Psychotechnik*
Leipzig. (Not translated into English.)
1914 *Psychology, General and Applied*
New York: Appleton.
1918 *Business Psychology*
Chicago: La Salle Extension University.
(In the series of texts on Business Administration issued to students of the Business Administration Course.)

Dexter Simpson Kimball
(1865-1952)
United States

Dean Dexter Kimball's earliest contribution to management, of the many he made in a long life of service to the American engineering profession, was his decision in 1904 to offer an elective course of lectures in works administration to senior students in mechanical engineering at Cornell University. This was the first course in any American university to teach the principles of management with full reference to the pioneering work accomplished up to that time by F.

W. Taylor. As Kimball himself recognized in his autobiography, the course was the fruit of his immediate appreciation of Taylor's paper *Shop Management,* read to The American Society of Mechanical Engineers the previous year. Kimball recorded his view that 'this remarkable paper was . . . the first effort to apply logical methods to the problems of production and management. No other single document has had such a profound effect upon American industry and management'.[1]

He had wished to call his new course at Cornell 'economics of production'.

'but Dean Smith thought that was a little high-brow, and so we settled on works administration as more likely to get by the Committee on Courses. For the first time I as a teacher experienced the skepticism that many educators display toward new educational ideas. One of the older professors remarked that he saw no reason why I should not offer such a course, but for the life of him he could not see what I could put in it . . . Anyway, the Committee on Courses agreed that no serious harm could be done by my course in works administration . . . So far as I know, these were the first lectures on the economics of production given in any university in this country. There had been books and lectures on shop systems, costs, etc., but I believe this was the first effort to inform engineering students of the economic basis of modern ,production.'[2]

The lead which Cornell University thus took in teaching the new science of management was long maintained. Four years later, in 1908, the new Harvard School of Business Administration hesitated for some time before deciding to adopt the Taylor system as the basis of its teaching on shop management.

Kimball's book which grew out of these lectures at Cornell, *Principles of Industrial Organization* (1913) was a pioneering effort in management literature and long remained a standard textbook. Almost forty years later it was still being issued in a new edition to meet the steady demand from students and from practising engineers and managers. Scholarly yet practical in its review of the whole field of management principles and practice, it has been the basis of many engineers' management education in Europe as well as in America.

Kimball was a happy example of that blend of practical experience with academic work which has enriched American teaching of management. He lived to a ripe old age and rendered outstanding services to American engineering, to engineering education, and to the science

---

[1] Dexter S. Kimball: *I Remember,* page 84.
[2] *ibid,* page 85.

of management. At Cornell University he influenced hundreds of undergraduates, among them many future leaders of industry. In his public and consulting work he was in contact in speeches and writings with very many teachers, college administrators, and engineers, and he actively participated in most of the societies and organizations concerned with the advancement of management. His achievement may be measured by the many honours which came to him and the unique collection of management medals of which he was the recipient.

Curriculum Vitae

1865   Born on 21st October in New River, New Brunswick, Canada. His family went to California to settle during his boyhood.

1881-7   Apprentice and journeyman with Pope & Talbot, Port Gamble, Washington, D.C.

1887-93   In shops of Union Iron Works, San Francisco.

1893-6   Studied mechanical engineering at Stanford University. 1896 A.B. in Engineering, 1913 M.E.

1896-8   In engineering department of Union Iron Works, San Francisco.

1898-1901   Assistant professor of machine design, Sibley College, Cornell University.

1901-4   Works manager, Stanley Electric Manufacturing Co., Pittsfield, Mass.

1904-5   Professor of machine construction, Sibley College, Cornell University.

1905-15   Professor of machine design and construction, Cornell University, also undertaking consulting work in industry.

1915-20   Professor of industrial engineering, Sibley College, Cornell University.

1920-36   First Dean of the unified College of Engineering, Cornell University, subsequently Emeritus.

1918 &   Acting President, Cornell University.
1929-30

1941   Chairman, Tools and Equipment group, Priorities Division, Office of Production Management, Washington.

1944   Special lecturer in industrial organization and management in the Federal War Training programme, and also in the Postgraduate School of the U.S. Naval Academy.

1952   Died on 1st November aet. 87.

He held the following degrees: LL.D., Rochester University, 1926; D.Sc., Case School of Applied Science, 1930; D.E., Kansas State

College (1933), Northeastern University (1934) and Lehigh University (1939).

He was President of The American Society of Mechanical Engineers (1922) and Honorary Member from 1939; President of the American Engineering Council (1926-8); and President of the Society for the Promotion of Engineering Education (1929). He was awarded the following Medals:

1933 Lamme Gold Medal of the Society for the Promotion of Engineering Education.

1933 Worcester Reed Warner Gold Medal of The American Society of Mechanical Engineers.

1943 Gantt Medal of The American Society of Mechanical Engineers and the American Management Association ('for outstanding attainment in the teaching and practice of industrial management and for distinguished contributions to its literature').

1948 Taylor Key of the Society for the Advancement of Management.

Personal Characteristics

'... There exists in memory a portrait of this dynamic dean. He enters with cheery welcome and quick, sure step. He perches his active and slender body on the corner of a desk or table, one foot dangling and swaying to and fro. From his hands hangs a not too elegant hat. He chuckles good naturedly, head cocked on one side. The intense piercing eyes sparkle with interest and good humor. His manner and language are simple, unaffected. Here is a warm, genial, kindly and friendly person, repeating like Homer of old, stories that are dear to him.

One such story called for a bit of acting. It was the Dean's impersonation of the serious-minded but dreary college professor at a faculty meeting. Standing behind a table and leaning on his right arm, the Dean would begin a finely spun academic argument with the opening words, "On the one hand". After covering all the points on that side of the case he would shift his weight to the left arm and take a new lease of his theme by saying "But on the other hand". Thus the objective and analytical mind of the professor would exhaust all the possibilities of debate on both sides of the question without arriving at a single clear-cut conclusion ...

Here, in these and other stories, is wisdom disguised in homespun, and the best of life recaptured and retold by an optimist who had found most things and most people good and hid from his friends the memories of events that were evil or sad ... With stories told and farewells spoken, there was a quick movement of the hand to put in place the sparse locks across a balding head, and he was gone, having refreshed and enriched the lives of those he left behind.'[1]

Selected Publications

BOOKS

1909 *Elements of Machine Design* (with John H. Barr)
New York: John Wiley & Sons Inc.
1911 *Industrial Education*
Ithaca: Cornell University Press.
1913 *Principles of Industrial Organization*
478 pages. New York: McGraw-Hill Book Co.
1914 *Elements of Cost Finding*
New York: Alexander Hamilton Institute.
1919 *Plant Management*
New York: Alexander Hamilton Institute.
1929 *Industrial Economics*
New York: McGraw Hill Publishing Co.
1953 *I Remember*
259 pages. New York: McGraw Hill.

ARTICLES

A complete list of the 269 pamphlets, magazine articles, etc., written by Dexter S. Kimball is given in his autobiography *I Remember*.

[1] From *Mechanical Engineering*, December 1952. (New York: The American Society of Mechanical Engineers).

Karol Adamiecki
(1866-1933)
Poland

Karol Adamiecki distinguished himself among the pioneers of management by his original contribution to management theory, by the part he took in the Polish and international movements for scientific management, and by his striking practical success.

His original contribution to management theory was contemporary with, but initially quite independent of, that of F. W. Taylor. From 1895 onwards he was using his experience as an engineer in Polish and Russian rolling mills to formulate principles of organization and in particular his 'theory of harmonization', which set out a law governing the planning and control of teamwork in production. To apply this theory he developed the 'harmonogram', a graphical device for simultaneously charting several complicated operations and thus ensuring the harmonization of a large number of activities. He constructed the first harmonogram in 1896. In rolling mills and mechanical engineering factories in the chemical industry, agriculture and mining, within Poland and abroad, the introduction of harmonograms led to increases in output between 100 and 400%. Adamiecki continued to develop his theory with remarkable results until his death. He described it and the results of its application for the first time in 1903 before the Society of Russian Engineers in Ekaterinoslaw; it caused a sensation in Russian technical circles. Its general principles, as well as the techniques associated with their application, follow the same lines that Taylor laid down for scientific management. Thus in the same year when F. W. Taylor was establishing a landmark in the management movement of the West with his paper *Shop Management,* Adamiecki was preparing the East to receive the new ideas, although the name of Taylor was yet unknown either to himself or to his audience. Had this contribution been made in a language more accessible to the West, it would have achieved the yet wider recognition that it well merited.

From 1903 onwards, Adamiecki was the pioneer of the Polish management movement. While continuing his work as an engineer and a consultant he pursued his self-appointed task for some years by the writing of articles on aspects of organization and management. Then in 1919 he was appointed as a lecturer in Management at Warsaw Polytechnic, later becoming the first Professor of Management. In the same year he set up an Institute for Propaganda in favour of Rationalization. Between 1919 and 1924 he fostered, in a large number of towns in Poland, the establishment of groups of engineers for the study of scientific management, and in 1925 his efforts resulted in the foundation of the Polish Institute of Scientific Management in Warsaw. He became the first chairman and director of the Institute.

Already by the end of the First World War Adamiecki's reputation had spread far beyond the frontiers of Poland, and in 1926 the International Committee for Scientific Management (CIOS) appointed him its first Vice-President. Soon after, he was offered a seat on the Board of the International Management Institute which was set up in Geneva in 1927.

At the Fifth International Management Congress in Amsterdam in 1932, he received the Gold Medal of the International Committee. It would have made Karol Adamiecki sad to know that Poland, a country in the vanguard of the management movement of his generation, no longer takes her lace among the members of the International Committee for Scientific Management.

Curriculum Vitae

1866   Born on 18th March in Dabrowa Gornicza, Poland, son of a mining engineer. He was educated at the Higher Technical School, Lodz, and took an engineering degree in St Petersburg, Russia, in 1891.

1891-99 Engineer in the Bank Smelting Works, Dabrowa Gornicza, working from 1896 onwards on the problem of increasing rolling mill output.

1899-   In charge of the rolling department of the Hartman Smelt-
1905   ing Works, Lugansk, and then technical director in the rolling mills for pipes and iron in Ekaterinoslaw. During this period he carried out technical research incorporated in various papers, and designed several important constructional installations.

1906-18 Worked in Poland and Russia as a consulting engineer, and was at the same time a director of a smelting works in Ostrow (1906) and managing director of The Ceramic Works Ltd. at Korwinow (1907-11). During this period he built several ceramic furnaces of his own design.

1919-22 Lecturer at Warsaw Polytechnic.

1922-33 First Professor in the newly-created Chair of Industrial Organization and Management, Warsaw Polytechnic.

1825-33 Co-founder, first Chairman of the Board and first Director, Polish Institute of Scientific Management, Warsaw.

1933   Died 16th May act. 67, after a long illness.

He held the Commodore Cross of the Order of Polonia Restituta, and the Czechoslovakia Order of the White Lion. He was a member *honoris causa* of the Masaryk Academy of Arts (Czechoslovakia 1928) for his theory of harmonization, and of the Academy of Technical Science, Warsaw. He was President of the Executive Committee of the Association of Organizing Engineers in Poland.

Personal Characteristics

Adamiecki's career was one of unusual struggle, for it was not politically easy for a Pole of his generation to achieve a leading position in the industry of Eastern Europe, and in his later years he was tragically afflicted with the physical infirmity of paralysis. The illness which was to cause his death prevented him from coming to Amsterdam to receive his Gold Medal in person in 1932.

The memory which his friends retain of him was of a man of great courage. He is remembered also for his perfect courtesy and broadmindedness, as a teacher, as a friend, and lastly, as a citizen of Europe by virtue of the wholehearted support he gave to the international management movement.

Selected Publications

From 1903 onwards Adamiecki contributed a very large number of papers and articles to Polish and foreign reviews on the social and economic effects of rationalization, on the part played by the engineer in industry, on methods of wage payment, and on the humanization of work; for instance:

1903 'Principles of Collective Work'
To Society of Russian Engineers, Ekaterinoslaw.
1909 'The Graphical Method of Organization of Work in Rolling Mills'
Nos. 17-20. *Przeglad Techniczny.*

He was also very active in an editorial capacity, from 1925 onwards as director of the Polish Institute of Scientific Management, in promoting the translation into Polish of foreign works on management, particularly the writings of Taylor.

BOOK

1948 *Harmonizacja Pracy* (Harmonization of Labour)
Posthumously published collection of articles by Adamiecki on his theory of harmonization. 118 pages. Warsaw: Instytut Naukowy Organizacji i Kierownictwa.

Alexander Hamilton Church
(1866-1936)
United States

A. Hamilton Church's contribution to management is the more
worthy of mention in this book because it has been neglected. It was
twofold. Church was, first, a pioneer in both Britain and America of
modern cost and works accounting, and secondly, author of one of
the earliest standard textbooks on scientific management.

Church spent his early career in England before going permanently
to the United States. In 1901, while still living in England, he published a series of articles in the *Engineering Magazine* of New York
entitled: 'The Proper Distribution of Establishment Charges'. These
articles took rank as a work of reference in accounting literature both
in Britain and the United States.[1] At that time the rudimentary costing methods in use for allocating overhead charges were beginning
to be displaced by the 'machine hour rate' method, whose adoption
has been described years later as the greatest single step forward in

[1] See preface to the articles, which were reprinted in book form in 1916.

111

modern times in costing technique.[1] Church made important improvements in the machine hour rate and combined with it his 'supplementary rate' and his 'general establishment charges'.

Subsequent application of his methods in the Hans Renold concern in England and elsewhere proved that they were not in practice the solution in line with future development. But his pioneering work has been acknowledged by a sometime President of the Institute of Cost and Works Accountants (England and Wales) who has said that Church 'probably did more than anyone, both directly and indirectly, to promote costing as it is now known, chiefly because he promoted thought'.[2] In effect Church had, in these articles, been the first to define the real aims of cost accounting, and in his emphasis on the conception of normal costs and abnormal losses had pointed the way to the technique of 'standard' costs on which cost accounting is so extensively based today.

Church had from the outset of his career been interested in the more general questions of organization and management. No doubt his interest was in part aroused by his early association with J. Slater Lewis. At B. & S. Massey in England between 1898 and 1900 he is credited with having introduced into the office something closely resembling work study as we know it today. For example, he had castors fixed on the juniors' chairs to ease the task of sorting Job Cards in the Works Order Bins. In 1900 he published his first article on organization. By 1906 he was probably living in the United States and was enthusiastically supporting the work of F. W. Taylor. A little later he was undertaking consultancy work in management in all its aspects, and in 1914 he published his book *The Science and Practice of Management*.

On this work rests Church's second claim to the title of pioneer. It has been called on high authority 'in every sense of the word a pioneering effort of fundamental importance and value'.[2] In it Church explained that, just as in his earlier articles on establishment charges he had been endeavouring to ascertain the fundamental facts of production from the viewpoint of *costs*, he was now pursuing the same aim from the viewpoint of *management*, and seeking to substitute, for the disconnected ideas initially represented by the elements of scientific management, an approach to the reduction of the regulative principles of management to their simplest terms. In his preface to the book, Church claimed that these principles, in the form he presented them jointly with L. P. Alford in an article in 1912, were

1 Hopf: *Soundings in the Literature of Management: Fifty Books the Educated Practitioner should Know* (details of publication in Appendix II).
2 Roland Dunkerley: 'A Historical Review of the Institute and the Profession'. To the Institute of Cost and Works Accountants, Great Britain. 1946.

afterwards adopted by the well-known committee appointed by The American Society of Mechanical Engineers to investigate the new systems of management in its report, 'The Present State of the Art of Industrial Management'. It appears that Church's book did not attract lasting attention, owing perhaps to lack of aggressive publicity. It deserved a better fate, for it presents an early and most remarkable synthesis of management.

A better fate might also have attended the memory of Church himself. Although he is recognized as a pioneer of management both in Great Britain and in the United States, and although he lived to a ripe age, the facts of his life and work are hidden in obscurity.

Curriculum Vitae

1866   Born on 11th October in England.

There is no certain record of where he was born or who his parents were. One report would indicate he was born in the British West Indies. Another more probable report states he was born in Brooklyn, that his father was a wealthy ship merchant, that his family moved to England in Church's boyhood, and that he was educated at Oxford. He practised as an electrical engineer, worked for the National Telephone Company, and then for P. & R. Jackson & Co. Ltd., Salford, Lancs., working with J. Slater Lewis from whom he learnt a great deal.

He then became a consultant and a specialist in costing systems.

1898-1900   With B. & S. Massey Ltd., Manchester where he reorganized the costing and financial accounting methods used, and made some improvements in office management.

1900-05   Introduced his own costing methods into Hans Renold Ltd., Manchester.

He had already transferred his chief activities to the United States and probably about this period became resident in America. He became an early supporter of Scientific Management and spent the rest of his career as a consultant and a writer on management.

1912-15   Consultant engineer with Patterson, Teale & Dennis of Boston.

late 1920's   Consultant to the Mt. Hope Finishing Company, North
or early   Dighton, Mass., converters of cotton cloth, where he set
1930's   up the production lines and established a realistic cost system.

1936   Died on 11th February aet. 70, in Taunton, Mass.

Personal Characteristics

Much patient research by The American Society of Mechanical Engineers has shed new light on the memory of this well-nigh forgotten pioneer of the management movement. Church was an exceptionally timid and lonely man. Though he was an authority on accounting and on management, he never joined any of the recognized accounting societies, or the Taylor Society, ASME, or any other engineering society. He refused all invitations to speak in public for he lacked the courage to face a group of people. Yet those few who knew him say he was an unusually charming man, one with whom it was a pleasure to work, and that he had gifts, not shared by all the early 'efficiency experts', for drawing out useful contributions from these with whom he worked and for finding compromise solutions which won general satisfaction. He was a perfectionist in work, almost an artist. He could not bear daily routine. Sometimes he would vanish for weeks at a time and then reappear with a new, constructive idea.

He never married. Gradually as he grew older, he became more and more a recluse. It was rumoured that he had wealthy relatives, but there is no indication that he ever saw them, or they him. He died alone, with no obituary notices either in the local or in the metropolitan journals. Yet his contribution to management was as great or greater than that of many whose names are famous in the movement. This shy, lonely and forgotten man takes a place in The Golden Book of Management that he doubly earned.

Selected Publications

BOOKS

1914 *The Science and Practice of Management*
535 pages. New York: Engineering Magazine Co. Later published by John R. Dunlop.

1916 *The Proper Distribution of Expense Burden*
144 pages. New York: Engineering Magazine Co. (Reprint in book form, with an added preface, of the series of articles published in 1901 with the title 'The Proper Distribution of Establishment Charges').

1917 *Manufacturing Costs and Accounts*
New York: McGraw Hill Publishing Co.

1923 *The Making of An Executive*
New York: D. Appleton & Co.

1930 *Overhead Expense in Relation to Costs, Sales and Profits*
New York: McGraw Hill.

ARTICLES

1900 'The Meaning of Commercial Organization'
New York: *Engineering Magazine*, Vol. 20. No. 3 December,
pp. 391-8.
1901 'British Industrial Welfare'
New York: *Cassier's Magazine*, Vol. 19, pp. 404-408.
1901 'The Proper Distribution of Establishment Charges'
New York: *Engineering Magazine*, Vols. 21 and 22 (articles in
six issues).
1906 'Cost and Time-Keeping Outfit of the Taylor System'
New York: *American Machinist*, Vol. 29, pt. 2, pp. 761-763.
1910 'Organization by Production Factors'
New York: *Engineering Magazine*, Vol. 38 (in 6 parts).
1910 'Production Factors in Cost Accounting and Works Management'
New York: Engineering Magazine Co.
1911 'Distribution of the Expense Burden'
New York: *American Machinist*, Vol. 34, pt. 2, pp. 991-992,
999.
1911 'Has "Scientific Management" Science?'
New York: *American Machinist*, Vol. 35, pp. 108-112.
1911 'Intensive Production and the Foreman'
New York: *American Machinist*, Vol. 34, pt. 2, pp. 830-831.
1911 'The Meaning of Scientific Management'
New York: *Engineering Magazine*, Vol. 41, pp. 97-101.
1912 'The Principles of Management', with L. P. Alford
New York: *American Machinist*, Vol. 36, pp. 857-861.
1913 'Practical Principles of Rational Management'
New York: *Engineering Magazine*, Vols. 44 and 45 (3 parts in
each Vol.).
1913 'Premium, Piece-Work and Expense Burden'
New York: *Engineering Magazine*, Vol. 46, pp. 7-18.
1914 'The Scientific Basis of Manufacturing Management'
New York: Efficiency Society. *Journal*, Vol. 3, Feb., pp. 8-15.
1914 'What are Principles of Management?'
New York: Efficiency Society. *Journal*, Vol. 3, Feb., pp. 16-18.
1916 'Industrial Management with Discussion'
San Francisco: *Transactions* of the International Engineering
Congress, San Francisco, 1915.

John Lee
(1867-1928)
Great Britain

John Lee was the editor of an outstanding work of reference on management published in Great Britain—Pitman's *Dictionary of Industrial Administration* (1928).

This massive two-volume 'Comprehensive Encyclopaedia of the Organization, Administration and Management of Modern Industry'

116

contained contributions from over a hundred of the best-known contemporary authorities on management both in Britain and America. The work marked an epoch. Its only fault was to be in advance of its time. A reprint did not prove commercially possible and much of the influence it could have had was lost by the fact that copies were not easily to be found. It continues to be used today by those fortunate enough to possess it.

The editorial task of codifying the best management thought of the day was congenial to John Lee, who was particularly gifted in clear exposition. Himself the author of several of the articles, he handled with great skill the problem of harmonizing the contributions of so many authorities without imposing a meaningless conformity. His editorial preface was an illuminating analysis of the interest in management to be observed at the time. The compilation of the work must have absorbed the greater part of the leisure time of his last years, for he retired from executive work only in 1927.

While this editorial feat was Lee's greatest single achievement, he had long been a writer of originality on management. His books had a philosophical quality too often lacking in management literature. His writings on organization, administration and personnel subjects were a serious contribution to thinking, particularly in interpreting American scientific management into British industrial terms. He reinforced the influence of his books and articles by much public speaking. He lectured regularly at the Rowntree Management Conferences and elsewhere, and was active in the Institute (now Royal Institute) of Public Administration in its early days. His pronouncements carried respect by virtue of his own practical achievement. He was manager of a large-scale enterprise with many international connexions—the Central Telegraph Office of the British Post Office.

In the advancement of truth, the clear definition of terms is an important phase. In making his final contribution to management in this field, Lee rendered a substantial service.

Curriculum Vitae

1867   Born on 16th June in Liverpool, of Irish parents.
        MA and MComSc (Belfast).
1883   Entered Post Office as a telegraphist in Liverpool.
1901   Assistant superintendent.
1907   Assistant traffic manager for telephones, at Post Office Headquarters, London.
1909-10 Helped to re-organize the Indian Railway Telegraph System.
1916   Deputy chief inspector of telegraph and telephone traffic.

1916	Member of Committee on High-Speed Telegraphy.
1917	Helped to organize the employment of women as telegraphists and telephonists behind the Allied lines in France.
1918	Postmaster of Belfast, where he introduced a system of staff consultation on the Whitley model.
1919	Controller of the Central Telegraph Office.
1920	Member of the Post Office delegation to a European conference on the restoration of communications, organized by the League of Nations.
1925	Head of British delegation to the International Telegraph Conference, Paris.
1926	Member of International Committee investigating code language in telegrams.
1927	Retired and joined the Boards of the Automatic Telephone Company and of some of its associated companies.
1928	Died on 24th December aet. 61, on the ship Laconia returning from the United States.

He was made a C.B.E. in 1923. He was a founder member of the Institute (now Royal Institute) of Public Administration and Chairman of its Council (1925-6).

Personal Characteristics

'Joined to a quick and perceptive mind, Lee possessed imagination and a rare gift of sympathy, which won for him in a high degree the affection of subordinates and colleagues and of a wide circle of friends. He possessed a native and genuine eloquence, and few could tell a story better.'[1] His conciliatory spirit and balanced outlook were of immense service to many younger men who were struggling to realise the new concepts of management in industrial practice.

He was interested in the applications of psychology to administrative problems. Another special interest was the reconciliation of the demands of industrial efficiency with the principles of Christianity and he wrote several important books on this subject. His activity in management was additional to his full-time duties in the Post Office (where he had risen from the ranks to a leading executive position) and it is certain that his ceaseless activity led to the permanent impairment of his health. When he retired he received remarkable personal tributes from business colleagues in Australia, Canada, America, France, Italy and Germany.

---

[1] The Times. 28th December. 1928 (obituary).

Selected Publications

BOOKS

1913 *Pitman's Economics of Telegraphs and Telephones*
93 pages. London: Pitman.

1917 *Telegraph Practice: A Study of Comparative Methods*
111 pages. London: Longmans.

1921 *Management: A Study of Industrial Organization*
134 pages. London: Pitman.

1921 *Plain Economics: An examination of Essential Issues*
118 pages. London: Pitman.

1923 *Industrial Organization: Developments and Prospects*
130 pages. London: Pitman.

1924 *The Principles of Industrial Welfare*
124 pages. London: Pitman.

1925 *An Introduction to Industrial Administration*
202 pages. London: Pitman.

1928 *Letters to An Absentee Director*
112 pages. London: Pitman (first published in *The Times
Trade and Engineering Supplement*).

1928 (Editor) *Dictionary of Industrial Administration*
London: Pitman. 2 vols. Vol. 1, 543 pages; Vol. 2, 607 pages.
Author of articles under the following headings: —
Discipline
Specialization and Co-ordination
Employee Shareholding
Significant Reports
Labour Banks
Trade Schools
Distribution of Processes
By-Products
Census of Production
Migration of Industries

ARTICLES

He was a frequent contributor to *The Economist* and to *The Times
Trade and Engineering Supplement*, and editor of the *Journal* of the
Institute (now Royal Institute) of Public Administration.

1922 'Works Councils and Similar Institutions in America, France,
Germany and England'
Papers of the Rowntree Lecture Conference, Oxford, 21st-25th
September.

1922 'Ideals of Industry' with Sydney Pascall
Papers of the Rowntree Lecture Conference, Oxford, 21st-25th
September.

1923 'The Ethics of Industry'
Papers of the Rowntree Lecture Conference, Oxford, 20th-24th September.
1926 'The Developments of Industrial Administration in Europe: An Attempt at Comparison'
Papers of the Rowntree Lecture Conference, Oxford, 30th September to 4th October.
1928 'The Pros and Cons of Functionalization'
Papers of the Rowntree Lecture Conference, Oxford, 27th-30th September. Reproduced as a chapter in *Papers in the Science of Administration* by Gulick and Urwick, New York, Columbia University, 1937.

Walther Rathenau
(1867-1922)
Germany

Walther Rathenau is chiefly remembered in Germany as a captain of industry who became a government servant and a statesman. But he was also an important forerunner of the German management movement by virtue of his writings on industrial organization and on the place of industry in society.

Rathenau was preoccupied by the economic problems of Germany arising out of her great increase in industrialization at the turn of the century. He became prominent before 1914 as a writer with radical though constructive political views. An able administrator in the industries which he controlled, he showed himself equally able as a government administrator during the war, and his writings on economic and social subjects in 1917-18 made him a passionately discussed figure and drew him into the political life which was to end in his assassination.

Rathenau set out his theories on industrial organization in his books *In Days to Come* (1917) and *The New Economy* (1918). It was through changes in the management of industry that Germany's economic and social problems could be solved. In the structural aspect of industrial organization, all the unnatural barriers (such as monopolies and customs tariffs) to the rational interplay of industrial forces must be removed. When this had been done, the rational application of scientific method and planning and the use of the new power-driven machinery, whose advent was yet recent in Germany, would permit the creation of limitless industrial wealth and by this means many political problems could in turn be solved.

But the effectiveness of industry could not be built on mechanized efficiency alone. There was needed an inspiration for industry's workers, a soul to infuse industry's life. So in the dynamic aspect of industrial organization, Rathenau urged the sublimation of the profit motive by depersonalizing the ownership of industry; enterprises were to be transformed to democratic institutions by giving the workers a share in the management.

'As there is so little room for the rise of responsibility within the actual limits of his labour, the worker must be able to find this outside those limits by having a share in the management. The provisional solution of the problem is the co-operation of the workers and officials in the conduct of the undertaking.'

The final solution was to be the form of organization that Rathenau postulated as the foundation of all industrial progress—the uniting of each industry into a self-governing body in which each worker has a voice. The transformation was to be gradually and peaceably carried out by the state.

It is instructive to compare these suggestions of Rathenau with the subsequent evolution of industrial organization in Germany. In 1919, self-governing corporations were set up in the coal and potash industries under the new German constitutions. In the inter-war period 'joint management' (Mitbestimmungsrecht) or the representation of workers on the top executive board in important German industries, became law and was further extended after 1945. Rathenau's method for 'motivating' industrial groups, although it has made little impact on the theory of industrial organization in Anglo-Saxon countries, accurately anticipated German development.

As a thinker on industrial organization, Rathenau differed from the Frenchman Fayol in looking outwards to the community around him rather than inwards to the administrative processes he directed, and he differed from the American Mary Follett in leaving untouched the psychological foundations of management in favour of its social implications. He was however at one with both these thinkers in perceiving that the rational organization of industry according to principles of social responsibility holds the secret of progress for a democratic community.

Curriculum Vitae

1867   Born, of a well-connected Jewish family, son of Emil Rathenau, the founder of the Allgemeine Elektricitäts-Gesellschaft (General Electric Company).
Educated in classics at a Gymnasium, and obtained a doctor's degree at the University of Berlin after studying mathematics, physics and chemistry.

1890   Continued his studies in mechanical and electrical engineering in Munich.

1891-3   Employee of the 'Aluminium-Industrie A.G.', Neuhausen, Switzerland.

1893-9   In charge of the 'Elektro-chemische Werke G.m.b.H.' with administrative headquarters at Bitterfeld, Sachsen.

1899-   Member of the Board and Head of Department for
1902   construction of power stations, Allgemeine Elektricitäts-Gesellschaft.

1902-07   Member of the Board, 'Berliner Handels-Gesellschaft'.

by 1909   He was associated, as Director or Managing Director, with over 80 large concerns centering mainly on the Allgemeine Elektricitäts-Gesellschaft.

1914   Appointed to the War Office to organize the German system of raw material supply.

1915   President of the Allgemeine Elektricitäts-Gesellschaft.

1919   Shared in preparations of the German Government for the Versailles negotiations.

1920   German expert at the conference at Spaa.

1920-21   Member of the Socialization Commission for the reorganization of Germany's economic system.

1921   Reichminister of Reconstruction.
1922   Reichsminister of Foreign Affairs in the Wirth Cabinet.
1922   Assassinated on 24th June aet. 55, by a nationalist extremist.

Personal Characteristics

Strangely enough, Rathenau was not popular in democratic circles in spite of his radical advocacy of democratic principles both for politics and for industry. Probably he was an incomprehensible figure—a business man who preached the need of a soul; a rich man who built himself an expensive villa and yet attacked luxury; a captain of industry whose political views were more socialist than those of any of the agitators among the employees of his own factories. His family have said that at heart he was much more a poet and philosopher than a man of affairs, and that he entered business life more through feelings of duty than because he really wished it. The highlights of his later political career were his speech as Foreign Minister at the Genoa Conference in 1922 when he obtained the first diplomatic concessions for Germany, and the conclusion of the peace treaty with Russia the same year. His assassination was a tragic end for one who had been the pioneer of an idealist philosophy for German industry and society.

Selected Publications

BOOKS

1902   *Impressionen* (Impressions)
        255 pages. Leipzig: Hirzel-Verlag.
1908   *Reflexionen* (Reflections)
        270 pages. Leipzig: Hirzel-Verlag.
1912   *Zur Kritik der Zeit* (Contemporary Criticism)
        260 pages. Berlin: S. Fischer-Verlag.
1913   *Zur Mechanik des Geistes* (Mechanics of the Mind)
        348 pages. Berlin: S. Fischer-Verlag.
1916   *Deutschlands Rohstoffversorgung* (Supply of Germany's Raw Materials)
        52 pages. Berlin: S. Fischer-Verlag.
1917   *Eine Streitschrift vom Glauben* (A Polemic of Faith)
        42 pages. Berlin: S. Fischer-Verlag.
1917   *Vom Aktienwesen* (Shares)
        62 pages. Berlin: S. Fischer-Verlag.
1917   *Von kommenden Dingen* (Things to Come)
        344 pages. Berlin: S. Fischer-Verlag.

1917	*Probleme der Friedenswirtschaft* (Vortrag) (Peacetime Economic Problems) 56 pages. Berlin: S. Fischer-Verlag.
1918	*An Deutschlands Jugend* (To Germany's Youth) 126 pages. Berlin: S. Fischer-Verlag.
1918	*Die neue Wirtschaft* (The New Economy) 86 pages. Berlin: S. Fischer-Verlag.
1918-25	*Gesammelte Schriften (Werke) in 5 Bänden* (Collected Writings—Works in 5 Volumes).
1919	*Der Kaiser* (The Emperor) 60 pages. Berlin: S. Fischer-Verlag.
1919	*Der neue Staat* (The new State) 74 pages. Berlin: S. Fischer-Verlag.
1919	*Kritik der dreifachen Revolution (Apologie)* Criticism of the triple Revolution (Defence) 125 pages. Berlin: S. Fischer-Verlag.

ARTICLES AND LETTERS

Rathenau was a prolific writer and his articles and letters fill five volumes (published as *The Collected Works of Walther Rathenau*).

These writings deal with problems of social and industrial organization, political issues, reflection of German aspirations and their implications, and so on. A representative selection of titles is given in Count Kessler's biography (see details of publication in Appendix II).

Sanford Eleazer Thompson
(1867-1949)
United States

Sanford E. Thompson was one of the group of associates who helped
F. W. Taylor to develop the principles and techniques of his system
of management. The independent contribution of Thompson was
substantial. Among its most significant aspects were, first, the application of the Taylor system of management to the building industry,

126

and, secondly, the development of time study as a management tool.

It was at the suggestion of Taylor that Thompson began his work in the building industry. Taylor had developed his ideas of management in terms of the engineering shops in which he himself had always worked. From the beginning, nevertheless, he had been concerned to prove that his methods had general application in any industry, and he even hoped to bring about the publication of a series of books on management, each written in terms of a different basic industry. The building industry was a suitable one with which to start, since many of its processes were already repetitive and detailed time study could at once be put in hand.

In 1896 Thompson, acting as an independent consultant but guided by Taylor, began the study of work in the building industry which he was to pursue with infinite thoroughness for almost seventeen years. By 1903 Thompson's material for a book was well advanced. In his paper *Shop Management* Taylor said:

'Mr. Sanford E. Thompson, C.E. (Civil Engineer) started in 1896 with but small help from the writer, except as far as the implements and methods are concerned, to study the time required to do all kinds of work in the building trades. In six years he has made a complete study of eight of the most important trades—excavating, masonry (including sewer-work and paving), carpentry, concrete and cement work, lathing and plastering, slating and roofing and rock quarrying.'

and further on . . .

'The writer's chief object in inducing Mr. Thompson to undertake a scientific study of the various building trades and to join him in a publication of this work was to demonstrate on a large scale not only the desirability of accurate time-study, but the efficiency and superiority of the method of studying elementary units as outlined above. He trusts that his object may be realised and that the publication of this book may be followed by similiar work on other trades and more particularly on the details of machine shop practice, in which he is especially interested.'

The two books incorporating the results of these studies were *Concrete Plain and Reinforced* (1905) and *Construction Costs* (1912), published under the joint authorship of Thompson and Taylor. Their success was immediate and their effect revolutionary. They put forward, to replace the pure guesswork which was the only existing method of computing building labour costs, an analysis and a method which was to constitute the turning point of modern development in this field.

The technique most used by Thompson in the building industry was time study. To him belongs the credit for perfecting this 'tool' of management, and to him is attributed the invention of the decimal-dial stop-watch. The stop-watch became, years afterwards, a symbol hated by the opponents of Scientific Management. It is important to record here that throughout Thompson's career he was repeatedly called upon by labour groups to give professional advice in problems relating to the measurement of work. His and Taylor's integrity in their attitude to the use of the stop-watch was shown in 1908, when Dean Gay of the new Harvard School of Business Administration suggested that the teaching of the Taylor system should begin with a course on time-study conducted by Thompson.

'This idea Taylor combatted with vehemence; he said it would be like teaching architecture by putting cornices on houses.'[1]

The idea was abandoned. Thompson did not teach time-study until 1910, and then only to advanced students and in the context of building operations. The accusations made against Scientific Management can often be refuted most easily by reference to the words of the pioneers themselves.

Like several of Taylor's other followers, Thompson became in later life a management consultant, advising on many different aspects of management and being entrusted with several assignments of public importance. An anecdote may illustrate the genuine idealism which motivated him as it did the others of the Taylor group. In 1913 the magazine *Collier's Weekly* was running a series of articles on 'everyday heroes'. Taylor received a letter suggesting that he himself would be a suitable subject. He replied:

'My feeling is that the heroes such as are called for by *Collier's Weekly* are men who are really making great sacrifices for the good of their kind . . . I have always in my work had the satisfaction of seeing tangible results accomplished within a reasonably short time, and having these results appreciated at least by the men whom they most concern.

It is a very different story for a man to work through a term of years . . . with no recognition whatever. In fact, my friend Sanford E. Thompson, of Newton Highlands, Mass., who for a great many years worked in a tireless manner and for a very small salary, and refused to publish any of his colossal time study until it was in really a very magnificent form, is far more of a hero than I ever was.'[2]

[1] Copley: *Frederick W. Taylor*, Vol. ii, page 290.
[2] Copley: *op. cit.* vol. ii, page 434.

Curriculum Vitae

1867	Born on 13th February in Ogdensburg, New York.
1889	Graduated from Massachusetts Institute of Technology with a B.Sc. degree in Civil Engineering. Later took graduate course in chemistry.
1889-90	Engineer and draftsman on design and construction, Moosehead Pulp and Paper Company, Solon, Maine.
1890-93	Superintendent of Construction and Assistant Superintendent of Production, Manufacturing Investment Company, Madison, Maine.
1893-94	In charge of operating department, Mt. Tom Pulp and Paper Company.
1894-95	Resident engineer, water-works construction, Arlington, Massachusetts.
1895-96	Assistant engineer on hydraulic and mill design, J. P. Frizell, Boston, Massachusetts.
1896-1917	Private practice as consulting engineer and executive, Newton Highlands, Massachusetts.
1917	Lieutenant Colonel, Army Ordnance Department.
1917-49	Senior Partner, Thompson and Lichtner Co. Inc., Brookline, Massachusetts—a management and engineering consulting firm; President of the Company from 1925 onwards.
1921	Member, Hoover Committee on Elimination of Waste in Industry.
1922	Member, Economic Advisory Board to the President of the United States' Unemployment Conference.
1931	Member, Elimination of Waste Committee of the National Construction Conference.
1938	Representative of the International Industrial Relations Institute at the Oxford Management Conference.
1942-43	Consultant to Secretary of War.
1949	Died on 25th February in Phoenix, Arizona, aet. 82.

Sanford E. Thompson was a President of the Taylor Society (1932); Fellow of The American Society of Mechanical Engineers; Honorary Life Member of The American Society of Civil Engineers, and an Honorary Member and Vice-President (1917-19) of the American Concrete Institute.

Personal Characteristics

Sanford E. Thompson was a man of medium height, thin yet broad-shouldered. His real energy and imagination were sometimes hidden by a New England reticence and he was not a commanding speaker. The special quality that F. W. Taylor valued in him was his tireless patience. This was shown in the earliest days of his association with Taylor at the Manufacturing Investment Co., when Thompson was at one time assigned a forty-hour observation stretch of a woodpulp 'cooking' process. When the results proved unsatisfactory, Thompson at once cheerfully volunteered for another stretch. This demonstration of a capacity for sustained application, together with infinite thoroughness, gained him Taylor's permanent friendship.[1]

He was a devoted family man, and known for his high ethical standards.

Selected Publications

BOOKS

1901 *Taylor Differential Piece-work System*
New York: Engineering Magazine Co.

1905 *Concrete,Plain and Reinforced*, with F. W. Taylor
New York: John Wiley and Sons.

1907 *Reinforced Concrete in Factory Construction*
New York: Atlas Portland Cement Co.

1909 *Concrete in Railroad Construction*
New York: Atlas Portland Cement Co.

1912 *Concrete Costs*, with F. W. Taylor
New York: John Wiley and Sons.

1939 *Reinforced Concrete Bridges*, with F. W. Taylor and E. Smulski
New York: John Wiley and Sons.

ARTICLES

1902 'Quality of the Production in Piece Work'
New York: *Cassier's Magazine*, Vol. 23, pp. 233-237.

1913 'Time Study and Task Work'
New York: *Industrial Engineering and Engineering Digest*, Vol. 13, pp. 347-350.

1914 'A Study of Cleaning Filter Sands with no Opportunity for Bonus Payments'
New York: Trans. ASME, Vol. 36, pp. 693-706.

1915 'Construction Management', with W. O. Lichtner
Chicago: *Journal* of the Western Society of Engineers, Vol. 20, pp. 109-151.

1916 'Scientific Methods in Construction', with W. O. Lichtner
Pittsburgh: *Proceedings* of the Engineers Society of Western Pennsylvania, Vol. 32, pp. 433-465.

[1] Anecdote from Copley: *op. cit.* vol. i, page 376.

1928 'Smoothing the Wrinkles from Management, Time Study the Tool'
Bulletin of the *Taylor Society,* Vol. 13, pp. 69-86.
1935 'Opportunities for Cost Reduction in Textile Manufacturing and Selling'
Rayon and Melliand Textile Monthly, Vol. 16, pp. 314-316, 435-436, 549, 576 and 585.
1936 'Improved Pulp and Paper Quality Through Incentives'
Paper Trade Journal, Vol. 102, March 19, pp. 39-43.
1937 'Brief Survey of Management Methods in Paper Mills'
Paper Trade Journal, Vol. 104, March 11, pp. 31-36.
1938 Part-author of 'History of Scientific Management in America'
Prepared for the 1938 International Management Congress.
New York: Mechanical Engineering, Vol. 69, pp. 671-675, September 1939.
1939 'Standards in Their Relation to Production Control'
Paper Trade Journal, Vol. 109, pp. 31-35, November 9.
1940 'Increased Production for Defense Needs'
Advanced Management, Vol. 5, pp. 153-158.
1941 'Synchronized Arms Production'
Army-Ordnance, Vol. 21, pp. 475-476, March-April.
1944 'Post War Cost Reductions'
Paper Trade Journal, Vol. 119, pp. 40-47, August 17.

Mary Parker Follett
(1868-1933)
United States

Mary Parker Follett was a political and social philosopher of the first rank. Her contribution to management, among the most outstanding recorded in this book, was to apply psychological insight and the findings of the social sciences to industry and through this, to offer a new conception of the nature of management and of human relationships within industrial groups.

Before Mary Follett, industrial groups had seldom been the subject of study of political or social scientists. It was her special merit to turn from the traditional subjects of study—the state or the community as a whole—progressively to concentrate on the study of industry. In this context she not only evolved principles of human association and organization specifically in terms of industry, but also convinced large numbers of business men of the practicality of these principles in dealing with their current problems. Her approach was to analyze the nature of the *consent* on which any democratic group is based by examining the psychological factors underlying it. This consent, she suggested is not static but a continuous process, generating new and living group ideas through the interpenetration of individual ideas.

Starting from this conception of the pattern which social relationships should take within human groups, she showed that *conflict* can be constructive. It can be harnessed to the service of the group much as an engineer uses friction. The most fruitful way of resolving conflict, she said, is not domination nor even compromise, but *integration* in which the parties concerned examine together new ways of achieving their conflicting desires. Again, she showed that *authority,* in terms of the subordination of one man to another, offends human emotions and cannot be the foundation of good industrial organization. The concept of final authority inhering in the chief executive should be replaced by an authority of function in which each individual has final authority for his own allotted task. By this means, personal power gives place to 'the law of the situation' in which a *decision,* though it may appear to crystallize in an act of the chief executive, is only a 'moment in a process' which may have started with the office boy. *Leadership* is not a matter of a dominating personality. The leader should be the one most able to secure interpenetration within the group of the best ideas of both leader and led. He must have the insight not only to *meet* the next situation but to *make* it. Moreover, leaders are not only born but can also be made, through training in the understanding of human behaviour.

It will be seen that with Mary Follett the key words in the terminology of industrial organization, which up to now had been static or structural words, became active and dynamic. The four principles of organization at which she finally arrived were all active, providing for the need of four kinds of co-ordination as the basis of good management:

co-ordination by direct contact of the responsible people concerned
co-ordination in the early stages
co-ordination as a reciprocal relation of all the features in a situation
co-ordination as a continuous process

These ideas are clearly of great importance for the problems of industry, where possibilities of conflict are so numerous and where the authority concept has been so highly developed.

Her final principles were expressed in terms of industry alone, and she thus earned a place among the philosophers of management. But her contribution was more significant still in that for her the principles of organization were universal and the choice of industrial groups as the subject of study was incidental. She found more liveliness of thinking, more courage for experiment, more impulse for 'integration' in her sense of the word among business managers than among administrators of any other kind of group. But her philosophy was equally valid for any kind of purposeful human association. She was thus one of the earliest political scientists to enable those whose lot is cast in business to see their work, not only as a means of livelihood, not only as an honorable occupation with a large content of professional interest, but as a definite and vital contribution towards the building of that new social order which is the legitimate preoccupation of every thinking citizen.

Her thinking was and still remains in advance of the times. Her influence has yet to reach its peak. The extent of her immediate practical influence on many business men must however also be mentioned here. From 1924 onwards she was lecturing to business audiences in both the United States and England, and many business men sought her advice on their problems of securing and maintaining human co-operation in their concerns. She had a strong bent for the practical. The illustrations with which her writings are liberally scattered are drawn from almost every phase of life. Business men learned from her, in forthright and lucid suggestions how to approach their difficulties by taking into account the motivating desires of individuals in relation to their working groups, and how to aim in their businesses, as government must do in the larger community, at the integration of points of view. Many successful business administrators, not least B. S. Rowntree, have testified to the help afforded them in their immediate difficulties by this modest spinster lady who had never managed a business in her life.

Curriculum Vitae

1868	Born in Boston, Mass., of a Boston family.
	Educated at Thayer Academy, Boston.
	Studied Philosophy, History, Law and Political Science at Radcliffe College, Massachusetts, USA. and Newnham College, Cambridge, England, and did some graduate study in Paris.
1891	On returning to the United States she took up an active life of social work in Boston.
1900	Set up the Roxbury Debating Club in the Roxbury

	Neighbouring House in Boston, later expanding it into centres providing social, recreational and educational facilities in this poor locality.
1909 onwards	Chairman of a group renamed in 1911 the Committee on the Extended Use of School Buildings. This Committee developed the well-known 'Boston Evening Centres' for educational and recreational activities, which were taken as a model by other cities throughout the country.
1912	Member of the first Boston Placement Bureau Committee which became later the municipal 'Department of Vocational Guidance'; then Member representing the public on the Massachusetts Minimum Wage Board.
1920	Gained wide recognition as a political philosopher on the publication of *The New State*.
1924	Began giving papers on industrial organization, especially to the annual conferences for business executives in New York by the Bureau of Personnel Administration. As her experience of industry grew she came to be consulted by many business men on problems of organization and human relations.
1926 & 1928	Visited England to read papers at the Rowntree Lecture Conference and to the National Institute of Industrial Psychology.
1929	Returned to live quietly in England until shortly before her death. She shared a home in Chelsea, London, with Dame Katherine Furze of the Girl Guide Movement.
1933	Died on 18th December aet. 65, in America.

Personal Characteristics

Although Mary Follett was so distinguished a philosopher, and although she never married, she was no blue-stocking. She left in her social work in Boston a practical achievement as signal as her contribution in the realm of ideas. Her outstanding characteristic was a facility for winning the confidence and esteem of those with whom she came in contact; she established a deeply-rooted understanding and friendship with a wide circle of eminent men and women on both sides of the Atlantic. The root of this social gift was her vivid interest in life. Every individual's experience, his relations with others and with the social groups—large or small—of which he was a part, was food for her thought. She listened with alert and kindly attention, she discussed problems in a temper which drew the best out of the indi-

135

vidual with whom she was talking. She did not force her learning on the business men who called on her to assist them with their problems. 'Often,' she is reported to have said, 'they could only spare time for luncheon, but I never had such interesting meals. One of those men gave me . . . the threads of a tangle he had with his employees. He wanted me to straighten it out. I answered him straight from Fichte; he didn't know that, of course, but . . . it seemed to meet the case.'[1]

She was in herself an example of the principle which she found basic for every form of human organization, from each individual life to world relations—co-ordination. For she was a person of universal mind and viewpoint, rounded culture, combining an interest in religion, music, painting, nature, history and travel with her consuming lifetime absorption in her work. She had no taste for power or prestige at all. Even her intellectual output was limited by her rigid self-criticism, her determination to be simple and understandable at all costs, her great modesty and her wish to be of practical use in quite humble capacities.

Selected Publications

BOOKS
1909 *The Speaker of the House of Representatives*
New York.
1920 *The New State*
New York and London: Longmans, Green.
1924 *Creative Experience*
New York and London: Longmans, Green.

PAPERS ON BUSINESS ORGANISATION AND ADMINISTRATION

The majority of these papers, given between 1924 and 1933, have been collected in two books as follows:
Dynamic Administration: The Collected Papers of Mary Parker Follett. Ed H. C. Metcalf and L. Urwick. 320 pages. London: Pitman, 1941. This volume contains the following papers, given to audiences either in the United States or Great Britain.
'Constructive Conflict'
'The Giving of Orders'
'Business as an Integrative Unity'
'Power'

---

1 Quoted by F. M. Stawell in her Memoir in the Newnham College Letter for January 1935.

'How Must Business Management Develop in Order to Possess the
Essentials of a Profession'
'How Must Business Management Develop in Order to Become a
Profession'
'The Meaning of Responsibility in Business Management'
'The Influence of Employee Representation in a Remolding of the
Accepted Type of Business Manager'
'The Psychology of Control'
'The Psychology of Consent and Participation'
'The Psychology of Conciliation and Arbitration'
'Leader and Expert'
'Some Discrepancies in Leadership Theory and Practice'
'Individualism in a Planned Society'
Freedom and Co-ordination: Lectures in Business Organization by
Mary Parker Follett. Ed L. Urwick. 89 pages. London: Pitman,
1949. This volume contains the following papers, the first given to the
Taylor Society in New York, and the remainder to the London
School of Economics, London.
'The Illusion of Final Authority'
'The Giving of Orders'
'The Basis of Authority'
'The Essentials of Leadership'
'Co-ordination'
'The Process of Control'

Frank Bunker Gilbreth
(1868-1924)
United States

Frank Bunker Gilbreth's distinctive contribution was to develop 'motion study' as a primary tool for managers and as a basis for new thinking about some of the aims of management.

Scientific Management, as Taylor and Gantt developed it, was a series of principles for analysing the routines and procedures surrounding the worker on his job. Gilbreth began his contribution to management with the publication of 'Field System' and 'Concrete System' in 1908, where he described the lines of authority and the responsibilities of different jobs within his own business as a building contractor. His earliest work was thus in the wider field of general management. His unique contribution was, however, his emphasis on human effort and the methods he devised for showing up wasteful and unproductive movements. He felt that if the 'one best way to do work' could be discovered for each and every element in a worker's movements and surroundings, the resulting gains in productivity could add significantly to the gains which Taylor was making by revising the system of management in the productive unit as a whole.

Gilbreth had already, as a builder, proved the truth of this theory. He had simplified the motions used in brick-laying, reducing their number from 18 to 5, increasing the hourly number of bricks laid from 175 to 350 and thus increasing productivity 100% over the previous system. During the First World War, he was later to have similar success in using his methods for training recruits and for rehabilitating disabled men. From 1912 until his death in 1924, he devoted himself to the steady development of the science of motion study. He was the first to apply the motion picture camera to the recording and analysis of performance, the first to classify the elements of human motions, or 'therbligs' (the word Gilbreth spelt backwards). Out of this work grew the laws of motion economy, looking to the systematic elimination of inefficiencies and waste, and the idea of estimating performance times as the sum of the times normally taken for the performance of the elementary motions used in the operation.

Thus far the contribution of Gilbreth has been described as pertaining to the mechanics of management. Motion study was, however, the means by which he made a contribution of the greatest importance to the dynamics of management. For while Taylor's emphasis had been primarily on the external factors effecting the worker, Gilbreth began by looking at the worker first, and this led him to apply the knowledge available from all the social sciences—physiology, psychology, education and the rest—to the task of improving and broadening the worker's capacity to contribute to the productivity of industry. This search for 'the one best way' was no narrow regimentation of the worker's movements. It was the means by which each man's personal potential could be maximized with benefit both to himself and to the unit in which he worked. It included his training, the methods he used, the tools at his disposal, and the physical and mental environment which surrounded him.

Gilbreth's particular contribution was therefore to develop management as a social science with the human being the centre of interest, round which research and experiment revolve and towards whose development they are directed. In 1916 he and his wife contributed jointly to the Annals of the American Academy of Political

139

and Social Science an article on the 'Three Position Plan of Promotion'. It was based squarely on the proposition that 'no organzation can hope to hold its members that does not consider not only the welfare of the organization as a whole, but also the welfare of the individuals composing that organization'. They stated that they wished to emphasize three points:

1 The necessity of attracting desirable applicants
2 The necessity of holding, fitting and promoting those already employed
3 The interdependence of these two necessities

And they insisted that 'no worker who is constitutionally able to become a permanent member of an organization will wish to change, if he is receiving adequate pay *and* has ample opportunity for advancement'. The Gilbreths' plan for achieving this objective practically, with its 'man in charge of promotion', its 'master promotion chart', its 'individual promotion charts' or 'fortune sheets', and its regular meeting between promotion man and worker to discuss the latter, was—allowing for differences in nomenclature—precisely the plan so often sold to corporations in the 1950's as something of a novelty under the title of executive or management development.

That he should have loved and married a woman who was herself a psychologist and a teacher was an event which can only be described as 'providential'. As he fired her enthusiasm and strengthened her self-confidence, so she broadened his outlook on management and widened the scope of management enquiry to include the whole range of the social sciences. In awarding its Gold Medal in 1954 to Lillian Moller Gilbreth on the occasion of its Tenth Congress, the International Committee for Scientific Management paid tribute to the work of her husband to whom she owed her initial inspiration.

Curriculum Vitae

1868   Born on 7th July in Fairfield, Maine, into a family drawn from New England farming stock.
        Though his father died in his early childhood, F. B. Gilbreth had a good schooling at Andover Academy and then at Boston Grammar School. He qualified for entry to the Massachusetts Institute of Technology but decided to start practical work at once.

1885   Apprenticed to a building contractor. Within 10 years he had become chief superintendent of the company. He also achieved technical distinction in a new design for scaffolding, a new method of water-proofing cellars, and several innovations in concrete construction.

1895   Resigned to set up his own contracting business in Boston. He patented many technical inventions and perfected many administrative improvements in the methods of the business. One of his successes was his share in rebuilding California after the earthquake in 1905.

The business tended to develop from contracting to consulting work in construction. On this basis he could run not only a busy New York office with American branches, but also a London office. His first three books on building were based on this experience. He also began to be interested in the general science of management.

1903   Became Member of The American Society of Mechanical Engineers.

1910   Became intensely interested in the Eastern Rates Case and joined the group who were developing Scientific Management. In this year he was also one of the team from The American Society of Mechanical Engineers who paid a formal visit to the Institution of Mechanical Engineers in England.

1912   Gave up his contracting business and turned to 'management engineering' specializing in physical working methods. He became friendly with Gantt and Taylor, and in collaboration with his wife began to develop the distinctive Gilbreth contribution to the science of management. The New England Butt Co. of Providence was the scene of his experimental work during the next five years. There he established the Taylor system of management as a whole and carried out his own research into motion study. He quickly gained a reputation as an expert on management.

1917-18   Major of engineers in US army, on the general staff concerned with the training of recruits. He also did special work for the rehabilitation of crippled soldiers, but his war effort was cut short by a severe illness.

1919-24   Returned to management consultancy and to developing motion study.

1924   Died on 14th June aet. 56, when preparing to attend the Prague International Management Congress.

In 1943 the award of the Gantt Medal was made to Lillian M. Gilbreth and Frank B. Gilbreth jointly, by The American Society of Mechanical Engineers and the Institute of Management, 'in recognition of their pioneer work in management, their development of the principles and techniques of motion study, their application of those techniques in industry, agriculture and the home, and their work in spreading that knowledge through courses of training and classes at universities'.

Personal Characteristics

Because two of his children have written one of the most amusing books in modern American literature which has been made into a film that has enjoyed a wide popularity, there is a real danger that the depth and value of Frank Gilbreth's achievement may be underestimated by future generations. Both families and films need laughter. That the originality of his mind and his total lack of self-consciousness added to the gaiety of life should never be allowed to diminish appreciation of his high seriousness of purpose or of the courage, energy and devotion which he brought to the service of management and of society. That as a man of 44, with a large and growing family, he should have abandoned his very lucrative and successful contracting business in order to concentrate on the new science of management, because he believed it was of importance to the community, is in itself, evidence of an unusual depth of character and indifference to personal advantage where it appeared to conflict with social purpose. In a very real sense his was a 'dedicated' life. That he won and held the abiding love of one of 'the first women of America' is witness to his qualities as a man. Though his children may have often laughed with him and at him, and sometimes found his forthright enthusiasm extremely embarassing, the picture of a small boy sobbing his heart out because 'he had lost his Daddy' is a truer record of their relations. Frank Gilbreth was loveable as well as laughable and, above all, a real pioneer who added greatly to our knowledge and understanding of management in the early days when its novelty as an idea was often deeply suspect.

Selected Publications

BOOKS

1908 *Concrete System*
New York: The Engineering News Publishing Co.
1908 *Field System*
New York & Chicago: The Myron C. Clark Publishing Co.
1909 *Bricklaying System*
New York & Chicago: The Myron C. Clark Publishing Co.
1911 *Motion Study*
New York: D. van Nostrand Co.
1912 *Primer of Scientific Management*
108 pages. New York: D. van Nostrand Co.

1916 *Fatigue Study*
      New York: Sturgis & Walton Co.
1917 *Applied Motion Study*
      New York: Sturgis & Walton Co.
1920 *Motion Study for the Handicapped*
      New York: The Macmillan Co.; London: Routledge.

CONTRIBUTIONS TO THE PROCEEDINGS OF LEARNED SOCIETIES

1910 'Fires: Effects on Building Material and Permanent
      Elimination'
      New York: *Journal* of ASME, Vol. 32, p. 754 and Vol. 33,
      p. 577.
1915 'Motion Study for the Crippled Soldier'
      New York: *Journal of* ASME, Vol. 37, p. 669.
1915 'What Scientific Management Means to America's Industrial
      Position' (with Lillian Gilbreth)
      New York: *Annals of The American Academy of Political and
      Social Science*, Vol. 61, p. 208.
1916 'Graphic Control of the Exception Principle for Executives'
      New York: Trans. ASME, Vol. 38, p. 123.
1921 'Process Charts' (with Lillian Gilbreth)
      New York: Trans. ASME, Vol. 43, p. 1029.
1921 'Symposium. Stop-Watch Time Study. An Indictment and a
      Defence' (with Lillian Gilbreth)
      New York: *Bulletin of The Taylor Society*, Vol. 6, p. 97.
1922 'Ten Years' Progress in Management' (with Lillian Gilbreth)
      New York: Trans. ASME, Vol. 44, p. 1285.
1924 'Scientific Management in Other Countries than the United
      States' (with Lillian Gilbreth)
      New York: *Bulletin of The Taylor Society*, Vol. 9, p. 132.

Robert Franklin Hoxie
(1868-1916)
United States

Robert F. Hoxie published in 1915 a book entitled *Scientific Man-agement and Labor*. This book is significant in the history of management because it was the first attempt to define the relationship between scientific management and organized labour.

Formal labour opposition to scientific management crystallized immediately the movement became popular. This was perhaps inevitable, for the movement had thereby gained numerous adherents whose understanding of its principles was imperfect and who lacked both the social outlook of the early pioneers and their practical skill in dealing with people. The labour strike at the Watertown Arsenal precipitated a strong political movement to ban the use of the stopwatch in all Government factories. This was followed by the congressional enquiry of 1912. In 1914 public feeling on the matter was so aroused that the Federal Commission on Industrial Relations decided to make a special investigation into scientific management in relation to labour, and entrusted this to Hoxie, a professor of economics at Chicago University who had made a special study of labour problems although he had not hitherto been concerned with scientific management.

Scientific Management and Labor records the results of Hoxie's investigations and is full of interest. He attempted two things: first to define formally 'Trade Union Objections to Scientific Management' and 'The Labor Claims of Scientific Management': and secondly, to persuade the parties concerned to arrive at a reconciliation of the points of conflict which he had elicited. His success on the first count was noteworthy. For his statement of labour objections he obtained the official approval of the American Federation of Labor. For his statement of the scientific managers' side of the case he obtained the approval of Harrington Emerson and other practising exponents of the new management, with the exception of one person who would not give his approval—the father of scientific management himself. After protracted discussion an appendix had to be added: 'The Labor Claims of Scientific Management according to Mr. Frederick W. Taylor'. Taylor's opposition was based on his distrust of the well-meaning efforts of Hoxie and his colleagues to reconcile the aims of scientific management with these of trade-unionism, for Taylor believed that Hoxie did not see the issues correctly. Although he did not agree with Hoxie's proposed solutions, he is known, however, to have fully appreciated the importance of the investigation and he is quoted as saying that he and his associates would use every possible effort to make good come out of it.

The impartial reader of *Scientific Management and Labor* must conclude that it is a fair and penetrating analysis of the issues between management and labour as they then appeared, documented by many facts exhaustively investigated. As a first attempt to take stock of issues which were new in 1914 but which have remained fundamental in our society down to the present time, the book merits a place in the history of management. One significant phrase shows the quality of Hoxie's understanding of the issues at stake:

'Because of its youth and the necessary application of its principles to a competitive state of industry, it (scientific management) is, in many respects, crude, many of its devices are contradictory of its announced principles, and it is inadequately scientific. Nevertheless, it is to date the latest word in the sheer mechanics of production and *inherently in line with the march of events*.'[1]

Curriculum Vitae

1868	Born on 29th April at Edmeston, New York State.
	He graduated PhB at Cornell University in 1893 and subsequently PhD at Chicago University in 1905.
1896-8	Instructor in Economics at Cornell College, Iowa.
1898-1901	Instructor in Economics at Washington University, St Louis, Mo.
1901-2	Instructor in Economics at Washington and Lee, Lexington, Va.
1903-6	Instructor in Economics at Cornell University, Ithaca, NY.
1906-16	Associate Professor of Political Economy, Chicago University.
1914-16	Special investigator, United States Commission on industrial Relations.
1916	Died on 22nd June aet. 48.

Personal Characteristics

'Hoxie was an inquirer. He could not satisfy a demand for honest truth by accepting authority: he had to test what the books say by reference to the facts. Yet he was no devotee of mere description; he dealt with facts in relation to problems, and demanded both facts and consistent theory. He was painstaking in analysing his problem. diligent in gathering data, and painfully conscientious in determining what it all meant. In his mind there was endless conflict between the cautious student and the bold adventurer.

. . . He cared little for public reputation or academic recognition. His students were his public; to him inquiry and teaching were inseparable; he was forever following the quest wherever it led, in utter disregard of academic frontiers, with a pack of cubs at his heels. His distinctive work was in raising questions, in blazing trails, in sending youngsters adventuring.'[2]

---

1 *Scientific Management and Labor,* page 137, first edition, 1915. The italics are those of the editor of The Golden Book.
2 *Dictionary of Modern Biography.*

He suffered from ill health almost all his life. This made him subject to moods of deep depression, and it was during one such mood that he ended his own life at the age of 48.

Selected Publications

(Professor Hoxie also wrote several books on sociological subjects.)
1915 *Scientific Management and Labor*
 New York: D. Appleton & Co.
1916 *Scientific Management and Social Welfare*
 New York: Survey.
1916 *Why Organized Labor Opposes Scientific Management*
 Chicago: Journal of Political Economy.
1917 *Trade Unionism in the United States*
 Posthumous collection of lectures delivered at the University of
 Chicago, edited by E. H. Downey.

Hugo Diemer
(1870-1939)
United States

Hugo Diemer was the author of a classic textbook, published in 1910, on factory management. He was also a pioneer in the teaching of management in American colleges.

He was an early and original writer on management subjects, as is shown by a comparison of the titles of his books and articles with their dates. His early perception of the new principles of management, supported by experience as a consulting engineer in applying the management methods of F. W. Taylor supplemented by his own into a number of factories, made his textbook of 1910, *Factory Organization and Administration,* an immediate and sustained success. It ran through many editions. In the 1935 edition Diemer wrote:

'The author has had many letters from readers stating that after they had mastered the interrelation and universal application of management principles this has affected every important action in their lives as well as their outlook and attitude in their work and even their private lives and personality. Numerous executives and officials attribute less waste, more profits, and better understanding of employees to their mastery of management principles, science and philosophy. Surely the study is worthwhile.'

The later books which he wrote and edited, those on foremanship in particular, were similarly in the vanguard of management thinking.

Diemer occupied an important place in the American management movement over many years. A self-made man, he became a professor but retained an active connection with industry. In 1909 as a professor in Pennsylvania State College, he was one of the early pioneers in sponsoring a course in which industrial management was the centre of the syllabus. Soon after came vocational courses for foremen, again very early in the field.

He spent the last nineteen years of his career at LaSalle Extension University, Chicago (a correspondence institution) as Director of Management Courses and Personnel. At LaSalle, dealing with thousands of men educating themselves 'the hard way' in the theory of management while keeping up their full-time jobs in its practice, he had an important influence on the development of management education in America. The publicity engendered by his writings, original experiments in teaching, platform speaking to management organizations, and consultancy work did much to stimulate national interest in management education and to gain eminence for LaSalle as a teaching institution in this sphere.

In 1938 Diemer's long and pioneering services to management were recognized by the award of the Taylor Key by the Society for the Advancement of Management.

Curriculum Vitae

1870	Born on 18th November in Cincinnati, Ohio.
1888-92	Addyson Pipe & Steel Co. Cincinnati.
1892-6	Studied at Ohio State University (ME Electrical Engineering), University of Chicago, and Pennsylvania State College (History and Political Science).
1896-1900	Production Engineer, Bullock Engineering & Manufacturing Co., and Westinghouse Electric & Manufacturing Co.
1900-1	Assistant Professor of Mechanical Engineering, Michigan

149

	State College.
1901-4	Associate Professor of Mechanical Engineering, University of Kansas.
1904-7	Consulting Engineer, Indianapolis and Chicago. Also Superintendent, National Motor Vehicle Co. Indianapolis (1904-6).
1906-8	Production Manager, Goodman Manufacturing Co., Chicago, Ill.
1907-9	Professor of Mechanical Engineering, Pennsylvania State College.
1909-19	Professor of Industrial Engineering, Pennsylvania State College.
1917	Major, Ordnance Dept., in charge of US Cartridge Co. Lowell, Mass, and then on the staff of the commanding officer at Bethlehem Steel Co., Bethlehem, Penna. Later Lt Colonel in the Reserve Co.
1919-20	Personnel Superintendent, Winchester Repeating Arms Co.
1920-21	President and Director, Indianapolis Furniture Co.
1920-39	Director, Management Courses and Personnel, LaSalle Extension University, Chicago.
1939	Died on 3rd March aet. 69, in Chicago.

Diemer served as President of the Chicago Chapters of The American Society of Mechanical Engineers and of the Taylor Society; he was also a National Director and Vice-President of the Society of Industrial Engineers and a National Vice-President of the Society for the Advancement of Management.

Personal Characteristics

Col. Diemer was a kind and likeable man who made friends easily and who did not obtrude his formidable engineering and managerial gifts in his personal relationships. He gave much leisure time to neighbourly work in his community—the Beverly Hills area of Chicago, and was an active church-worker. He is remembered for his constant interest in people, and one of his colleagues has used the lately-coined term 'a human engineer' of him as a happy epitome of his personality.

Selected Publications

BOOKS

1910 *Factory Organization and Administration*
412 pages. New York: McGraw Hill Publishing Co.

1918 *Industrial Organization and Management*
308 pages. Chicago: LaSalle Extension University.
1920 *Personnel Administration* (with Daniel Bloomfield)
560 pages. Chicago: LaSalle Extension University
1921 *Modern Foremanship and Production Methods* (with Meyer and Daniel Bloomfield)
1036 pages. Chicago: LaSalle Extension University.
1925 *Principles of Production*
449 pages. Chicago; LaSalle Extension University.
1927 *Foremanship Training*
56 pages. Chicago: LaSalle Extension University.
1929 *Wage Payment Plans That Reduced Production Costs* (Editor)
275 pages. New York: McGraw Hill Publishing Co.
1930 *How To Set Up Production Control for Greater Profits* (Editor)
312 pages. New York: McGraw Hill Publishing Co.

ARTICLES
1899 'Functions and Organization of the Purchasing Department'
New York: *Engineering Magazine.*
1902 'Aids in Taking the Machine Shop Inventory'
New York: *Engineering Magazine.*
1903 'Essentials of Shop Management'
New York: *American Machinist,* Vol. 38.
1905 'A Combined Bonus and Premium System'
New York: *Engineering Magazine.*
1912 'The "Efficiency Movement" in 1911'
New York: *Iron Age,* Vol. 89.
1912 'Factory Organization in Relation to Industrial Education'
Annals of American Academy of Political and Social Sciences, Philadelphia, Vol. 44.
1912 'Industrial Management'
New York: *Journal of Accountancy,* Vol. 3.
1915 'Education in Scientific Management'
New York: *Efficiency Society Journal.*
1917 'Executive Control in the Factory'
Chicago: *Factory.*
1917 'Industrial Organization and Management'
Chicago: LaSalle Extension University.

Carl Köttgen
(1871-1951)
Germany

Carl Köttgen was a leader of the 'rationalization' movement in Germany in the 1920's and a founder of the Reichskuratorium für Wirtschaftlichkeit (German Institute of Management, or RKW).

He was an electrical engineer who, entering at the bottom, won his way to the position of chief executive in the firm of Siemens, the greatest concern in the German electrical equipment industry, while also gaining a high reputation in the technical field through his published work. As an engineer and a sometime president of the Verein Deutscher Ingenieure (Association of German Engineers, or VDI), Köttgen viewed the responsibilities of his profession in their broadest terms. Like the early members of The American Society of Mechanical Engineers in the United States, he became concerned to urge the close relationship between engineering and executive management, whether in business or government. He himself had accomplished the transition from one activity to the other. A visit after the First World War to the United States gave him the opportunity to observe Scientific Management as it was being applied there. He returned determined to introduce 'rationalization' into Germany. By persuading Carl Friedrich von Siemens to interest himself in rationalization and by enlisting the support of the German government and of important industrial firms, Köttgen brought about in 1921 the creation of RKW backed by sufficient support to ensure its progress. The introduction and early development of the rationalization movement in Germany was therefore, through the pioneering work of RKW, in great measure inspired by this distinguished engineer. He became RKW's Vice-Chairman, then its Chairman (1930-34), and upon its reconstitution after the Second World War he was awarded its honorary membership (1950).

Curriculum Vitae

1871   Born on 29th August at Barmen, the son of an engineer.
        He was educated at Barmen Realgymnasium (technical school) and at the Polytechnic Academy of Berlin-Charlottenburg (student of Professor Slaby).
1894   Joined the firm of Siemens.
1897   In charge of the power transmission office of Siemens.
1903   Confidential clerk to the lately-formed Siemens-Schuckert-Werke (SSW).
1905   Deputy member of the executive board of SSW.
1907   In charge of the British heavy current plant of Siemens Brothers.
1914-19 Interned in Great Britain during the First World War.
1919   Returned to Germany to take charge of the central administration of SSW.
1920   Chief executive of Siemens-Schuckert-Werke.
1939   Retired.
1951   Died on 12th December aet. 80, in Düsseldorf.
He was an honorary Doctor of Engineering of Berlin Polytechnic

Academy (1920); President of the Association of German Electrical Engineers (1926-7), of the Association of German Engineers (1929-31), and of the Third World Power Conference in Berlin (1930).

Personal Characteristics

Dr. Köttgen was a man who devoted most of his waking hours to his work. Notwithstanding its heavy claims, he always had time for the enjoyment of conversation and for various hobbies. He was a keen gardener and a skilled amateur photographer, and was fond of hunting.

Selected Publications

BOOKS

1897 *Elektrotechnik und Landwirtschaft* (Electrical Engineering and Agriculture)
Berlin: Paul Parey.

1925 *Das wirtschaftliche Amerika* (Productive America)
Berlin: VDI (Society of German Engineers).

1928 *Das fliessende Band* (The Assembly Line)
Berlin: J. Springer.

ARTICLES

1925 'Rationalization of Economic Activity'
Industrie und Handelszeitung, 24th June.

1925 'The Tasks of German Rationalization in Government and in Private Business'
Technik und Wirtschaft, No. 5.

1926 'Rationalization'
Address to the Association for the Promotion of Industry, *Gewerbefleiss* No. 3.

1927 'The Assembly Line'
Report to the Berlin Chamber of Industry and Commerce, October.

1929 'Fundamentals of Assembly Line Work'
ZVDI (Journal of the Society of German Engineers), p. 125.

Benjamin Seebohm Rowntree
(1871-1954)
Great Britain

B. Seebohm Rowntree was the British management movement's greatest pioneer. If his manifold contributions had to be summed up in a few words, it could be said that he gave purpose to the search for effective management. He had two underlying principles in his approach to the problems of industry. First, 'Whatever may be the motives which induce any given individual to engage in industry, its true basic purpose must be the service of the community'. And second, 'Industry is a human thing, in which men and women earn the means of life, and from which men and women are entitled to expect the means to a life worth living'. Rowntree's career was devoted to realising this philosophy, in his own family business and in British industry as a whole.

His early work was primarily social, directed towards improving industrial welfare. His discoveries in his first famous study of poverty (1901) led him, as labour director of Rowntree & Co. Ltd., the chocolate and confectionery manufacturers of York, to introduce there what was probably the most advanced provision for employee

155

welfare of any factory in Britain. During the war, he founded at the Ministry of Munitions a new Welfare Department offering an advisory service to employers in difficulties over the unfamiliar human problems arising out of war production. Largely through Rowntree's work and influence in this capacity there became firmly established in British industry, by the end of the war, an interest in industrial welfare and in the human aspects of industry.

After the war his work for industrial welfare expanded. Within his own firm he had early set out to remove the principal 'fears' which depress the outlook of employees, and to achieve that enhanced status for the working man which he knew, as a sociologist, was among the the most important of the satisfactions arising from work. This covered a wide range of developments. As early as 1904 he had established a Medical Department. Then, in the year 1905, there was established a day continuation school. In 1919 there was introduced a 44-hour, 5-day week, the question of whether the 44 hours should be worked in 5 or 5½ days being left to a ballot of employees. In 1919 there was established a comprehensive system of Works Councils. Many pioneering measures introduced into the Cocoa Works in the 1920's included family allowances, unemployment pay, higher education, the employment of trained industrial psychologists, and further provision for health, canteens and recreation. In 1919 he had put in hand a comprehensive investigation of all profit-sharing experience up to that time and as a result of this, in 1923 there was introduced a profit-sharing scheme which again was widely regarded as a model. Beyond the confines of his own firm he gave substantial support to the foundation of the Industrial Welfare Society and the National Institute of Industrial Psychology. He continued his research into social problems. He devised a 'human needs standard' which was used for every social survey made in Britain between the two wars. Although he had no political ambitions he had considerable political influence, and he came to enjoy the firm trust of the trade unions and to mediate significantly in more than one national industrial dispute. He played a leading part in the Liberal Industrial Inquiry of 1927/28 which published 'Britain's Industrial Future'.

Rowntree was, however, never paternalist in his industrial philosophy. He insisted from the outset that industry could not afford to pay a high level of wages and to provide good conditions of employment unless it was efficiently organized and managed. Because of this conviction he became a pioneer also of the science of management. From 1923 onwards the Rowntree Works were systematically reorganized according to the new principles of Scientific Management which Rowntree culled from every source available to him both in Britain and the United States. Much of this work became the

156

foundation for accepted textbooks in the study of management,[1] and it should not be forgotten that Mary Parker Follett chose the Rowntree Works as one of the 'cases' for her study of the social philosophy of business. Rowntree's energy for advancing Scientific Management overflowed into the national movement in Britain. In 1919 he founded the conferences for works directors, managers and foremen which became the annual 'Oxford Management Conferences'. Beginning with the theme of industrial relations, they came to be a national forum for the widest exchange of knowledge bearing on the principles and practice of management. In 1926 Rowntree founded the Management Research Groups with a different aim—the exchange of confidential management information for mutual benefit among senior executives from non-competing firms. The Groups have become a permanent institution. These two movements started by Rowntree marked virtually the inception of the study of 'scientific management' in Great Britain. There was moreover no organization connected with the advancement of management formed between 1918 and the Second World War which did not owe much of its origin and progress to Rowntree's enthusiasm and interest.

Separate mention should be made, finally, of B. S. Rowntree's work in a sphere halfway between 'welfare' and 'scientific management'—that of communications in industry. The immediate post-war years were the era of the Whitley Councils and of new gospels of the ideal relationship between management and worker. Rowntree led the way in the York Works towards a new conception of successful joint consultation, setting out this conception in his book *The Human Factor in Business: Experiments in Industrial Democracy* (1921). A full-time company-paid shop steward; a works council; a joint appeal committee for disciplinary matters; and the regular supply of management information to the employees: these were only a few of the innovations which made the Rowntree organization the model of good industrial relations which it has remained. The joint appeal committee in particular was a lone instance of a recognition in industry of the distinction between the executive and judicial aspects of authority.

Rowntree was a force, the full impact of which is yet to be felt, for better relations between managers and workers. Some of the experiments which he initiated and applied with outstanding practical success still read like 'moonbeams from the larger lunacy' to the more

[1] O. Sheldon: *Philosophy of Management*, London, Pitman, 1923.
C. H. Northcott and others: *Factory Organization*, London, Pitman, 1927.
W. Wallace: *Business Forecasting and its Practical Application*, London, Pitman, 1927.
L. Urwick: *Organizing a Sales Office*, London, Pitman, 1929.

conservative element among business managers. He was, in the considered judgment of the editor of this book (whose chief he was during important formative years), a greater influence than any other business man who has lived in our time towards guiding his country to a wider, wiser and more enlightened view of the task of business leadership.

Curriculum Vitae

1871   Born on 7th July, the second son of Joseph Rowntree, founder of Rowntree & Co. Ltd., the chocolate and confectionery firm at York.
Educated at Bootham, the Quaker School at York, and trained in chemistry at Owen's College, Manchester.

1889   Began his career as a chemist at the York Works, soon becoming a departmental manager.

1897   Labour Director. In this position he was able to undertake experiments directed towards improving the conditions of the workers.
Responsible for the establishment of a pension fund for workers in the company.

1913-14   Member of the Land Enquiry Committee of Lloyd George.

1916-18   Director of a new Industrial Welfare Department created by Lloyd George at the Ministry of Munitions, London.

1917   Member of the Government's Reconstruction Committee.

1918   Organized at Scarborough the first of a series of week-end lecture conferences for works executives and foremen, which settled down in 1922 to two conferences a year at Balliol College, Oxford.

1919   Founded the Central Works Council at Rowntree & Co., Ltd.

1919   Standard factory hours reduced to 44, and a five-day week subsequently established by workers' ballot.

1921   Visited USA, and repeated the visit almost annually up to 1939.

1923   Succeeded his father as Chairman of Rowntree & Co., Ltd., but retained the post of labour director until 1936.

1927   Founded the first Management Research Group in Britain, an association of non-competing firms.

1931   Adviser to Lloyd George on a study of unemployment under Ramsay Macdonald's government.

1936   Relinquished executive responsibilities, remaining Chairman of the Board.

1941   Retired from the Board.

158

1954   Died on 7th October aet. 83, at his home in High Wycombe,
        Buckinghamshire.
He was made a Companion of Honour in 1931. He was a holder of
the Royal St Olaf Order of Norway, was a Justice of the Peace, an
Honorary LID of Manchester University, and the first Honorary
Fellow of the British Institute of Management.

Personal Characteristics

'. . . for those of us who were privileged to work alongside him—and
with him it was always "alongside" and never "under"—it is the memory of the man, the human being, that endures like a spring of water
in a thirsty land. I have known a few men in my lifetime (my own
father was another of them) whose attitude to life was so ordered that
one was never tempted, even for an instant, to doubt their integrity,
to start that search for a secondary motive behind the outer pattern
of their deeds and words which implies that their yea is not wholly
yea and their nay means "it depends". He was a man, too, of perfect
loyalty. To these may be added other virtues—a kindliness to others,
a generous and sensitive sympathy with their feelings, a readiness to
share in the ordinary joys and sorrows of every man, regardless of
rank or station, which made him a very able practitioner of what he
preached. That sounds dull, "unco' guid". But the whole was ir-
radiated by a most delightful and constantly unexpected sense of
humour.

'I am sure that the last thing he would have wished is that our
proceedings should be in any way saddened by the thought of his
passing. Rather it would accord with his lifelong attitude, that we
should go forward with renewed vigour in the task of developing
better management as an essential preliminary condition to better
relations not only between the parties to industry but also between
the nations—the task to which he devoted the major portion of his
working life.'[1]

Selected Publications

BOOKS
1901 *Poverty: A Study of Town Life*
      437 pages. London: Macmillan.
1910 *Land and Labour: Lessons from Belgium*
      633 pages. London: Macmillan.

[1] From the text of the short address given by L. Urwick at the European
Management Conference, Torquay, 20-23rd October 1954, as Gold Medallist of the International Committee for Scientific Management.

1911 *Unemployment: A Social Study* (with Bruno Lasker)
318 pages. London: Macmillan.
1913 *How the Labourer Lives* (with May Kendall)
342 pages. London: Thos. Nelson.
1914 *The Way to Industrial Peace*
1918 *The Human Needs of Labour*
168 pages. London: Longmans Green.
1921 *The Human Factor in Business: Experiments in Industrial Democracy*
188 pages. London: Longmans Green.
1921 *The Responsibility of Women Workers for Dependants* (with F. D. Stuart)
68 pages. London: Oxford University Press.
1922 *Industrial Unrest: A Way Out*
48 pages. London: Longmans Green.
1930 *The Agricultural Dilemma* (with Viscount Astor)
101 pages. London: P. S. King & Son Ltd.
1939 *British Agriculture* (with Viscount Astor)
284 pages. London: Penguin Books.
1941 *Poverty & Progress—A Second Social Survey of York*
540 pages. London: Longmans Green.
1946 *Mixed Farming and Muddled Thinking* (with Viscount Astor)
143 pages. London: Macdonald.
1951 *Poverty and the Welfare State—A Third Social Survey of York* (with G. R. Lavers)
104 pages. London: Longmans Green.
1951 *English Life and Leisure: A Social Study* (with G. R. Lavers)
482 pages. London: Longmans Green.

ARTICLES, ETC.

B. S. Rowntree wrote many articles for English and American periodicals, and addressed numerous conferences. Many of his articles and papers have been reproduced in pamphlet form. The following small selection of titles will give some idea of the subjects covered.

'The Board of Directors and the Purpose of a Business'
'Christianity and Industrial Relations'
'The Conditions of the People'
'Economic Conditions in Industry'
'Industrial Unrest—A Way Out'
'The Prospects and Tasks of Social Reconstruction'
'A Solution of the Unemployment Problem'

160

Robert Grosvenor Valentine
(1872-1916)
United States

Robert G. Valentine was, like Robert F. Hoxie, one of the earliest persons to endeavour to interpret Scientific Management in a form acceptable to organized labour.

Many of F. W. Taylor's closest adherents had become troubled, about the year 1912, by the absence of any provision for the role of labour unions in Taylor's conception of management. Taylor believed that the advantages of scientific management were, if correctly and systematically pursued, mutually beneficial to both employers and workers, but that the employers alone should be responsible for applying scientific management in their concerns. The labour unions, by their tendency to restrict output and their insistence on collective bargaining, were in his view in opposition to his principles. Valentine was a sincere admirer of Taylor and had been practising as a consultant introducing the Taylor system into manufacturing plants. Valentine however came to hold the view that the interests of employer and worker are not necessarily identical in the matter of dividing the profits arising from increased production, and thus that workers need the collective bargaining power provided by union organization. He therefore voiced the criticism that scientific management was misguided in not enlisting the co-operation of the unions.

Valentine was able, because of his sympathy with both Taylor and the labour union movement, to mediate in some of the potential conflicts with labour of Taylor's last years. In his own consultancy work he specialized in the labour relations aspect of any changes in management. In some assignments he acted as the agent jointly of the employers' association and the union and was able to devise practical patterns of co-operation, furnishing the necessary assurance of protection to the workers while promoting the advantages to be obtained from improved management. He devised a technique for a 'labour audit' which was an early approach to a body of principles of personnel management. He assisted Hoxie in the Federal enquiry which led to the publication of Hoxie's *Scientific Management and Labor* (1915), a landmark in the effort to reconcile the two philosophies involved.

Finally, Valentine himself published papers as contributions to this vital issue. The title of one, 'The Progressive Relationship of Efficiency and Consent' indicates him as a thinker of vision in that transitional period in industrial philosophy. Studying the controversy today, one can recognize that the criticisms of Taylor reported by Valentine in his articles were less than just and that Valentine's hopes for 'joint control' by employers and labour in dividing the production surplus were too far ahead of the times. Yet the part played by Valentine and his collaborators in exploring the common ground between management and labour, and in working for the development of co-operation instead of conflict in industrial relations generally, was a contribution of importance.

Curriculum Vitae

1872	Born on 29th November in West Newton, Mass.
1896	AB, Harvard University.
1896-9	Assistant in English, Massachusetts Institute of Tech-

162

nology.
1899-1901	With the National City Bank, New York, part of the time in the accounting department.
1901-2	Instructor in English, Massachusetts Institute of Technology.
1902-4	With Farmers' Loan and Trust Co., New York.
1905-8	Private secretary to commissioner Francis E. Leupp of the Indian Service.
1908	Supervisor of Indian Schools.
1909-12	Assistant commissioner for Indian Affairs.
1912-16	Investigator and consultant in labour problems, Boston.
1913	Voluntary Chairman of first Massachusetts Minimum Wage Board, during the economic depression of the period.
1916	Died on 15th September aet. 44.

Personal Characteristics

Robert G. Valentine is remembered as a man of deep sincerity who had a liberalizing and democratizing influence over those with whom he came in contact. He is said to have so influenced several of the other pioneers commemorated in this book.

Selected Publications

1915 'New Certificates of Character for Manufacturers'
New York: *Industrial Engineering and Engineering Digest.*
1915 'Progressive Relation between Efficiency and Consent'
Hanover N.J.: Society to Promote the Science of Management.
1915 'Scientific Management and Organized Labor'
Hanover N.J.: Society to Promote the Science of Management.

Charles Samuel Myers
(1873-1946)
Great Britain

Charles Samuel Myers was the pioneer of industrial psychology in Great Britain. His practical contribution was to found and develop the National Institute of Industrial Psychology.

Until the First World War Myers had been an academic psychologist at Cambridge University, and had gained repute in his development of experimental psychology. In 1918, following on his wartime work of promoting applications of psychology in the Armed Services, he delivered two important lectures to the Royal Institution of Great Britain in which he declared that the time had come to 'take psychology out of the laboratory and carry it over into the field of everyday life', in particular into industrial life. One of his listeners was H. J. Welch, a business man, who had for some time been wondering whether psychological methods could not be applied to industry and commerce along the lines described by Hugo Münsterberg in some of his popular American writings. The two men decided to collaborate in organizing the subscription of funds for this project and in 1920 their efforts met with success in the foundation of the National Institute of Industrial Psychology.

Since its foundation the National Institute of Industrial Psychology (NIIP) has been one of the focal points in Great Britain for the study and application of better methods in dealing with the human factor in management. Its object was defined as the application of psychological and physiological knowledge to the problems of industry and commerce. Its activities include research, advisory services to individuals and firms, training, and dissemination of information through lectures, discussions, publications and the maintenance of a reference library. Its growth was Myers's lifework. Gaining recognition from British industry was no easy matter. The quiet life devoted to scientific research which had always been Myers's ambition was exchanged for a plunge 'into the arduous task of organization, administration, making contacts with private individuals, public bodies and commercial firms, securing financial support, and seeking to introduce scientific ideals and methods into the world of commerce and manufacture . . . Much of the support the Institute received was the direct result of his capacity for communicating to others his own enthusiastic belief in the great part industrial psychology has still to play in the life of the nation'.[1] By the end of the interwar period, the Institute had helped to build up a remarkable corpus of knowledge in regard to the work and reactions of the human being in industry and commerce, and its programme was wider than that of any comparable body in the world.

Myers's conception had been noble from the outset. While he had given full weight to the specialized techniques which psychology could contribute to management in such fields as vocational selection and training, he did not restrict the claims of industrial psychology to narrow confines. Industrial psychology in his view was the means by which the whole process of management could be thought through in order to take its rightful place as a social science. It was with this

165

aim in mind that he mastered the principles of F. W. Taylor and F. B. Gilbreth, that he made himself familiar at first hand with every aspect of industry, and that he undertook so wide a programme for the Institute. In his earlier years he had helped to take psychology from the lecture-room into the laboratory. In his later career he took it from the laboratory into the manager's office and on to the factory floor.

Curriculum Vitae

1873	Born in London on 13th March. His father and grandfather were business men in the City of London. He was educated at the City of London School.
1891-8	At Cambridge University (Gonville and Caius College) taking BA and then a medical degree.
1898-9	Member of the Cambridge Anthropological Expedition to New Guinea and Borneo.
1899-1900	House physician at St. Bartholomew's Hospital, London.
1900-02	In Egypt for health reasons.
1902	Assistant to W. H. R. Rivers at Cambridge in his classes in experimental psychology.
1906	Part-time Professor of Psychology, King's College, London.
1909	University lecturer at Cambridge in Experimental Psychology. His important *Text Book of Experimental Psychology* was published in this year.
1912	Director of the Psychological Laboratory, Cambridge University.
1915	Commissioned in the Royal Army Medical Corps in France.
1916	Consultant psychologist to the British Armies in France.
1918-22	Reader in Experimental Psychology at Cambridge.
1918-29	Active member of the Industrial Fatigue Research Board.
1919	Organized at Cambridge under the auspices of the University Laboratory a Summer School on Industrial Administration.
1922-38	Left academic life to become full-time Director of NIIP; became Principal in 1930, and retired in 1938 with the title of Honorary Scientific Adviser.
1941	Member of War Office Advisory Committee on personnel selection.
1946	Died on 12th October aet. 73, at Winsford, Somerset.

[1] Obituary by Professor Sir Cyril Burt: *Occupational Psychology*, London, January, 1947, page 4.

He was a Fellow of the Royal Society (one of the first elected for psychological work) (1915); President of the British Psychological Society (1920); President of the Psychology Section of the British Association (1922 and 1931); and President of the seventh International Congress in Psychology (1923). He served on the Education Committee of the British Management Council throughout its existence (1937-1947).

He was made a Companion of the British Empire in 1919 and held the following academic degrees: MA, MD, ScD (Cantab), Hon DSc (Manch), Hon LLD (Calcutta), Hon DSc (Pennsylvania). He was an Honorary Fellow of Gonville and Caius College, Cambridge.

Personal Characteristics

Myers is remembered with affection by his fellow-psychologists. He radiated good humour and enthusiasm. Proud of his Jewish race, he was 'a humane cultured scientist'[1] of the eighteenth century British tradition, combining scientific integrity with many social graces, and possessing a large circle of friends into which he readily welcomed newcomers, especially the young. The turning point in his life was his abandonment of the gracious way of living he had followed at Cambridge, to instal himself in two rooms in Holborn and set out to establish relations with the world of business. At times the setbacks of his new activities caused him depression, for he was modest and not by nature assertive. 'Indeed, it was his personal qualities, which he himself often regarded as defects rather than as assets, that enabled him to succeed where the more usual kind of pioneer would have failed. His quiet and cultured manner, his diffident speech, his complete freedom from push or gush, his self-criticism and reserve, his amazing kindliness and tolerance, combined with a dogged resistance wherever the interests of the Institute were threatened, enabled him, in spite of much opposition and scepticism, to win his way alike in the world of business and the world of high science. From the first to the last, the key to his succes was his own unflagging self-sacrifice.'[2]

[1] Obituary by Professor Sir Cyril Burt: *Occupational Psychology*, London, January, 1947, page 6.
[2] Memoir by Professor T. H. Pear: *British Journal of Educational Psychology*, London, February 1947, page 5.

Selected Publications

BOOKS

1918 *Present-Day Applications of Psychology* (Originally two lectures given to the Royal Institution)
47 pages. London: Methuen.

1921 *Mind and Work*
176 pages. London: University of London Press.

1925 *Industrial Psychology in Great Britain*
164 pages. London: Jonathan Cape.

1928 *Industrial Psychology* (editor)
252 pages. London: Home University Library of Modern Knowledge series: Oxford University Press.

1932 *Business Rationalization*
76 pages. London: Pitman.

1932 *Ten Years of Industrial Psychology* (by H. J. Welch and C. S. Myers)
146 pages. London: Pitman.

ARTICLES

Myers contributed numerous papers to scientific journals. He was one of the founders, in 1904, of the *British Journal of Psychology*.

John Howell Williams
(1873-1941)
United States

John Howell Williams was an early thinker on scientific management and the originator of 'the flexible budget' as an instrument of
general administrative control.

His first contribution to management was his concept of 'visualiza-
tion of management'. In papers to the Taylor Society in 1915 and

1916 he drew attention to the importance of *recording* in the development of a body of knowledge. Just as in engineering the drawings and plans precede the physical work and make it easier to execute, so in the Taylor system of management, said Williams, it was becoming customary to make indexes and instructions of increasing precision which could be executed in the same way as an engineer executes the blueprints of the drawing office. The science of management could in this respect learn from engineering and the efforts of those in the movement should be directed towards increasing the precision of the indexes, instructions and symbols used. Williams himself originated several devices in this spirit which were subsequently found useful in practice.

Williams first put forward his concept of 'the flexible budget' in 1922, and published the authoritative statement in 1934. The flexible budget has proved one of the most effective devices of general administrative control in the management of enterprises.

He was the subject of a new development, interesting when viewed after the lapse of time, in the admission policy of The American Society of Mechanical Engineers for its Members. In 1920 he was the first person to be admitted to the Society entirely on evidence of managerial ability, and without the possession of an engineering qualification.

Curriculum Vitae

1873	Born on 22nd January, in Baltimore, Md. He had no formal education and his early life was marked by economic struggle.
1899-1900	Started a small printing business in Baltimore; this prospered through his efforts and evolved into Williams, Wilkins & Co., the leading business of its kind in Baltimore, later noted as an example of scientific management.
1900-07	Moved to New York and was for a period connected with different aspects of the printing business.
1907-17	Investigator for the Trust Company of America of new enterprises seeking loans.
circ 1909	Began undertaking management consultancy work.
1917-21	In charge of organization and methods in the Quartermaster Corps of the United States Army.
1921-35	New York manager for Day and Zimmerman Inc., of Philadelphia.
1928	Retained to report to the Interstate Commerce Commission on Railroad costing procedures. This report

disclosed important new information on costs and was
widely read.

1935-41   Retired because of severe ill-health.

1941   Died on 23rd May aet. 68.

Personal Characteristics

Distinguished management friends have recorded that Williams'
upbringing in the school of hard knocks made of him a rugged, energetic individualist, depending almost too much on himself. Yet he
was an outstandingly honorable and dependable personality, charming, a loyal and appreciative friend, sensitive to beauty in every
form, tolerant in argument, and unusually courageous in the face of
failing health.

Selected Publications

BOOK

1934   *The Flexible Budget*
New York: McGraw-Hill Publishing Co.

ARTICLES

1915-16 'The Index as a Factor in Industry'
Bulletin of the Taylor Society, Vol. I, No. 3, pp. 2-6, May,
1915, and Vol. II, No. 2, pp. 6-14, July 1916.

1922   'A Technique for the Chief Executive'
Bulletin of the Taylor Society, Vol. VII, No. 2, pp. 47-68,
April.

1923   'The Ways and Means of the Chief Executive'
Bulletin of the Taylor Society, Vol. VIII, No. 2, pp. 53-58,
April.

1924   'Management as an Executive Function'
Bulletin of the Taylor Society, Vol. IX, No. 2, pp. 66-71,
April.

1926   'Top Control'
Bulletin of the Taylor Society, Vol. XI, No. 4, pp. 199-206,
October.

1928   'The Budget as a Medium of Executive Leadership'
Bulletin of the Taylor Society, Vol. XIII, No. 4, pp. 166-169
August.

1929   'General Administrative Control'
Chapter XIX in *Scientific Management in American In-
dustry,* edited by H. S. Person for the Taylor Society. New
York: Harper and Brothers.

Ernst Streer (Ritter von) Streeruwitz
(1874-1952)
Austria

Ernst Streeruwitz was the founder of the Austrian Board of Efficiency (1928) and the author of one of the classics of management literature in the German language.

This book, *Rationalization and the World Economic System* (1931), was a picture of contemporary affairs so comprehensive as to merit the term encyclopaedic. As founder-director of the Austrian Board of Efficiency, Streeruwitz was in the closest touch with every activity of management in his country and with the international management movement. In the course of his varied career he gained a wealth of experience from every field of economic life, to which he could apply the yardstick of rationalization obtained from his close contact with the management movement. It is not surprising that he should have applied this standard to the highest and widest field of his manifold activities--national and international statecraft. *Rationalization and the World Economic System* was written by the founder and leader of the Austrian Board of Efficiency, but it was the politician and statesman (for Streeruwitz had been Federal Chan-

172

cellor of Austria) who guided the pen. Much of the book was controversial in both its technical and its political aspects, but the whole was illumined by a powerful personality, by a wide general knowledge not cramped by specialization, and by an enthusiastic temperament.

The author's chief aim was to lead the reader through the successive stages from the narrower rationalization of undertakings and national industries to the rationalization of the world economic system and of politics. That a rationalization expert should adventure into the realm of general politics was novel in 1931. 'Politics and rationalization—is there any connection between the two things? There is, for politics may hinder and hamper economic rationalization' (p. 147).

In this view Streeruwitz was in agreement with the ideas underlying the discussion on 'the Pros and Cons of Rationalization' at the Second Conference of the International Management Institute in July 1931. His view was that the leaders and experts in the rationalization movement had 'the right to concern ourselves with bigger things than conveyors, automatic lathes and stop watches, and thereby (to) lift the discussion of rationalization to a higher plane and give it a wider scope, namely the rebuilding and reorganization of the world as a whole by leading it back to the source from which our movement took its name—*ratio* or reason' (pp. 356-7).

In 1928 Streeruwitz devised the constitution of the Austrian Board of Efficiency (Osterreichisches Kuratorium für Wirtschaftlichkeit). This constitution has not only stood the test of time in Austria, but at the International Rationalization Conference in Geneva in 1931 mentioned above, it was specially commended as a model which other countries might adopt in creating their own Institutes. The OeKW, during the years up to the Second World War, accomplished significant work under Streeruwitz's leadership, applying the principles of rationalization to trade, the health and insurance services, timber and coal utilization, and road and rail transport.

Curriculum Vitae

1874   Born in Mies, Bohemia.
        Educated at Grammar School, Vienna; Military Academy, Wiener Neustadt, Vienna University (Law) and Vienna Technical High School (Engineering).
1900-02 Steward of the Lissa Estate, Bohemia.
1902-03 Director, Franz Leitenberger Textile Mills, Bohemia.
1904-13 Director, Cosmanos A.G. Textile Mills, Bohemia.
1914-19 War volunteer, cavalry captain and major.

1919	Director of Neunkirchner Druckfabriks A.G., textile printers.
1923	Christian Socialist Deputy to the National Assembly.
1928	Founder-President of the Austrian Board of Efficiency (Oesterreichische Kuratorium für Wirtschaftlichkeit).
May-Sep 1929	Federal Chancellor of Austria.
1930-8	President, Vienna Chamber of Commerce until his retirement. Parliamentary Rapporteur for the reform of the Austrian Federal Railways.
1952	Died aet. 78.

He was a Doctor of Political Science, Vienna University (1939) and during the First World War was decorated with the Franz Joseph Order, Signum Laudis with Cross D, and Iron Cross.

Personal Characteristics

Streeruwitz was an idealist and a nobleman in the best sense of the term. His closing years were devoted to the consolations of private study in the uncertain surroundings of the danger-centre of post-war Western society in which he lived. The sage remark of the old Austrian philosopher Carneri, with which Streeruwitz closed his book of 1931, reflected the philosophy of this statesman of pre-war Austria.

'There are times when the proper leader cannot be found and in which conscience fails to act. But a people is not on that account doomed. The work is taken over by necessity, and it never fails. But before necessity can accomplish anything it must grow—grow until, like a horrible spectre, it brings men to their senses, so that the idle are aroused from their idleness, the cranks cured of their perversity and the despairing imbued with fresh courage. Then folly and incompetence are driven out of the field, and the world once more resumes, as it always has done, its steady forward march.'

Selected Publications

1931 *Rationalisierung und Weltwirtschaft* (Rationalization and the World Economic System)
Vienna: Julius Springer.
1934 *Wie es War* . . . (The way it was . . .)
Vienna.
1937 *Springflut über Oesterreich* (Springtides over Austria)
Vienna.

George De Albert Babcock
(1875-1942)
United States

George D. Babcock pioneered in introducing the Taylor system of management into the American motor vehicle industry between 1908 and 1912. This work, begun by Carl Barth as a consultant and continued by Babcock as a plant executive, was the first application of scientific management in a major American industry.

Babcock made several original contributions to the Taylor methods: the earliest known employee counselling programme of the kind later made famous by Elton Mayo; an improved formula for

175

base wage rates; and an integrated planning system visualized from a single control board. His employee counselling programme in the Franklin Company was developed as an integral part of his system of management. An early and original experiment, it anticipated the 'Hawthorne Investigations' by many years, and has been called 'management's first attempt to direct human processes within an industrial structure.'[1]

Of the wage rate formula which Babcock introduced into the plant manufacturing the Franklin automobile, Carl Barth wrote: 'In Mr. Babcock's formula in determining a man's base rate, we have the first attempt to consider this matter from all possible angles with a view to absolute justice.'[2] The formula automatically adjusted the base wage rate in accordance with changes in the cost of living and the personal record of the employee.

Babcock's visualized planning system made use of a control board showing the exact location of every project in the plant. It introduced such features as the use of pneumatic tubes for issuing and returning orders, and the preservation by photography of progress records. The net result of the system in the Franklin plant was a great saving of capital through reduction of the volume of work in progress. Later in his career Babcock put into practice other remarkable applications of his system. In a tractor and road machinery plant he laid out a two-year time schedule for over two million detailed operations, each one of which was without exception completed to time. In his work for the Rural Electrification Administration he codified a very large number of government construction projects on a single sheet of paper, producing the first clear picture to be obtained of this heterogeneous field. His methods here saved the Government several million dollars in construction costs.

The work of Babcock, combining pioneering advances in the science of management with advances in the field of morale and human relations, is yet another piece of evidence refuting those who accuse the Taylor group of having dehumanized management.

Curriculum Vitae

1875   Born on 18th October in Corinne, Utah. Educated at public school in Syracuse, NY, and later attended Fairfield Military Academy, NY.

1897-1900   Instructor in physics, chemistry and mechanical drawing

---

1 Quoted from the article on Babcock in the *National Cyclopaedia of American Biography*, Vol. 31. The present outline is largely based on that article.
2 Preface to *The Taylor System in Franklin Management* by Babcock.

	at Fairfield Military Academy.
1900-04	Attended Purdue University graduating with BS degree in electrical engineering.
1904-07	Associated with William Kent as professor of mechanical arts and industrial engineering at Syracuse University.
1907-17	Assistant Superintendent (1907-12), then factory superintendent and general production manager (1912-17), H. H. Franklin Automobile Manufacturing Company, Syracuse.
1917-19	Chief Ordnance Supply Officer of the American Expeditionary Force in liaison with the General Staff.
1919-25	Manufacturing executive of the Holt Manufacturing Company, Peoria, Ill, producers of caterpillar tractors and road machinery. In 1921-2 he also collaborated with others in organizing the Division of Simplified Practice in the US Department of Commerce.
1925-28	Manufacturing Engineer and Assistant to the Vice-President of Manufacture, Dodge Bros., Inc., automobile producers, Detroit.
1928-34	Operated his own lumber manufacturing plant in Fletcher, NC.
1934-37	Entered service of US Government as regional engineer with the Civil Works Administration, holding various positions of increasing authority.
1937-39	Management engineer for the Rural Electrification Administration.
1939-42	Director of Engineering Management, Federal Works Agency.
1942	Died on 12th January aet. 67, in Washington, DC.

He was a charter member of the Taylor Society, and a lecturer on industrial management at the University of Chicago, Harvard University and other American colleges, as well as in Germany, France and Czechoslovakia.

Personal Characteristics

While George D. Babcock was a protagonist of the scientific approach to management, he was also noted for his capacity for seeing management as a whole. Science, in his outlook, occupied only its due place and was harnessed to a sincere interest in the welfare of his workers and to a kindly and generous personality.

Selected Publications

BOOK

1917 *Taylor System in Franklin Management*
245 pages. New York: Engineering Magazine Co.

ARTICLES

1914 'Results of Applied Scientific Management'
New York: *Iron Age,* Vol. 93 and 94 (series of 7 articles).

1914 { 'Routing Schedule and Despatch'
{ 'Making an Efficient Plant More Efficient'
New York: *Industrial Engineering and the Engineering Digest,*
Vol. 14, pp. 228-233, 275-283 and 427-431.

1915 'Exact Control of Manufacture in Practice'
New York: *Iron Age,* Vol. 96, pp. 1410-1413.

1916 'Fixing Individual Wage Rates on Facts'
New York: *Iron Age,* Vol. 97, pp. 1375-1379.

1921 Part editor of 'Waste in Industry', published by the Federated
American Engineering Societies.
New York: McGraw Hill Publishing Co.

1924 Section on production and control in *Management Handbook*
(ed L. P. Alford).

Edward Tregaskiss Elbourne
(1875-1935)
Great Britain

Edward Tregaskiss Elbourne was the pioneer in Great Britain of management viewed as a profession in its own right. To this end he founded the Institute of Industrial Administration, a body which has striven in Great Britain through many years and against many obstacles to establish recognized professional standards. The Institute's qualification has long been the sole British equivalent to the many degrees to which the student of management may aspire in other countries, notably the United States.

Elbourne's own career demonstrated the logic upon which his aims for management were based. If management was a science (and he early became convinced that it was, in the course of his work as an engineer and factory manager), its principles and practice could be the subject of analytical definition. So in 1914 he published *Factory Organization and Accounts,* perhaps the most comprehensive one-man textbook on the whole field of management (excluding selling) to appear in any country up to that time. Largely through the instrumentality of a high official in the Ministry of Munitions, some 10,000 copies of this book were sold during the course of the war, principally to the executive staffs of government contracting firms. Elbourne's principles of management were thus provided with an avenue leading to their immediate translation into practice, and the book may well have been among the main stimuli giving rise to the marked progress in applied scientific management which was one of the features of British industry between 1914 and 1920. Moreover, the book has endured. A comprehensive British textbook of management published in 1953 included it in a list of authoritative books on management restricted to seven publications.[1]

If management was a field which could be analytically defined, it was a 'subject' that could be taught and could be made the basis of a professional qualification. Elbourne conceived a plan of creating a corporate body devoted to the study and teaching of management; the body would be designed also to impart that special responsibility associated with the word 'profession' to the status of those practising management. In 1920 he founded the Institute of Industrial Administration. Essentially concerned with education, the Institute from the outset took as one of its objects the development of a syllabus and the awarding of a qualification to those attaining a required standard of knowledge, training and experience in management. In 1928, Elbourne's advocacy resulted in the initiation by the Regent Street Polytechnic, London, of a four-year part-time course in industrial administration according to the Institute's syllabus—the most extensive syllabus so far in existence.

The focal point having been established for the development of management as a profession, Elbourne's remaining years were spent in the endeavour to gain support for the Institute from a sceptical industrial world. His vision proved justified although progress was slow. In 1924 the Institution of Mechanical Engineers adopted the subject 'Engineering Economics' as part of its professional examination scheme. In 1934 the Institution of Electrical Engineers joined the older Institution in a common syllabus for this subject, of which the title was now changed to 'Fundamentals of Industrial Administration'. Elbourne lived to see other bodies—the Federation of

---

[1] *Principles and Practice of Management* ed E. F. L. Brech. 750 pages. London: Longmans Green, 1953. (See page 742.)

British Industries and the University of London for example—recognize management as a valid subject for systematic study.

Finally, he was the precursor of a second major stage in education for management: the provision for a period of mental reinvigoration for experienced executives midway through their careers at a 'staff college for industry' on the army parallel. His ten full-time study conferences for executives at Loughborough College in 1934 foreshadowed many of the essential features of the Administrative Staff College, which was not founded until more than a decade later.

Elbourne had chosen the most difficult task among those who strove to found Institutes in the field of management in Britain. For while others were successful in specialized fields (for example Myers in industrial psychology), he was seeking recognition for the study of management viewed as a whole. In so doing he had to struggle against the many prejudices of managers who had 'learnt the hard way' and who found it difficult to accept that younger men might train themselves in management by more systematic and rational means. In Great Britain there are still those who refuse to recognize that the art of business can be based on science; but many younger managers have cause to be grateful to Elbourne for the start he gave them in making their business careers not only more effective but more satisfying and creative.

In 1951 the Institute of Industrial Administration established the Elbourne Memorial Lecture, to be given periodically, at the Institute's invitation, by an individual whom the Institute would thus honour in association with the name of its founder.

Curriculum Vitae

1875   Born in Hampshire, on 12th June.
        Educated in Birmingham; apprenticed successively in three engineering concerns; became an Associate Member of the Institution of Mechanical Engineers in 1896.
1896   Began his engineering career as a draughtsman.
circ 1900 Visited USA to study machine tools and factory organization.
1900   Works organizer and accountant, John I. Thorneycroft & Co. Ltd., moving progressively to higher posts. Assistant General Manager to Mr (later Sir) Harry Brindley at the Ponders End Shell Factory at the same company.
1919   Partner with Brindley in consultancy work in engineering and factory administration. In June-July Elbourne gave three series of lectures on Industrial Administration to audiences of industrial executives.

181

1920	On Brindley's death, Elbourne continued the consultancy practice alone until his death, relinquishing the technical side and concentrating on organization.
1920	First Honorary Secretary and Honorary Director of Education of the Institute of Industrial Administration.
1925	Visited the United States to study marketing and publicity.
1927	Joint Director of Studies, IIA. Lecture Course at Regent Street Polytechnic, London.
1935	Died on 18th October aet. 60.

He received the MBE in 1919 in recognition of his work at Ponders End.

Personal Characteristics

Elbourne was a man more interested in ideas than in money-making. He needed a colleague to give a practical direction to his visionary plans and the early death of his friend Sir Harry Brindley was a setback not only to his work but also to the development of the Institute which they had founded together. His intellectual endowments were so abundant that they sometimes tripped him in matters of exposition. The thoughts tumbled over each other. He could see what he meant: he did not always succeed in making other people see it.

That almost single-handed he should have succeeded as an unpaid officer in establishing the Institute while continuing to practise his own consultancy work is a tribute to his unflagging energy and patient courage in the face of difficulties and disappointments. On his death the management movement in Britain sincerely lamented the loss of one of its most devoted pioneers.

Selected Publications

BOOKS

1914 *Factory Administration and Accounts*
654 pages. London: Library Press Ltd. Revised and much enlarged in 1921 and subsequent editions as: *Factory Administration and Cost Accounts,* 831 pages.

1919 *The Costing Problem*
148 pages. London: Library Press Ltd.

1920 *The Management Problem*
153 pages. London: Library Press Ltd.

1926 *The Marketing Problem*
216 pages. London: Longmans, Green & Co.

1934 *Fundamentals of Industrial Administration*
660 pages. London: Macdonald & Evans. Ed. H. Macfarland Davis, 1947.

ARTICLES

1918 'The Story of Ponders End Shell Works: Its Labour Problems and Their Solution'
The Engineer. Series of 13 articles, later circulated privately in book form.

1921 'Staff Organization in Factories'
Journal of the Institute of Industrial Administration, October.

1924 'The Organization of Brains in Industry'
Papers of the Rowntree Lecture Conference (No. 19)
Oxford, September.

1927 'Trade Association Statistics'
Paper read before the Royal Statistical Society (1927)
The Accountant. Vol. LXXVII, p. 437, October 1st.

1928 'The Technique of Industrial Administration'
Series of articles under this title published in *The Accountant.*
January-October.

Friedrich-Ludwig Meyenberg
(1875-1949)
Germany

The name of Professor F. L. Meyenberg is linked, like that of Kurt Hegner, with the formative period of the Reichsausschuss für Arbeitszeitermittlung (German Institute of Work and Time Study, or REFA).

Professor Meyenberg was one of the earliest pioneers of management in Germany. From 1919, by which time he was an engineer of mature industrial experience, he began publishing articles on management, popularizing the work of F. W. Taylor in the United States and interpreting it in terms applicable to German industry. In 1925 he became the first managing director of REFA, founded the previous year. In this capacity he made many contributions to the dissemination in Germany of the science of work study and of management. In particular, he was among the first in Germany to insist on giving foremost place to 'the human factor' in management. He was part-editor of the successful 'Second REFA Book', a manual of the principles and practice of work study, which sold over 100,000 copies within a short time of its publication in 1933. During his period with REFA (until 1933) he was also a Professor of Industrial Administration and took a leading part in different societies for the furtherance of the German management movement.

184

In 1933 Professor Meyenberg left his native country and emigrated to Great Britain. This major change did not stop his career in management. By 1938 he had become a management author in the English language and published thenceforth in England four management books on the subjects on which he was an authority—work study and management, particularly from the engineering viewpoint. He lectured in technical colleges and took an active part in the management group of the Institution of Mechanical Engineers. He helped to found the Institute of Economic Engineering, an association of work study engineers.

After the Second World War he returned to Germany to forge a new bond with his old colleagues of REFA. He helped them to set up their organization again after the changes caused by the war, and in the year of his death in Germany he was awarded an honour which must have meant much to him—REFA's honorary membership.

Curriculum Vitae

1875	Born at Hanover on 22nd October.
	Educated at the Goethe Gymnasium and the Polytechnical Academies of Hanover and Berlin. Graduated Dipl.Ing.
1894-8	Served apprenticeship during his college vacations at Royal Railway Main Works, Hanover.
1898-1900	Assistant to Professor Eugen Meyer at the Institute of Physical Engineering, University of Göttingen.
1900-25	Designing engineer in the Gasmotorenfabrik Deutz.
	Tending and shipping engineer, Maschinenbau AG Balcke, Bochum.
	Chief Engineer, Eisenbahn-Signal-Bauanstalt Max Judel & Co., Brunswick.
	Technical Director, Waffenwerk Oberspree Kornbusch & Co.
	Director of Factory Management, Knorrbremse AG, Berlin-Lichtenberg.
	Technical Director, Riebe Kugellager-und Werkzeugfabrik, Berlin-Weissensee.
	In charge of internal organization, business statistics, standardization, Deutsche Werke AG, Berlin.
1925-33	Managing Director, Reichsausschuss für Arbeitszeitermittlung (German Institute of Work and Time Study, or REFA).
1926-33	Professor of Industrial Administration and Head of the Institute for Scientific Management at the Polytechnical

1933	Academy of Brunswick. Emigrated to Great Britain, and later became a naturalized British subject.
1934-5	On the technical staff of the British Iron and Steel Federation.
1935-41	Work study engineer and management expert with Appleby-Frodingham Iron & Steel Co., then with Samuel Fox & Co. Ltd., Stocksbridge.
1941-9	Author, translator, and lecturer on work study and management at Polytechnics, etc.; 1946, member of a British BIOS. technical mission to Germany.
1949	Died in Frankfurt on 1st October aet. 74.

In Germany he was Chairman of the Committee on Practical Application of Standards, German Standards Association; Chairman of the Committee on Industrial Accounts, Association of German Engineers; and Member of Council, German Institution of Production Engineers. In Britain he was a full Member of the Institution of Mechanical Engineers (1939 onwards) and an Honorary Member of the Institute of Economic Engineering (1941 onwards).

Personal Characteristics

A man of first-class intellect who won the respect of the engineering profession in both Germany and Great Britain, Meyenberg had many of the traditional characteristics of the professor—modesty, a quiet manner of speaking, short sight, indifferent health during the last years of his life, and a simple manner of living. The start of a new life in England, made necessary by departure from Germany, was not easy for him; it disturbed his work and brought economic difficulties which he never entirely surmounted. His return home after the Second World War was a great joy to him, and one must admire the fortitude with which he adapted himself and pursued his lifework in England during these troubled years.

Selected Publications

BOOKS

1924	*The Place of Standardization in the Organization of an Engineering Plant* Berlin: Julius Springer.
1938	Co-author of *The New Management* by H. T. Hildage, T. G. Marple and F. L. Meyenberg. 358 pages. London: Macdonald and Evans.
1942	*Economic Control of Iron and Steel Works*

332 pages. London: Chapman and Hall Ltd. The book is based on two series of articles originally published in *Metallurgia* and *Iron and Steel* (see below, 1938-40 and 1940-41).

1945   *Time Study and Rate-fixing*
Published by the Institute of Economic Engineering.
London: Pitman.

1951   *Industrial Administration and Management* (posthumously published)
London: Pitman.

ARTICLES

1919   'The Basic Principles of Scientific Management—an Aid in Economic Reconstruction'
Technik und Wirtschaft. Vol. 12, pages 353-65.

1921   'A critical review of Taylorism. An analysis in the light of two new publications in the managerial literature'
Technik und Wirtschaft. Vol. 14, pages 402-13.

1924   'Factory Management and Factory Organization'
ZVDI, Vol. 68, page 34.

1925-33 Editor of the journal *Maschinenbau*, published by the Verein Deutscher Ingenieure.

1929   'The Adoption of standards in practice'
Masch-Bau Betrieb. Vol. 8, pages 465-66.

1929   'Training of Engineers at Technical High Schools'
Masch-Bau Betrieb. Vol. 8, pages 3-6.

1930   'The Significance of Scientific Management'
Technik und Wirtschaft. Vol. 23, pages 1-3.

1931   'The Finances of a Technical-Scientific Association and Publishing House'
Technik und Wirtschaft. Vol. 24, pages 141-146.

1931   'The Human Factor in Factory Operation'
Masch-Bau Betrieb. Vol. 10, pages 614-16.

1931   'Industrial Costing; the Engineer and Industrial Costing'
ZVDI, Vol. 75, pages 61-62.

1932   'Evaluation of Operating Costs Per Electric Truck Conveying'
Der Betrieb. Vol. 11, page 95.

1938-40 'Industrial Administration and Production Control'
Series of articles in *Metallurgia* (England).

1940-41 'Features of Costing and Accountancy in Iron and Steel Industry'
in *Iron and Steel* (England).

1945-7 Editor of *The Engineers' Digest*, London.

William Henry Leffingwell
(1876-1934)
United States

W. H. Leffingwell was the first person to demonstrate that the principles of Scientific Management as they had been applied to production could be applied with equal success in the office.

His writings are still standard works. His first major contribution was his book *Scientific Office Management* (1917), the forerunner of all modern studies in office management. In 1921 he published his eight principles of scientific office management. In 1925 came *Office Management Principles and Practice,* a comprehensive treatise presenting his philosophy of management and expounding its application to office work. This book earned a place also in the general literature of management.[1] His third book, *Textbook of Office Management* (1932), was included in H. A. Hopf's selection of fifty leading management books in 1945.[2]

Leffingwell's influence through his books and his many articles was widened by much practical success, from his first application in his own office of the methods of F. W. Taylor, throughout his later distinguished career as a consultant. The essence of the new attitude he brought to office management was the replacement of forms and systems by the intelligent application of universal management principles. He was a prominent figure in the management movement at home and abroad, and his work was recognized in 1933 by his election to an important general management honour in America—the presidency of the Taylor Society.

Leffingwell endowed a medal during his presidency of the National Office Management Association. It is awarded annually, not for inventing a machine, appliance or device, not for writing a book, but for outstanding accomplishment of practical value in office management. This criterion was the one by which he also measured his own achievement.

Curriculum Vitae

1876   Born on 14th June in Woodstock, Ont, Canada, of a family whose ancestors came from England to settle in Connecticut in 1637. His father was a woodworker.
He attended high school in Grand Rapids, Michigan.

1893   Started work as a stenographer.

1895   Stenographer in an engraving house in Chicago.

circ 1897   Stenographer in a stockyards commission house.

1900   Private secretary to a manufacturing superintendent; then he worked in the advertising business in Erie, Pennsylvania.

1903-10   Stenographer in a mail-order publishing house in New

---

[1] Its importance is noted, for instance, in 'A History of Scientific Management in the United States of America' by H. P. Dutton, in *Advanced Management,* October, 1953.

[2] Hopf: *Soundings in the Literature of Management,* 1945 (details of publication in Appendix II).

York, where he became successively circulation manager, office manager and general manager.

1910-14   In England, France, Belgium and Germany, establishing branches for his employer and studying management practices and office methods.

1914   Returning to the United States, he joined the management engineering firm of L. V. Estes Inc., becoming manager of their office efficiency department in 1916.

1918-34   Head of the W. H. Leffingwell Co., a professional consulting organization, after 1920 called the Leffingwell-Ream Company.

1934   Died on 19th December aet. 58.

He was a member of The American Society of Mechanical Engineers, the Taylor Society (President 1933 and 1934), The American Management Association, and the National Office Management Association (President 1929-32). In 1927 he was Chairman of the Society of Industrial Engineers' national committee on the elimination of waste in offices.

Personal Characteristics

W. H. Leffingwell is remembered for his generosity in sharing the results of his researches with others, and for his unfailing good will and courtesy. One cannot but admire the man who, beginning his career as a male shorthand typist, succeeded by his independent endeavour in originating a whole new branch of management knowledge, and in becoming an internationally-known authority on its practice.

Selected Publications

BOOKS

1917 *Scientific Office Management*
262 pages. Chicago: A. W. Shaw Co.

1918 *Making the Office Pay* (Editor)
389 pages. Chicago: A. W. Shaw Co.

1918 *Automatic Letter Writer and Dictation System* (Editor)
308 pages. Chicago: A. W. Shaw Co.

1925 *Office Management Principles and Practice*
850 pages. Chicago: A. W. Shaw Co.

1926 *Office Appliance Manual* (Editor)
836 pages. Chicago: A. W. Shaw Co.

1932 *Textbook of Office Management*
Revised in 1943 and 1950 by E. M. Robinson.
649 pages. New York: McGraw Hill Publishing Co.

Beginning in 1916 and continuing to the time of his death, Leffingwell contributed many articles on scientific office management to management periodicals, especially the Taylor Society *Bulletin* and to *System* Magazine and its successor publications. His first published article, entitled 'My Plan for Applying "Scientific Management" in Offices' appeared in *System* in October 1916. Nearly all his addresses to national and international management societies were published, including three to Congresses of the International Committee of Scientific Management.

A comprehensive bibliography of Leffingwell's writings appears on pages 14-15 of *A Bibliography on Office Management,* compiled by Dorothy B. Goldsmith and published by the National Office Management Association in 1931.

Leon Pratt Alford
(1877-1942)
United States

L. P. Alford was the pioneer of 'management handbooks'. These handbooks, edited by Alford who was a distinguished engineer and published by the Ronald Press Co., interpreted the work of the earlier management pioneers and did much to disseminate knowledge about management at a time when few textbooks were available for the use of engineers. The handbooks aroused interest at all levels of industry and became standard works both in the United States and in Europe.

Alford's second major contribution was his work for The American Society of Mechanical Engineers. From 1912 until his death he was continuously serving on ASME committees. He was the first chairman of the Management Division on its creation in 1920. Two years later he produced the first of the decennial reports of ASME on 'Ten Years Progress in Management'. He was the author of the second in 1932 and his preparations for the third were well-advanced when his death occurred in 1942. These reports, covering a period of thirty years and prepared under the unifying influence of a mind deeply versed in management literature and practice, form a unique contribution to our knowledge, a brief yet authoritative guide among the many more ponderous volumes which exist.

Alford made several original contributions to literature on industrial economics, particularly on the collation of quantitative data, showing in this way how a qualified engineer could bridge the gap between technology and business affairs. Above all, however, his contribution was interpretative. He passed on to later generations through his handbooks and reports a better understanding of the work of the early pioneers. His wide influence was due to the singular breadth of view, balance of judgment, and clarity of expression with which he fulfilled this task.

In 1931 he was awarded the Gantt Medal 'for long and distinguished service in the field of industrial engineering'.

Curriculum Vitae

1877   Born on 3rd January of colonial ancestry at Simsbury, Conn.
           Educated at Plainville (Conn.) High School.
1896   BS in Electrical Engineering, Worcester Polytechnic Institute (ME in 1905).
1896-1907 Entered McKay Metallic Fastening Association, Winchester, Mass, rising from assistant machine-shop foreman to chief of the mechanical engineering departments of the various McKay companies, which united to form part of the United Shoe Machinery Company. In 1902 he was materially responsible for the design and building of the United Shoe Machinery Plant at Beverly, Mass, at that time the largest reinforced-concrete machine shop in the world.
1907-17   An editor of *The American Machinist*, becoming Editor-in-Chief in 1911.

1917-21	Editor of *Industrial Management*.
1921-42	With the Ronald Press Co. as Editor of the journals in the management field (*Management Engineering, Management and Administration*, etc): on the Board, 1925-42; Vice-President, 1922-34.
1935-7	Undertook two management studies for Government Departments as a consulting engineer.
1937-42	Professor of Administrative Engineering in New York University and head of the Industrial (later Administrative) Engineering Department.
1942	Died on 2nd January in New York aet. 65.

He was awarded by The American Society of Mechanical Engineers the first Melville Prize Medal (1927). He was a Member of the Society from 1900 and was elected an honorary Member one month before his death. He was made an honorary Doctor of Engineering by Worcester Polytechnic Institute in 1932.

Personal Characteristics

'L. P. Alford possessed the industrious and solid virtues of his New England background. His customary modest manner and softly spoken voice accentuated the sincerity and logic of clear thinking, lucidly expressed. The orderliness of his mind was fertile ground for the principles of management which he unearthed, studied, practised, formulated and taught. His fair, benevolent and bespectacled countenance is best remembered as being lightened with an infectious and disarming smile . . . He spoke forcefully and lucidly with an economy of words and an abundance of sound sense and wrote in like manner.'[1] Above all, he knew how to stimulate and direct the best efforts of other men.

Selected Publications

BOOKS

1924 *Management's Handbook* (Editor)
1607 pages. New York: Ronald Press Co.
1928 *The Laws of Management Applied to Manufacturing*
266 pages. New York: Ronald Press Co.
1934 *Cost and Production Handbook* (Editor)
1544 pages. New York: Ronald Press Co.
1934 *Henry Laurence Gantt, Leader in Industry*
315 pages. New York: The American Society of Mechanical Engineers.

[1] Quoted from obituary in *Mechanical Engineering*, 1942.

1940 *The Principles of Industrial Management for Engineers*
531 pages. New York: Ronald Press Co.
1944 *Production Handbook* (Co-editor with J. R. Bangs)
1650 pages. New York: Ronald Press Co.

PAPERS

His contributions to the papers and reports of The American Society of Mechanical Engineers are too many to be enumerated. The scope of his papers included high-speed drilling, industrial relations, preferred numbers, factory construction and arrangement, production control, and the evaluation of manufacturing operation. In addition to all these he wrote papers for the Society for the Promotion of Engineering Education, the American Management Association and the American Engineering Council, and other papers which were given in England, Japan and Germany.

Henry Sturgis Dennison
(1877-1952)
United States

Henry Sturgis Dennison was an industrialist who between the two
world wars played a creative part in many aspects of the management movement, both in the United States and internationally.

He first became known for making the management of his own medium-sized manufacturing company among the most progressive in America. In 1911 he and his uncle put through a profit-sharing and management-sharing plan in the company. Two hundred employees were brought into partnership in the management as 'voting shareholders' with a share in choosing directors. Since then the destiny of the company has been completely in the hands of the current 'industrial partners', ie the principal employees. In the 1920's he pioneered with an unemployment insurance scheme and with an elaborate pattern of 'executive development'. Dennison's aim was to convince American business, through his own example, that it should give service to employees and to the community at large no less than to the shareholders, the traditional beneficiaries of business effort. He sought to establish high employee morale through teamwork, honourable dealing and the use of the scientific method. 'It is the Company as a Fellowship which alone is really worth dreaming and hoping for ... There can't be much fun very long in working for yourself alone; to work with and for others who are working with and for you is what can lift you and swing you along so that the Monday morning start of the week is as keen as the Saturday end ... The absolute measure of men is the extent to which they have operated to capacity—be that capacity what it may—in the service of their fellows.'[1] In preaching this philosophy Dennison helped to lead American business to a new conception of its place in society. He could, in this and other respects also, be called 'the Seebohm Rowntree of America'—the enlightened manager of a private business contributing his experience ever more prodigally to public affairs.

In 1924 he initiated the Manufacturers' Research Association with headquarters in Boston. This was a group of non-competing firms who established conjointly a small research staff as a centre on which to base the exchange of detailed information on their respective management methods. The Association represented a new conception of frankness of co-operation between businesses which was of lasting importance. Although it was dissolved in the depression of 1929-31, it served as the model for the Management Research Groups in Great Britain which have there become permanent.

Dennison was active in the organized management movement in America, particularly in the Taylor Society and the American Management Association. In the international sphere he was a prominent supporter of the International Management Institute along with his

---

1 From the *Memorial Booklet* published by the Dennison Manufacturing Co. in 1952.

friend E. A. Filene, and served as its Vice-Chairman throughout its six years' existence.

Dennison wrote, among other works, a short book—*Organization Engineering* (1931)—which had been called 'one of the clearest and most fundamental expositions of the subject of which our American literature may boast.'[1] His work was recognized in 1932 by the award of the Gantt Medal (by The American Society of Mechanical Engineers and the Institute of Management) as 'one of the leading contributors to the development of the science and art of management'; and in 1940 by the award of the Taylor Key (by the Society for the Advancement of Management).

Curriculum Vitae

1877	Born on 4th March at Roxbury, Mass.
	Educated at Roxbury Latin School and at Harvard University (A.B., 1899).
1899	Joined the family business, The Dennison Manufacturing Company, Framingham, Mass., a medium-sized concern producing paper products such as jewellers' boxes, tags, labels, sealing wax and crepe paper.
1906	Manager of Works, Dennison Manufacturing Company.
1917-52	President of Dennison Manufacturing Company.
1917-18	Advisor to the Chairman of the War Industries Board, and Assistant Director of the Central Bureau of Planning and Statistics.
1919	Member of President Wilson's Industrial Conference.
1921	Member of President Harding's Unemployment Conference.
1922-28	Director, Service Relations Division, the United States Post Office Department.
1926-52	Trustee of the Twentieth Century Fund.
1934	Chairman, Industrial Advisory Board, United States Department of Commerce.
1935-43	Adviser, National Resources Planning Board.
1935-9	First American Employers' Representative, International Labour Office, Geneva.
1937-45	A Director and Deputy Chairman, Federal Reserve Bank of Boston.

---

[1] by Harry Arthur Hopf, in a book review of *The Making of Scientific Management* by Urwick and Brech. *The Management Review* (American Management Association, New York), Jan-Feb 1947.

1951-2   Member, National Manpower Council, Columbia University.
1952   Died 29th February aet. 75 at Framingham, Mass.

He was a President of the Taylor Society and a Member of Council of the American Management Association. He was an honorary ScD of the University of Pennsylvania (1927) and honorary Doctor of Business Administration, University of Michigan (1929).

Personal Characteristics

'Henry S. Dennison . . . was certainly not a typical businessman . . . His business acumen built the paper products company . . . into one of the most successful of its kind in the world. Yet he never appeared to be interested in money or even power. It was the "operation" and the "team" behind it that concerned him. Like E. A. Filene who was his good friend, he had a strong bent for the social . . . He was a "liberal" in the old-fashioned usage of the word.'[1]

The many who were privileged to know him remember not only the kindness and vitality of a broad human character, but also the wisdom of a distinguished mind. Interested in every field of knowledge, whether philosophy, literature, or the arts, he was a man who understood the art and science of management not only in their application to business but, even more, in the living of a constructive and gracious life.

Perhaps the dominant impression left in the minds of many of his friends was the inexhaustible sense of fun with which he illuminated alike the most profound argument and the simplest social occasion. It was this which prevented his high seriousness of purpose from ever tempting him to become, even for a moment, pompous. It was fun to work with him and fun to play with him.

Probably it was this ultimate simplicity which left his memory enshrined in the hearts of many much younger people, in no way related to him, as 'Pop Dennison'.

Selected Publications

BOOKS

1926 *Profit Sharing and Stock Ownership for Employees*
(with others)
New York: Harper and Brothers.
1931 *Organization Engineering*
New York: McGraw Hill Publishing Co.

---

1 *The Boston Herald*, Editorial, March 3, 1952.

1938 *Modern Competition and Business Policy* (with others)
New York: Oxford University Press.
1938 *Toward Full Employment* (with others)
New York: McGraw Hill Publishing Co.
(The last three were anticipated, in briefer form, in the chapter on 'Management' in *Recent Economic Changes,* being the Report presented to President Hoover's Conference on Unemployment, 1929.)

ARTICLES
The following is only a brief selection from the very large number of papers and lectures delivered over a considerable period: —
1922 'Management and the Business Cycle'
Proceedings of the American Statistical Association.
1924 'Who Can Hire Management?'
Taylor Society *Bulletin.*
1925 'Business Management and the Professions'
Proceedings of the American Academy of Political and Social Science.
1926 'How Manufacturers Can Co-operate with Each Other to secure Maximum Efficiency in Industry'
Papers of the Rowntree Lecture Conference, Oxford, England.
1929 'Probable Effects on Mechanization in Industry'
Proceedings of the American Economic Association.
1931 Contributed chapter to *Restriction of Output among Unorganized Workers* by S. B. Mathewson. New York: The Viking Press.
1932 'Ethics in Modern Business'
Weinstock Lectures.

By courtesy of the National Cyclopaedia of American Biography

Horace King Hathaway
(1878-1944)
United States

Horace K. Hathaway was, along with Barth, Gantt and Cooke, one of the four close associates with whom over a period of years F. W. Taylor worked out his system of management. Taylor considered

Hathaway to be 'the best all-round man in the movement'.[1]

Hathaway's personal achievement was the application of scientific management to the Tabor Manufacturing Company of Philadelphia, manufacturers of moulding and other machine shop plant. When he went there in 1904 the company was in bad financial straits. In 1910 the remarkable improvement in its position was used by Brandeis in the Eastern Rates Case hearings (a law case dealing with a proposed rise in railway rates) as the strongest argument for the efficiency of scientific management. The material value of the company's output had grown to fully three times that of 1904, while the size of the factory and the amount of capital equipment had remained substantially the same and the labour force had been reduced. The Tabor plant became, with the Link Belt plant as managed by J. M. Dodge, 'the most celebrated demonstration ground and school connected with the scientific management movement'.[2]

This work was the essence of Hathaway's contribution to management and it was recognized in 1942 by the award to him of the Taylor Key from the Society for the Advancement of Management. He is to be remembered also, however, for important articles contributed to journals. Those on the planning department and on elementary time study were in particular regarded as classics.

Curriculum Vitae

1878	Born on 9th April in San Francisco.
	Educated at San Francisco public schools, Williamson trade school, and Drexel Institute, Philadelphia.
1896-1902	Associated with the Midvale Steel Company of Philadelphia, starting as an apprentice and working up to journeyman machinist, draftsman, inspector, gang-boss, and finally tool-room foreman.
1902-04	Superintendent of the Payne Engine Company, Elmira, NY, manufacturer of boilers, steam engines and special machinery.
1905	Engaged by James Mapes Dodge to assist in the installation of the Taylor System in the Philadelphia plant of the Link Belt Company.
1905-07	At the request of F. W. Taylor, and at first on loan from the Link Belt Company, installed the Taylor System in the Tabor Manufacturing Company of Philadelphia.

---

[1] Drury: *Scientific Management,* page 109 (details of publication in Appendix II).

[2] Drury, *op. cit.,* p. 148.

	Acted first as superintendent and later became works manager and vice-president.
1907-17	While continuing to be vice-president of the Tabor Manufacturing Company, he took up consulting practice in Philadelphia in association with Taylor. During this period, he also lectured regularly at the Harvard Business School, The Wharton School of the University of Pennsylvania and on various occasions at New York University and the Massachusetts Institute of Technology.
1917-19	Commissioned in the US Army and saw service in Europe.
1919-23	Resumed consulting practice in Philadelphia.
1923-26	Consulting engineer to the Industrial Association of San Francisco.
1927-28	General Manager of the Schlage Lock Co., San Francisco.
1929-41	Retained for a short period by Manning, Maxwell and Moore, New York City (railway and machine tools), and then for a number of years by the Mallinckrodt Chemical Works of St Louis. From 1937 to his death, he was also a consulting professor at the Graduate School of Business of Stanford University.
1941-44	Private consulting engineering practice in San Francisco.
1944	Died on 12th June aet. 66, in Palo Alto, Calif.

For his services in the First World War he was made an Officer of the Ordre de l'Etoile Noire by the French Government.

He was a member of The American Society of Mechanical Engineers and of the Society for the Advancement of Management.

Personal Characteristics

In the Taylor group Hathaway was, although the youngest member, perhaps the calmest and most evenly balanced. A tireless and meticulous worker, he was nonetheless gregarious and genial with a dry vein of humour. Able to gain the complete confidence of his workmen, he always seemed to be enthusiastically enjoying whatever he happened to be doing. A comment of Taylor's upon him in the early days was:

'For about three years past I have been very intimately thrown with Mr. Hathaway. Time after time, when the decision rested with him, I have seen him choose the straight-forward, honest and direct way of dealing with men and the square way of treating them. It is needless for me to add that I look upon Mr. Hathaway as one of the most able and brilliant young men that I know of.'[1]

Selected Publications

ARTICLES

1906 'Discussion of Mr. Taylor's "Art of Cutting Metals" '
New York: Trans. ASME, Vol. 28, pp. 287-290.

1911 'Prerequisites to the Introduction of Scientific Management'
New York: *Engineering Magazine,* Vol. 41. Reprinted in *Scientific Management,* ed. C. B. Thompson, Harvard, 1914.

1912 'Elementary Time Study as a Part of the Taylor System of Scientific Management'
New York: *Industrial Engineering,* Vol. 11, pp. 85-95.

1912 'The Planning Department, Its Organization and Function'
New York: *Industrial Engineering,* Vol. 12. Reprinted in *Scientific Management,* ed C. B. Thompson, Harvard, 1914.

1915 'Scientific Management and its Relations to the Foundry Industry'
Cleveland: Transactions of the American Foundrymen's Association, Vol. 24, pp. 83-120.

1916 'Proposed Plan for Activities of Machine Shop Sub-committee of ASME'
New York: *Journal* of ASME, Vol. 38, p. 972.

In his later years he was a frequent contributor of articles on applied scientific management to the transactions of various technical societies. Many of them were translated into foreign languages.

---

[1] Written by Taylor to the President of The American Society of Mechanical Engineers in 1907. See Copley: *Life of F. W. Taylor,* Vol. ii p. 181 (details of publication in Appendix II).

Gustave-L. Gérard
(1879-1949)
Belgium

Gustave-L. Gérard was a pioneer of the management movement in Belgium during more than three decades.

In his early career (from 1906) he was one of Europe's first professional management consultants, specializing in organization and in the encouragement of engineering standardization. This latter work led him to become the founder of the Belgian Standards Organization and then to be appointed to the Central Industrial Committee, a key policy-forming body in the industrial economy of Belgium. From this position Gérard played for many years an important part in the industrial development of his country.

To this engineer, imbued with a sense of order and logic, the development of better management in industry was a fundamental preoccupation. In 1922, with Edmond Landauer and Robert Caussin, he made the first contacts with a view to creating an organization devoted to management studies. In 1925, the year in which he was a chief organizer of the Second International Management Congress in Brussels, these contacts bore fruit in the creation of the Comité National Belge de l'Organisation Scientifique (CNBOS). The CNBOS had his influential support throughout the rest of his life, and from 1940 to 1948 he undertook its presidency. He aided its work also from outside. He was responsible for the creation of the Science-Industry Fund (1929), for ensuring co-operation between research establishments and the leaders of industry; of the Co-ordinating Committee for Distribution Studies (1932) under the aegis of the International Chamber of Commerce; and of the Committee for Professional and Technical Education (Comité de l'Enseignement Professionnel et Technique) (1926). He was the author of an excellent book containing a collection of recommendations on good management; the writer of regular articles on management for a wide audience over many years in the journal *L'Etoile Belge;* and the editor of a series of special publications on management subjects.

Gérard had all the genius required for making an individual and profound contribution to the principles and practice of management. He deliberately chose, nevertheless, to make a contribution of another kind. He was a born organizer, with the gift of enlisting support for projects of many kinds likely to benefit the Belgian economy on the national industrial level. He concentrated his energies on the constant creation of study groups, committees, research organizations, funds, and so on, staffing them with teams of individuals giving voluntary service and drawn from the same circles likely to benefit by the results of their efforts. In this way, inspiring enthusiasm in others while effacing himself, he set in motion over the years a volume of collective activity exceeding by far the compass of one man's possibilities. Since he was a man of high social purpose, this work did much to bring Belgian industry to a new realization of its social responsibilities. His work was, in a word, an example of good management as the art of 'getting things done through people'.

The Belgian management movement recognized his achievement in 1948 by appointing him to the honorary presidency of CNBOS and by instituting the Gustave-L. Gérard Prize, awarded for a contribution to the advancement of management.

Curriculum Vitae

1879   Born on 24th April in Liège.

1902   Diploma as Civil Engineer (Mines) at Liège University.

1902-06 Engineer in the design department of a large rolling stock and metallic structure manufacturing company, travelling several times to South Africa on the company's behalf.

1906-14 Consultant in mechanical engineering factories.

1918   Member of the Central Industrial Committee (Comité Central Industriel) of Belgium which became in 1946 the Federation of Belgian Industries; from 1927 to 1946 he was its managing director.

1919   Founder of the Belgian Standards Organization (Association Belge de Standardisation, after 1946 the Institut Belge de Normalisation). He was successively Secretary-General, Vice-President and President (1946-9).

1921-49 Secretary of the Belgian Committee of the International Chamber of Commerce.

1926   Technical Counsellor and (1928) Member of the Board of the International Labour Office (Bureau International du Travail), and subsequently part-founder of the Belgian Association of Industrial Employers (Association des Employeurs Industriels).

1949   Died aet. 70 on 11th January in Brussels.

He was a President of the Association of Engineers of Liège University (1934-7) and a President of the Federation of Belgian Engineers' Associations (1934-5).

Personal Characteristics

'What one noticed in him at once was his direct way of seeing things, of penetrating to the heart of a problem. This clarity of thought emanated from an upright character, from a complete integrity.

He gave himself inexhaustibly to his work and seemed never to pause for an instant, drawing his associates with him in his tireless drive, demanding much from them but more from himself. He called on industry for effort, effort in the economic sphere, effort in the technical sphere, effort towards science, effort towards progress.

The multiplicity of his interests did not give his work the stamp of careless improvisation. He practised his own maxim: "Everything worth doing is worth doing well", and this pride in a job well done showed itself in his writing, to the simplicity of which was added the charm of a naturally elegant style. If another trait characterized him it was his gift for synthesis. He would crystallize in a few words, objectively and accurately, the conclusions of a whole meeting's debate. As an employers' representative he was particularly appreciated for his humanity in social problems. And finally, he expended himself without stint in the moral and social purposes which guided his lifework.'[1]

Selected Publications

1929 *L'Art de l'Organisation* (The Art of Management)
    90 pages. Brussels: La Renaissance du Livre. Second ed 1943, revised, 102 pages.

From 1932 to 1947 with the aid of the Solvay Fund, Gérard edited some fifty publications entitled 'Studies of the Central Industrial Committee' (Etudes du Comité Central Industriel), among which were certain noteworthy contributions to management knowledge in Belgium, on the subjects of social security, factory hygiene and health, accident prevention, industrial organization, distribution, purchasing power and salaries, work qualification, budgetary control, technological unemployment, proportion of labour in different industries, professional organization and the activity of industrial federations.

He also published an article each week for 20 years (more than a thousand articles) in *L'Etoile Belge,* under the pseudonym 'Observer'.

---

[1] Extracts translated from 'Gustave-L. Gérard' by R. Caussin, in *Organisation Scientifique,* Monthly Bulletin of CNBOS, January 1949.

Wallace Clark
(1880-1948)
United States

Wallace Clark made one of the greatest single contributions of any American towards making American methods of management known and used outside his own country.

During many years he worked in European countries as a management consultant, advising both private and public concerns. That the older societies of Europe appreciated his exceptional understanding of their problems is shown by the offices and honours which came to him and by the number of languages into which his writings have been translated.

Americans also recognized his achievement. The Gantt Medal was awarded to him by The American Society of Mechanical Engineers and the Institute of Management in 1934 'in recognition of his distinguished service in the development and promotion of scientific management in the United States and abroad'. On his death four leading American management bodies[1] established the Wallace Clark International Management Award for 'a distinguished contribution to scientific management in the international field'.

The basis of the philosophy of management which Wallace Clark introduced into Europe was the principles and methods of Henry Laurence Gantt, under whom he had begun his career. He developed and adapted the work of Gantt, adding in his maturity contributions of his own. His industrial gospel for Europe was 'to remove all obstacles to a free flow of work, starting from the bottom up, considering nothing as static or impossible'. This implied, of course, more production and better quality in less time and at lower cost, but even more, it connoted better working conditions and the philosophy characteristic of Gantt towards human beings in their work. It was nothing else than the 'mental revolution' postulated by Taylor. In Europe it merged into the productivity drive which has become an integral part of the effort for economic recovery after the Second World War. Wallace Clark helped to lay the foundations on which the European productivity movement is based.

In 1952 his wife, Mrs. Pearl Clark, who had long been his business partner, retired to establish at New York University the Wallace Clark Institute of International Management, where the Reports and other records incorporating his international experience have been collected for use in research and education in the international management field.

Curriculum Vitae

1880   Born in Cincinnati, Ohio, 27th July. His great-grandfather Clark, born in England, was one of the first lawyers in Cincinnati. His maternal grandfather Robert Rankin, born in Scotland, was a contractor building reservoirs and canals.

1902   Graduated from University of Cincinnati, BA degree.

1902-08 Clerical position Cincinnati and the Philippines.

1908-13 Private secretary to the president of the Remington Type-

---

1 The American Society of Mechanical Engineers, the American Management Association, the Society for the Advancement of Management and the Association of Consulting Management Engineers. The Award is presented annually through the Council for International Progress in Management (USA).

writer Company, New York.
1913-15   In charge of office work. Attended night classes in Industrial Management at New York University.
1915-20   Member of Henry L. Gantt's management consulting staff; retained in this capacity by Remington Typewriter Company, 1915-17.
1918-20   Head of Scheduling Section of US Shipping Board.
1920-48   Head of his own consulting firm, Wallace Clark and Company.
1926   Industrial member of Kemmerer Finance Mission to Poland. He returned to Poland the following year at the invitation of the Polish Government to organize the modernization of several state industries.
1927-39   Offices in London and Paris installing his methods in private and government industries in 12 countries.
1939   Consultant to the French Purchasing Mission in New York.
1940-42   Consultant to US Signal Corps and several other government agencies in Washington.
1942-48   Resumed his private consulting practice, chiefly in the United States and Canada.
1946-48   Chairman of the International Committee of the National Planning Association which presented his Report and recommendations on 'The Export of Technology', preceding 'Point Four'.
1948   Died aet. 68 in New York.

Wallace Clark was awarded the Order of Polonia Restituta in 1926. He was an honorary Doctor of Engineering of the Stevens Institute of Technology; Fellow of The American Society of Mechanical Engineers; Fellow of the Society for the Advancement of Management; Member of the Institute of Industrial Administration (Great Britain); of the Institution of Civil Engineers (France); of the Masaryk Academy (Czecho-Slovakia). He served as adviser on Scientific Management to the International Labour Office, and as American representative on the International Committee of Scientific Management.

Personal Characteristics

Among many published tributes to Wallace Clark are the following:
'He was always the quiet, unassuming colleague and generous friend, never seeking the limelight or the transient glamor of public recognition, but always applying that penetrating intelligence and fine understanding to the consideration of problems presented, and striving for solutions which, when attained, owed much to his commonsense approach and marked powers of analysis.

211

'Wallace Clark possessed many of the natural attributes of leadership: poise, knowledge, simplicity of expression and bearing, helpfulness, objectivity, direct but tactful utterance, discretion, devotion to long-range aims, and carelessness of self. Small wonder, then, that he exercised a strong and lasting influence over thinking and planning in management and related fields.'

The above from a leading American engineer and consultant.

From an engineer in Europe:

'The greatest achievement of Wallace Clark, in my opinion, his greatest contribution, consists in the men he trained . . . the people who came under his influence in the various countries where he worked and who represent a living tribute to his great work. By his role as a guide and leader of men, Wallace Clark has ensured for himself a permanent place in the history of the Scientific Management movement.'

Selected Publications

BOOKS

1921 *Foremanship* (contributing author)
New York: The Association Press.

1922 *The Gantt Chart*
New York: Ronald Press. Since then, this book has been translated and published in 13 other countries and the 14th translation is in preparation.

1924 Chapter on 'Plant Layout' (with Fred J. Miller) in
Management's Handbook
New York: Ronald Press.

1925 *Shop and Office Forms*
New York: McGraw Hill.

1926 *Report on Polish Monopolies* (included in Report of the Kemmerer Commission to Republic of Poland)

1944 *Production Handbook* (Contributing Editor)
New York: Ronald Press.

A book on *Planning* (not yet published).

ARTICLES

Numerous articles in the Proceedings of various engineering and management societies, and in technical and management journals. A volume of these is to be published.

Raoul Dautry
(1880-1951)
France

The name of Raoul Dautry is to the French railways what the name of Fayol is to the French mining and metallurgical industries.

The extent of his great personal achievement in the railways is widely acknowledged in France. An able engineer and a born organizer, Dautry was an early convert to the science of management. Initial feats of his career were his completion in record time in 1918

213

of a strategic railway line, the reconstruction of the northern railway network using disabled men in 1919-21, and the rapid building of new homes for 60,000 railway employees and families. In 1928 as chief engineer of the Northern Railways, he created 'Management Commissions' instructed to reorganize the technical and administrative services. Appointed later in the same year director of the State Railways, he there instituted similar commissions. The State Railways had been the subject of much popular criticism. Dautry transformed administrative procedures and reorganized the management of stations, factories, depots and warehouses. When he retired in 1937 the State Railways had become among the most efficient of the different networks. His book *Métier d'Homme*, the record of talks given over a long period, has served as a textbook on management to many engineers both in his own industry and in others.

Dautry participated from the outset in the management movement. In 1926 he was among the first engineers to give support to the newly-created Comité National de l'Organisation Française (CNOF). In 1934, when CNOF instituted the School of Scientific Management, Dautry enrolled in the opening course a number of State railwaymen, and persuaded his colleagues in the private railway companies to do the same. Since then railwaymen have regularly attended the School. In 1935-7 he was a member of council of CNOF, and in 1948 he took a leading part in the CNOF International Management Conference.

He was also distinguished as a social reformer. His campaign for slum clearance, his famous garden cities for railwaymen, medical welfare services, children's holiday camps, apprenticeship centres, schools, testify, as also do many passages in his book, to the importance he attached to human beings in all his managerial work.

Curriculum Vitae

1903   Graduated from the Ecole Polytechnique and entered the Northern Railway Company.

1928-37   Director of the State Railway Company.

1931   Reorganized the General Transatlantic Co. and the Aeropostal Co.

1934   Chairman of Technical Public Works Commission for dealing with Unemployment.

1937   Retired and entered private industry for a short time (General Electricity Co.).

1939   Minister of Armaments.

1940   Retired from public life.

1944   President of the French Mutual Aid Movement.

1944-46 Minister of Reconstruction and Town Planning.
1944-51 Vice-President of the International Wagon-Lit Co.
1945-51 Mayor of Lourmarin (Vaucluse).
1946-51 French Government Delegate to the Atomic Energy Commission.
1948-51 President of Council, Cité Universitaire of Paris.
1951   Died aet. 71.
He was decorated in 1918 with the Legion of Honour.

Personal Characteristics

Dautry had an intense social consciousness in his organizing work. Sometimes his intimate colleagues would expect to surprise him by proposing to him some great new objective at which to aim. He would instead show them that their vision had not been great enough. When he had conceived one of his many ideas, nothing would shake his determination to realise it in record time. And although all his life he had no interest in wealth for himself, he found the most ingenious means of obtaining finance for the projects he had at heart. His door was open to the humblest, and his somewhat cold and severe manner hid much sensitivity to social misfortune.

He was not an orator, but spoke with clarity. He was a man of wide culture as a result of much reading especially during hours of insomnia. His capacity for work was great. He was first at his desk each morning when not out on sites and set the pace in this respect for all his fellow-workers. At the end of his life, at 71 years of age, he was still the most eager among his colleagues to make progress with the projects he had on hand.

Publication

1937 *Métier d'Homme* (A Man's Profession)
     Paris: Libraire Plon.

Waldemar Hellmich
(1880-1949)
Germany

Waldemar Hellmich's name is honoured by two great German organizations: the Verein Deutscher Ingenieure (Association of German Engineers or VDI) and the Organisation der Deutschen Normung (German Standards Association).

Hellmich was managing director of the VDI from 1916 to 1933, and guided it through the difficult years after the First World War in its work for the German engineering profession. Gifted both as an originator and as a stimulator of effort in others, Hellmich achieved progress for the VDI notably by the creation of many study groups and committees, both in the engineering and the management spheres. Among groups in the latter sphere owing their inception to him were the Arbeitsgemeinschaft Deutscher Betriebsingenieure (Study Group of German Efficiency Engineers), the Reichsausschuss für Arbeitszeitermittlung (German Institute of Work and Time Study, or REFA) and the Ausschuss für wirtschaftliche Fertigung (Study Group for Productivity). He is perhaps best known for his lead in establishing the conception of engineering as a profession with moral responsibilities not less than those of the medical profession. His publication 'The Cultural Mission of the Engineer' (1949) defined an ideal of which German engineers are justly proud.

Hellmich made many contributions to the progress of standardization. A year after he assumed directorship of VDI he became founder-director of the German Standards Association, and he set the movement securely on the path of progress by public speaking and writing. His publications 'Ten Years of Standardization in Germany' (1927) and 'Twenty-five Years of Standardization in Germany' (1942) were considered landmarks in the movement. Later in his career he received many tributes of honour from these two organizations, for his activity in the material aspects of their work, and for the spiritual leadership he gave to them and to the German engineering profession as a whole.

Curriculum Vitae

1880   Born in Berlin on 21st August.
       Educated at the Humanities Gymnasium, the University of Breslau and the Polytechnical Academy of Charlottenburg.
1910   Member of staff in the Association of German Engineers (VDI).
1916-33 Director of the Association of German Engineers.
1917-33 Co-founder and director of the German Standards Association, of the Study Group of German Efficiency Engineers, of the Study Group for Engineering in Agriculture and of the German Metallurgical Society.
1924   Awarded the honorary degree of Dr-Ing by the Polytechnical Academy of Braunschweig for his work in promoting the progress of industry.
1933   Managing Director of the German Hoffman-La Roche AG at Grenzach. Trustee of the German Standards Association.

1942	Awarded the Medal of Honour of the VDI for his contribution to engineering and to standardization.
1948	Honorary member of the Association of German Engineers and honorary president of the German Standards Association.
1949	Died at Grenzach on 1st October aet. 69.

Personal Characteristics

Vision, judgment, fertility of mind, ceaseless energy, and a noble spirit were the qualities which animated Hellmich's career and gained him his privileged place in the history of German engineering.

Selected Publications

1910 'Pension Schemes for Employees in Private Business'
Technik und Wirtschaft, Vol. 3, pp. 488-494.
1911 'The Question of the Competition Clause'
Technik und Wirtschaft, Vol. 4, pp. 39-43.
'Law Relating to the Terms of Association of Municipal Bodies'
Technik und Wirtschaft, Vol. 4, pp. 187-190.
'The Law Relating to Compulsory Vocational Training Schools'
Technik und Wirtschaft, Vol. 4, pp. 269-271.
'The Administration of Public Works in Prussia from 1900 to 1910'
Technik und Wirtschaft, Vol. 4, pp. 544-551.
1913 'State Control and State Intervention in Private Business'
Technik und Wirtschaft, Vol. 6, pp. 37-45.
1923 'The Concept of Labour-Value in the Production of Commodities in Germany'
ZVDI (Journal of the Society of German Engineers), Vol. 67, pp. 965-969.
1925 'Economic Conveying in Works with Particular Reference to the use of Trackless Haulage Trucks'
Masch-Bau Betrieb, Vol. 4, pp. 472-477.
1927 'Ten Years of Standardization in Germany'
ZVDI, Vol. 71, pp. 1525-1531.
'The Nature of German Standardization'
ZVDI, Vol. 71, No. 44.
1929 'The Professional Consciousness of the Engineer'
ZVDI, Vol. 73, pp. 1073-1074.
1930 'The Need for Research!'

ZVDI, Vol. 74, pp. 1525-1526.
'Ten Years' Co-operation among German Industrial Engineers'
Masch-Bau Betrieb, Vol. 9, p. 188.
1931 'The Responsibility of an Engineer'
ZVDI, Vol. 75, pp. 1-4.
1932 'Pros and Cons of Technology'
Der Betrieb, Vol. 11, No. 1.
1942 '25 Years of Standardization in Germany'
Stahl und Eisen, Vol. 62, No. 45, pp. 937-941.
1943 'The Meaning of Standardization'
ZVDI, Vol. 80, pp. 2-7.
1948 'The Spiritual Division among German Engineers'
ZVDI, Vol. 80, pp. 65-67.
1949 'The Cultural Mission of the Engineer'
VDI, Nachrichten, Jg. 3, No. 8, pp. 1-2.

George Elton Mayo
(1880-1949)
Australia

Elton Mayo's main contributions to management were his revelation of the importance of the human and particularly the social factors in industrial relationships, and of the immense difficulty of developing true scientific techniques applicable to the study of social behaviour.

Although he was by birth Australian, his most significant work was accomplished in the United States, at the Department of Industrial Research at Harvard between 1927 and 1947. The Hawthorne Investigations, conducted by a team which he led with the collaboration of the Western Electric Company and the financial support of the Rockefeller Foundation, were by far the most comprehensive study ever attempted of the attitudes and reactions of groups of workers under practical conditions. The material secured justified Mayo's new concept of the motives which influence industrial relationships.

This concept was that logical, economic factors are far less important even in economic relationships than emotional and non-logical attitudes and sentiments. Moreover, of the human factors influencing an employee's attitudes and sentiments, the most powerful are those arising from his participation in social groups. Thus not only must arrangements for work satisfy the objective requirements of accomplishing the purpose to which the effort is directed, but the arrangements will be effective only if, simultaneously, they satisfy for the workers concerned this subjective requirement of social satisfaction in the working process. Our society in the last 100 years, however, has changed its nature. Formerly it was an established society in which men acquired both technical skill and the capacity for collaboration slowly, by 'living into' a prescribed set of traditional routines—in short, through the apprenticeship system. For that society we have substituted 'an adaptive society', vowed to continuous technical change. These technical changes disturb the social routines of the primary working groups and rouse the deepest resentment among the workers. Our capacity to collaborate with each other appears to be diminishing steadily.

The remedy Mayo proposed is that we should learn new 'social skills'. 'If our technical skills are to make sudden and radical changes in our methods of working we must develop social skills that can balance these moves by effecting social changes in methods of living to meet the altered situation. We cannot live and prosper with one foot in the twentieth century and the other in the eighteenth.'[1] He pointed out that whereas high administrators have accepted responsibility for training workers in new technical skills, no one has taken[2] responsibility for training them in the new (adaptive) social skills.

And that involves primarily a new concept of authority, as dependent not on the formal right to require action of others but on the degree to which individuals assent to orders. That in its turn depends upon 'a co-operative personal attitude of individuals on the one hand and the system of communications in the organization on the other'.[3] Above all we must learn to study actual social situations, not theoretical formulations, we must practise what Mayo called 'the clinical approach'. While Mayo's work was based primarily on industrial examples it applies to any form of human co-operation.

[1] *The Social Problems of an Industrial Civilization*, p. 30.
[2] *Ibid* p. 32. [3] *Ibid* p. 50.

Curriculum Vitae

1880   Born on 26th December in Adelaide.
Educated at St. Peter's College, Adelaide, and at Adelaide University, where he took a degree in Logic and Philosophy. He studied Medicine in Edinburgh, Scotland, and was associated with W. H. R. Rivers in his work on psychopathology.

1911-19 Lecturer in Logic, Ethics and Philosophy, Queensland University. During the war he undertook in his spare time the psycho-therapeutic treatment of shell shocked soldiers, the first man in Australia to use this treatment.

1919   Chair of Philosophy, Queensland University.

1922   Went to United States.

1923-26 Undertook industrial research for the Rockefeller Foundation, as a Research Associate of Pennsylvania University.

1926   Associate Professor, Department of Industrial Research, Graduate School of Business Administration, Harvard University.

1929-47 Chair of Industrial Research, without limitation of tenure.

1949   Died on 7th September aet. 69, in Surrey, England.

He was a Fellow of the American Academy of Arts and Sciences, and held the title 'Emeritus' on retiring from his Chair in 1947.

Personal Characteristics

Many people who write of social skill are far from word perfect: in actual situations they require incessant prompting. Not so Elton Mayo. To watch him handle a strange, and sometimes initially suspicious audience was in itself an invaluable lesson in practical psychology. With his slight figure leaning against a table, his fingers busy interminably building up his cigarette holder of many quills and disassembling it again, he just talked: he never made speeches. It is hard to do justice to the quality of those 'talks'; their casualness, their clarity and their humour were the perfect expression of the charm, the persuasiveness and the humanity of the man himself.

A friend who worked as his assistant over a number of years wrote about him:

'My colleagues will understand me when I say that without Elton Mayo's genius for integrating the activities of a working group, and without his unfailing generosity in putting his ideas and wisdom at the disposal of his followers, some of us, I in particular, would have had no insight by which to approach the critical problem of a civilization committed for the first time to a continuous technological evolution with all that implies in the way of skilled social readjustment.'[1]

Selected Publications

BOOKS

1933 *The Human Problems of an Industrial Civilization*
Boston: Division of Research, Harvard Business School. 2nd ed, New York: Macmillan, 1946.

1945 *The Social Problems of an Industrial Civilization*
English edition by Routledge and Kegan Paul Ltd., London, 1952, with an Appendix on *The Political Problem,* reproducing two lectures delivered at Harvard in 1947.

1948 *Some Notes on the Psychology of Pierre Janet*
Cambridge: Harvard University Press.

ARTICLES

The following are some of the most noteworthy of Mayo's many articles:

1929 'Maladjustment of the Industrial Worker'
A chapter in *The Wertheim Lectures on Industrial Relations,* 1928, a volume of lectures on various phases of industrial relations published by the Jacob Wertheim Fellowship for the Betterment of Industrial Relations, Cambridge, Mass: Harvard University Press.

1929 'What is Monotony?'
The Human Factor. Boston: Massachusetts Society for Mental Hygiene, January.

1930 'Changing Methods in Industry'
The Personnel Journal, Vol. XX, No. 1.

1930 'The Work of Jean Piaget'
Ohio State University Bulletin, Columbus, Ohio, Vol. XXXV, No. 3.

1937 'What Every Village Knows'
Survey Graphic, New York, Vol. XXVI, No. 12.

1939 'Frightened People'
Harvard Medical Alumni Bulletin, Vol. XIII, No. 2.

1939 'Routine Interaction and the Problem of Collaboration'
American Sociological Review, Vol. IV.

1941 'The Descent into Chaos'
Privately printed, Harvard Business School.

---

[1] T. N. Whitehead: *Leadership in a Free Society.* University of London Press, 1936.

1945 'Group Tensions in Industry'
Approach to National Unity, a paper prepared for the fifth symposium of the Conference on Science, Philosophy and Religion in Their Relation to the Democratic Way of Life, Inc. Edited by Lyman Bryson, Louis Finkelstein and Robert M. Maciver, New York and London: Harper and Brothers.

1945 'Supervision and what it Means'
Studies in Supervision, lecture given at McGill University, Montreal, 30th January. Montreal: McGill University.

At least seven books on the 'Hawthorne Investigations' have been published. Among them may be mentioned:

Management and the Worker: F. J. Roethlisberger and W. J. Dickson. Harvard University Press, 1939, 10th printing 1950.

The Industrial Worker: T. N. Whitehead, London: Oxford University Press, 1938.

Management and Morale: F. J. Roethlisberger. Harvard University Press, 1942.

Leadership in a Free Society: T. N. Whitehead. University of London Press, 1936.

The Making of Scientific Management, Vol. III, The Hawthorne Investigations. Urwick and Brech. London: Pitman, 1948.

Charles Edward Knoeppel
(1881-1936)
United States

Charles Edward Knoeppel was one of the exponents of the Taylor system of scientific management in the years immediately following the most active period of Taylor and Gantt. In his understanding of management he was noticeably ahead of his time. He is to be remembered for adding several original contributions to the principles and methods already established. By 1907 he had done much work in cost accounting, including development of standard costs, in the foundry industry and elsewhere. By 1908 he had developed methods of factory organization and administration based on the Taylor system. In 1908-9 he is credited, as part of his original work in the use of graphs for management purposes, with probably the earliest use of the cross-over 'break-even' chart, now a standard tool of management. Later in his career he became the original exponent of 'profit engineering' and coined the name 'profitgraph', as more descriptive of the purpose of the break-even chart.

He was an early and prolific writer of books and articles on the science of management. As soon as he had satisfied himself of the practical worth of a development in management, he published a book or an article about it. A glance at the list of his titles is sufficient to show his originality. Since his publications were popular by reason of their lucidity, Knoeppel therefore had a significant share in focussing attention on the science of management at a crucial time in its struggle for acceptance by American industry.

As a contribution to public service Knoeppel played a remarkable part in the work of the Committee on Waste in Industry, organized under Hoover by the Federated Engineering Societies in 1920-1. To this committee he furnished, for the use of its engineers in making analyses of industry, a complete and specific questionnaire which he and his staff had evolved through years of study and practice. This was used by the committee as the basis for its method of work. Knoeppel was himself the author of the chapter of the committee's report entitled 'Purchasing and Sales Policies'.

Curriculum Vitae

1881   Born on 15th April in Milwaukee, Wisconsin.
            He was educated in the public schools of Buffalo, New York, and was prevented by economic difficulties from going to college, although he had prepared to do so.
1899-1904   His earliest employment was as a newspaper reporter; then successively as a labourer and moulder at the Ames Iron Works, Oswego, New York. He progressed to the positions of draftsman and then designer at the Buffalo Forge Company, Buffalo, New York, and soon to office manager, then systematizer at the Parkhurst Boiler Works, Oswego, New York.
1905   Member of the Expert Systematizing Staff of the Library Bureau, Boston, Massachusetts, and engaged in personal consulting work in cost accounting and industrial engineering.
1908   With his father, organized Knoeppel and Knoeppel, Foundry Specialists.
1909   Member of Staff, Emerson Engineers, New York.
1911   Member of Staff, Suffern and Son, New York.
1912   Organized Van Gelder, Knoeppel and Young, Cost Accountants and Industrial Engineers, New York.
1914   Organized C. E. Knoeppel and Co. Inc., Industrial Engineers, New York.
1917-18   Made an 8-month study of shipyard conditions for the Emergency Fleet Corporation and an investigation into

	the employment of women in war work.
1925-29	Associated with Bigelow, Kent, Willard and Co. Inc., Management Engineers, Boston, Mass, as Managing Director of their division, Waste Eliminators Inc.
1929-32	Organized Knoeppel Industrial Counsel, Cleveland, Ohio.
1933-36	Engaged in individual consulting practice in Philadelphia, Pennsylvania, advising on profit planning, economic pricing and variable budgeting.
1936	Died on 29th November aet. 55, in Philadelphia, Pennsylvania.

He was an active member of management societies, and one of the organizers of the Society of Industrial Engineers (1917). He lectured on Organization and Management for two years at New York University.

Personal Characteristics

A man who owed his worldly success to his own efforts from the time he began his working life as a labourer, C. E. Knoeppel deservedly earned the high esteem of his contemporaries. He was a man of charm and candour. Perhaps because his own early difficulties had imbued him with a feeling for the importance of the community, he had an acute sense of public duty and he gave very generously of his time and experience to many causes.

Selected Publications

BOOKS

1911 *Maximum Production in Machine Shop and Foundry*
365 pages. New York: Engineering Magazine Co.
1915 *Installing Efficiency Methods*
258 pages. New York: Engineering Magazine Co.
1916 *Industrial Preparedness*
145 pages. New York: Engineering Magazine Co.
1917 *Organization and Administration*
446 pages. New York: Factory Management Course, Industrial Extension Institute.
1920 *Graphic Production Control*
477 pages. New York: Engineering Magazine Co.
1921 *What Industrial Engineering Includes—for Industrial Executives: 101 Things to Do; 1001 Results Other Secured*
154 pages. New York: C. E. Knoeppel & Co. Inc.
1933 *Profit Engineering—Applied Economics in Making Business Profitable*

227

326 pages. New York and London: McGraw-Hill Publishing Co.

1937 *Managing for Profit—Working Methods for Profit Planning and Control* (with the collaboration of E. G. Seybold)
343 pages. New York and London: McGraw-Hill Publishing Co.

PAPERS
(Selected from a very much longer list)

1907 'Cost Reduction through Cost Comparison'
Series of three articles in March, April and May issues of *The Engineering Magazine,* New York.

1908 'Maximum Production through Organization and Administration'
Series of four articles in April-June issues of *The Engineering Magazine,* New York.

1918 'Industrial Organization as it Affects Executives and Workers'
New York: Trans. ASME.

1918 'Women in Industry'
Chicago, Ill.: *Miscellaneous Publications* of the Society of Industrial Engineers, Vol. 1, February.

1920 'The Future of Industrial Engineering'
Chicago, Ill: *Publications* of the Society of Industrial Engineers, Vol. 3, No. 5, February.

1928 'Human Development as Industry's Real Task'
Blue Ridge, North Carolina: *Proceedings,* 9th Annual Southern Conference on Human Relations in Industry, August.

1929 'Dividend Requirements from Waste Elimination'
Bulletin of the Society of Industrial Engineers, Jan. (An address delivered at the 15th National Convention of the Society, Rochester, NY, October, 1928.)

1930 The following series of seven articles appeared in *Factory Management and Maintenance.* New York: McGraw-Hill Publishing Co., in the months January through July, in the order stated:
'Wanted—the Profit Engineer'
'Profit Planning and Control'
'Profit-making Policies'
'Plotting the Profit Course'
'Isolating Industrial Loss Germs'
'Industrial Pilot House'
'Profit Engineering, The Cure for Marginitis'

228

Kurt Hegner
(1882-1949)
Germany

Kurt Hegner rendered services to the German management movement by his lifelong support of many management associations, and by his original contributions to the development of work study and of standardization.

The introduction of time study and method study into Germany, on the principles of Taylor and Gilbreth, was not easy and required years of team work by those who understood the potentialities of the new science. Hegner was a leader among them. He was from 1928 to 1945 chairman of the first work study organization to be created in Germany—the Reichsausschuss für Arbeitszeitermittlung (German Institute of Work and Time Study, or REFA).

In 1923, before the foundation of REFA, he had already adapted case study material on elementary management accounting from his own machine tool factory, to serve as the basis of short courses which he organized. In 1924, he published his book *A Manual of Standard Processing Time* which became the leading text on the principles and practice of time study. The book served as material for the extended teaching which he now undertook and in which he was the pioneer of the well known REFA teachers. He directly inspired the success-

229

ful 'First' and 'Second' REFA books (1928 and 1933 respectively), manuals of the principles and practice of work study.

Hegner took an active interest from the start in the German standardization movement. Himself chairman of the machine tool committee of the German Standards Association, he did much for the general progress of the movement, helping to overcome the considerable resistance with which it had to contend.

In addition to the above activities he gave service to the Reichskuratorium für Wirtschaftlichkeit (German Institute of Management or RKW), the Ausschuss für wirtschaftliche Fertigung (Study Group for Productivity) and the Arbeitsgemeinschaft Deutscher Betriebsingenieure (Study Group of German Efficiency Engineers).

Curriculum Vitae

1882	Born on 9th December at Zeitz.
1899	Apprenticed to Ludw, Loewe & Co., Berlin (machine tool manufacturers).
1908	Became works manager of the Standard products plant.
1919	Works manager of the milling machine manufacturing plant.
1926-49	Technical director of the company and member of the Board.
1949	Died in Berlin on 17th September aet. 67.

He was awarded the Gold Medal of Honour of VDI (Association of German Engineers) in 1941, in particular for his services as chairman of the Arbeitsgemeinschaft Deutscher Betriebsingenieure (Study Group of German Engineers).

Personal Characteristics

Hegner was a gifted speaker, and yet had the modesty necessary to be a good team worker. Though he was a busy executive in a great machine tool concern, his work for REFA was always of the nature of a crusade to him. He considered the great events in REFA'S progress as the highlights of his life. He died at his desk working at a speech for a REFA function, in which he demanded systematic principles for the conduct of REFA courses, and which he termed a 'sort of confession'.

Selected Publications

BOOKS

1924   *Lehrbuch der Vorkalkulation von Bearbeitungszeiten*

(Manual of Standard Processing Time)
Berlin: Springer.
1939   *Die Werkzeugmaschine*
(The Machine Tool)
Report to the 77th General Meeting at the Society of German Engineers at Dresden.
Berlin: Publishing House of the VDI (Association of German Engineers).

ARTICLES

1922   'Basic Time-Units for the Calculation of Operating Time'
Der Betrieb, Vol. 4, pp. 323-329.
'Means of Reducing the Cost of Assembly Work'
Der Betrieb, Vol. 4, pp. 244-249.

1923-24 'Costing Problems'
Masch-Bau Betrieb, Vol. 3, p. 701.
'The Costing Problem and Its Solution'
ZVDI, Vol. 68, pp. 821-824.

1926   'Manual on the Evaluation of Operating Times'
Masch-Bau Betrieb, Vol. 5, p. 176.

1928   'Piecework and Rate Fixing'
Masch-Bau Betrieb, Vol. 7, pp. 97-103.

1933   'A more Detailed Study on the Evaluation of the Operating Time'
Second REFA Book. Berlin: Beuth-Vertrieb GMBH.

1937   'Appraisal of Standard Values for Milling on the Basis of Practical Examples from Milling'
Report of the Milling Committee of the Corporation of German Industrial Engineers (ADB) Berlin, pp. 387-388 and pp. 437-438.
'Standardization in Machine Tool Making'
Der Betrieb, Vol. 19, pp. 169-172.
'Standard Values for Milling. Assessment of milling Examples'
Reports of the Mills' Committee of the Corporation of German Industrial Engineers (ADB) Berlin, pp. 287-88.
'The Working Committees of the Corporation of German Industrial Engineers (ADB)'
Der Betrieb, Vol. 21, p. 64.

1944   'New Operating Units in German Machine Tool Making'
ZVDI, Vol. 88, pp. 633-637.
'Future Tasks for German Machine Tool Making'
Werkstattstechnik und Maschinenbau. Berlin: Springer.

Harry Arthur Hopf
(1882-1949)
United States

Harry Arthur Hopf was an outstanding figure in the history of the management movement. His lifework was recognized in 1938 by the award of the Gold Medal of CIOS.

His was the contribution both of a doer and a thinker. In his chosen career as a management consultant, he was in his early days the pioneer, along with W. H. Leffingwell, in applying the methods of scientific management, hitherto confined to the factory, to the domain of the office. In life insurance companies between 1908 and 1917 he made some of the earliest studies and applications of techniques now universally adopted in scientific office management, such as: procedure analysis, standardization of clerical operations and output, production control and job analysis. Somewhat later, he did much original work on executive compensation. The advances made in many aspects of office organization and management during three decades (1918-48) were largely of his inspiration. In the final phase of his career he became a consultant of national and international repute in the broader field of business administration and organization.

As a teacher, Harry Arthur Hopf influenced many of those who are the leaders of today in the world of management. As a worker for the management movement, he helped to create many management societies now prominent in the United States. When these societies ultimately came together, largely through his influence, to found the National Management Council unifying the American management movement, he served as its first chairman from 1933-6. He was one of the founders of CIOS and contributed to its expansion, serving as deputy president from 1935 to 1938.

It was, however, as a scholar and philosopher of the science of management that Harry Arthur Hopf accomplished his most outstanding work. The booklets which he published between 1915 and 1947 surveyed the whole field of management thought and may be classified by subject as follows:

office management, compensation and incentives

the human factor in management

the evolution of management thought and future education for management

management engineering and means of measuring managerial accomplishment

the nature of management and of organization.

The last-named group entitled Harry Arthur Hopf to a place with Fayol and Mary Follett among writers of classics on the philosophy of management. His papers 'Adapting the Industrial Organization to Changing Conditions' and 'Evolution in Organization during the Past Decade' must, in particular, be read by all serious students of organization. Perhaps the best summary of his philosophy of management as a whole is contained in 'New Perspectives in Management'. His general approach was essentially simple: 'It is because of a profound conviction that, for an indefinite period to come the solution of the economic problems of this country will have to be sought through reconstitution of all types of organized human enterprise on levels of simplicity and scope low enough to permit readily of co-ordination and control, that consideration of the rôle of management and what it can and should do to create and preserve optimal conditions in the individual business enterprise appears to be a timely and worthwhile undertaking.' He emphasised the dynamic aspects of management and contributed to the analysis of leadership. Lastly, he put forward the all-inclusive concept of 'optimology, or the science of the optimum'.

It was his thesis that management, whether of individual enterprises or of social and political entities, should strive always for attainment of the optimum, or 'that state of development which, when reached and maintained, tends to perpetuate an equilibrium among the factors of cost, size and human capacity, and thus to promote, in the highest degree, regular realization of its objectives'.

In 1938, he founded the Hopf Institute of Management. 'The stimuli derived from the many activities to which I was devoting myself crystallized in a project that had long been germinating in my mind. It involved the creation of an institute that would devote itself to exploration of the scientific foundations of management, would contribute to the educational development of business executives, and would serve as a world center and clearing house for scholars in the field. These and certain collateral objectives appealed to me as goals of indispensable character in the advancement of the function of management.'

The Hopf Institute of Management has given and continues to give, under the direction of Mrs. Harry Arthur Hopf, valuable service to management along the lines of its founder's ideal.

It is a matter for regret that Harry Arthur Hopf's practical success and the responsibilities that came with it stood between him and that comprehensive book on management which should have collated his writings for easy access by future students. The works of Harry Arthur Hopf are classics of management literature and of great current interest. Their collection for publication would be a service to the movement. It would also be his most fitting memorial.

Curriculum Vitae

1882   Born on 3rd April in London, England. His parents were naturalized British citizens, his father being of German, and his mother of French-German parentage.
            Attended school London, England, and subsequently Kassel, Germany.

1898   Emigrated to the United States as a penniless youth. During the next few years, while earning his living, he managed to complete his education at evening classes, attending the following schools: New York University Schools of Commerce, of Law, and Graduate School of Business Administration; Columbia University School of Business. He obtained the degrees of Bachelor of Commercial Science (1906) (Master 1916) and Master of Business Administration (1922).

1898-1902   Minor clerical positions, including 3 years as junior clerk, American Sugar Refining Company.

1902-14   Germania (now Guardian) Life Insurance Company, New York, rising from foreign-language stenographer to Assistant to Vice-President, and head of Underwriting and Planning activities.

1914-17   Manager, Planning Department, Phoenix Mutual Life

Insurance Co., Hartford, Connecticut.

1917-18   Manager, Planning Department, Smokeless Powder Operating Department, E. I. Dupont de Nemours & Co., Wilmington, Delaware.

1919-22   Organization Counsel and Chairman, New Building Planning Committee, Federal Reserve Bank of New York; Adviser, Personnel Committee and Secretary, Pension Committee, Federal Reserve System.

1922-49   Head of H. A. Hopf and Company, Consulting Management Engineers, New York, and Ossining, New York. In his consulting work Hopf advised on problems of organization, management, compensation, special building planning, and clerical procedures. He also acted as consultant to many governmental agencies.

1938-49   Founder and President, Hopf Institute of Management, Ossining, New York.

1949   Died on 3rd June aet. 67, at Ossining, New York.

He was elected a Fellow of the National Office Management Association in 1936, and was awarded the Taylor Key of the Society for the Advancement of Management in 1947. He was a Knight of the Royal Order of the North Star, Sweden, and an honorary member of the Masaryk Academy, Czechoslovakia. He was a corresponding member of the management societies of Great Britain, France, Germany, and Switzerland; and held the honorary degrees of MSc of Bryant College and DEng of Rensselaer Polytechnic Institute, Troy, NY.

Personal Characteristics

A man of exceptional gifts of mind and character, Harry Arthur Hopf brought to his professional work the wisdom and humanity of the truly cultured man. The life he built for himself from the most humble beginnings, and the friends he made, may be judged from the memorial issue of *Net Results* which contains tributes from the first names in management in half a dozen countries. One of these calls him

'a battler against mediocrity . . . He demanded high standards of accomplishment of his associates and held himself to even stricter self-disciplines. Difficulty always challenged him . . . few men found so much stimulation and incentive in day-to-day living as he . . .

'His great contribution to the world in which he lived has been the heightened dignity and prestige which his accomplishments have earned for the profession which he graced. The art and

235

science of management in the United States and in the world are permanently the better because of him'.[1]

Selected Publications

BOOKS

1940   Chapter VII 'Administrative Co-ordination' in *Public Management in the New Democracy,* ed. by Fritz Morstein Marx.
New York: Harper and Brothers.

1946   *People and Books,* co-author with Henry C. Link.
Published by the Book Industry Committee of the Book Manufacturers Institute, New York.

PAPERS AND BOOKLETS (SELECTED TITLES)

1915   'The Planning Department As a Factor in the Modern Office Organization'
Efficiency Society Journal, Vol. 4, No. 8, November.

1917   'Home Office Organization'
Proceedings, 12th Annual Meeting, American Life Convention, Grand Rapids, Michigan.

1921   'Salary Standardization as an Aid to Industrial Stability'
Proceedings, Society of Industrial Engineers, Fall Convention, Springfield, Mass.

1923   'Physical Factors in Office Planning'
Series of eight articles in the *Office Economist,* Art Metal Company, Jamestown, New York.

1927   'Problems of Bank Organization'
Joint meeting of Taylor Society and American Society of Mechanical Engineers, *Bulletin* of the Taylor Society, Vol. XII, No. 2, April.

1930   'Housing Business Organizations for Efficient Operation'
Architectural Forum, New York, April and May, 1930.
Also *Proceedings,* Chicago Chapter, American Institute of Architects, February.

1931   'Whither Management?'
Proceedings, American Life Convention, Pittsburgh, Pa, 26th Annual Meeting.

1932   'The Evolution of Organization'

---

[1] Professor Erwin H. Schell: *Net Results,* October 1949, p. 49. Published by the Hopf Institute of Management Inc., Ossining, N.Y.

Proceedings, Annual Convention, National Association of Cost Accountants, Detroit, Michigan.

1933   'The Present Status, Responsibilities and Future of the Management Engineer'
Proceedings, Society of Industrial Engineers, 19th National Convention, Chicago, Ill.

1935   'Management and the Optimum'
Proceedings, Comité International de l'Organisation Scientifique, London, 1935, VI International Congress.

1937   'Business Management and the Scientific Point of View'
Joint meeting of Montreal Branch of Engineering Institute of Canada and 4 other Societies; *Engineering Journal* (Canada), Vol. XX, No. 12, December.

1943, 44, 45   'New Perspectives in Management'
A series of 15 articles in *The Spectator,* the Chilton Company, Philadelphia, Pa.

1944   'Organization, Executive Capacity and Progress'
Proceedings, Annual Conference, Life Office Management Association, Boston, Mass.

1945   'Executive Compensation and Accomplishment'
American Management Association, Financial Management Series, No. 78.

1945   'Soundings in the Literature of Management: Fifty Books the Educated Practitioner Should Know'
Hopf Institute of Management Publication No. 6; also *Advanced Management,* Vol. X, No. 3, September, 1945; also incorporated in G. T. Coman: *Sources of Business Information,* Ch. 9, 'Management', Prentice-Hall, New York, 1949.

1946   'Adapting the Industrial Organization to Changing Conditions'
New Brunswick: Rutgers University.

1947   'Evolution in Organization During the Past Decade'
Proceedings, VIII International Congress, Comité International de L'Organisation Scientifique, Stockholm; Hopf Institute of Management publication No. 10.
'Historical Perspectives in Management'
Management Review (American Management Association), New York, Jan, Feb, and Mar 1947; Hopf Institute of Management Publication No. 7.
'Incentives for Executives'
Proceedings, 40th Annual Meeting, American Pharmaceutical Manufacturers' Association, Boca Raton, Fla; also, Hopf Institute of Management Publication No. 9.

Alvin Earl Dodd
(1883-1951)
United States

Alvin Dodd was one of those most responsible for the development of the American Management Association from small beginnings into the front-rank management organization it is today..

The American Management Association was founded in 1923. Its early growth was much set back by the great depression, and when Dodd became its executive vice-president in 1933 it was no more than an obscure institution with some 1600 members. Dodd was a man of organizing and publicizing genius. He set out to establish high quality in the AMA's output, and then to bring its activities

238

prominently before the attention of the business community. His success during 14 years was triumphant. He considered that the services that the AMA offered met a direct need on the part of practical managers, no less urgent than the need for an essential product or service of their business. And so he used the same direct selling methods in promoting the AMA as those of the merchandizing industry in which he had previously worked. Through this approach, and through his systematic organization of activities, including a method for conference planning unrivalled of its kind, the American Management Association grew to attract annual attendances of upwards of 15,000 executives and to achieve the largest publication circulation of any management body in the world. Dodd's written work was not extensive. But as a 'public relations' man he was outstanding. Recognition of this contribution by his colleagues in the American Management movement brought him the Gantt Medal in 1947[1] 'for his leadership in stimulating greater recognition and acceptance of the social responsibilities of management; and for his success in building The American Management Association into an authoritative forum for collecting, analyzing and disseminating management knowledge'.

Curriculum Vitae

1883   Born on 11th March at Hudson, New York.

1905   Graduated from Armour Institute of Technology (now Illinois Institute of Technology) with a BSc degree in engineering.

1905-06 Assistant Principal, Fifth Ward Manual Training School, Allegheny, Pennsylvania.

1906-07 Head, Manual Arts Department, Massachusetts Normal School, North Adams, Massachusetts.

1907-08 President, Eastern Arts Association.

1908-12 Principal, North Bennett Industrial School, Boston, Massachusetts.

1912-16 Director, National Society for Promotion of Industrial Education. Largely through his efforts in this position, the Act was passed which began federally sponsored and financed public vocational education in the United States.

1917   Member, Committee on Classification of Personnel, General Staff, US Army. Here he helped to establish the Army's first programme of personnel management, testing, classification and placement.

[1] The Gantt Medal is awarded annually by The American Society of Mechanical Engineers and the American Management Association.

1917-21 Director, Retail Research Association and Associated Merchandising Corporation.
1921-27 Manager of Distribution Department, US Chamber of Commerce.
1927-29 Lecturer on trade and industrial problems, Northwestern University, University of Chicago, University of Washington, and Stanford University. Director General, Wholesale Dry Goods Institute.
1929-30 Assistant-to-President, Sears, Roebuck and Company.
1930-33 Vice-President in charge of merchandizing and sales, Kroger Grocery and Baking Company.
1933-48 With the American Management Association as Executive Vice-President (till 1936) then President (till 1948).
1949-51 Managing Director, U.S. International Chamber of Commerce.
1951 Died on 2nd June in New York aet. 68.

He was made Honorary President of the American Management Association in 1948. In that year he was also made an honorary Doctor of Laws by Temple University.

Personal Characteristics

Alvin Dodd had a special talent for knowing and liking people, and his sensitive and intuitive nature caused people to like him in return. To a marked degree the success of his many undertakings was due to his ability to put himself in the place of others.

His friend Harry Arthur Hopf called him a catalyst. John M. Hancock spoke of him as 'a man gifted in the ability to integrate into meaningful pattern the random concepts and accomplishments of many specialists in diverse tasks and industries . . . ' He was always interested in the human side of business, and he did a great deal to make management more aware of its social responsibilities.

Selected Publications

BOOKS

1940 *Planning the Package* (written in conjunction with others) New York: American Management Association.
1942 *How to Train Workers for War Industries* (with J. O. Rice) New York: Harper and Brothers.

ARTICLES

The following articles were selected from a much longer list:
1940 'The Ideal Boss in 1940'
Supervision, February.

1940 'What Management Faces'
Forbes, August 15.
1941 'Changing the Course of the Stream'
Dun's Review, August.
1942 'What to do about Salesmen with Little or Nothing to Sell'
Printers' Ink, January 16.
1945 'Negro Employment Opportunities—During and After the War'
Opportunity, April-June.
1947 'Nine Critical Problems Facing Management'
Dun's Review, July.
1948 'Management's Role in Shaping the Future'
Dun's Review, July.
1948 'Productivity—Prices and Markets'
Mechanical Engineering, February.

Edmond Landauer
(1883-1934)
Belgium

Edmond Landauer's name is closely linked with the history of CIOS and of the international management movement. He was one of the chief founders of CIOS, and later its first secretary-general and its vice-chairman. He was also a founder of the International Management Institute, and of the Belgian Committee of Scientific Management. His work was recognized by CIOS in 1935 by the posthumous award of its Gold Medal.

Landauer was a business man of conspicuous personal success.

For many years director of a Roumanian textile manufacturing firm, he brought about in his own managerial job an admirable realization of management principles. He wrote several articles on his methods, revealing clearly his understanding of the ideals and methods of F. W. Taylor, and of the right way to apply them in practice to a European concern. Since Landauer was himself wholly European in character and outlook, his assimilation and active dissemination of the best American management thought and practice were a valuable contribution to the international understanding of the subject.

He was a theorist of repute, as is evidenced by his theory of rational purchasing policy in the textile industry and his several studies on the science of management in general. As a thinker, as an enthusiastic co-ordinator of national efforts towards the growth of the international movement, and as an architect of CIOS, he has a permanent place in management history.

Curriculum Vitae

1883 Born in Brussels 19th November.
He took a doctorate of Science in Brussels, and then spent several years travelling in different countries including the United States and Canada. In the latter country he reorganized a firm with Belgian connexions.
He then took over management of a textile mill in Roumania, the 'Tessatoria Romana'. He was connected with this firm for 20 years and drew from it most of the material for his writings. He lived for several years in Roumania.
In his later years he acted as a textile consultant to firms in Belgium, France, England, Denmark. He led an energetic life of travel throughout Europe, continuing to manage the Roumanian mill from a distance.
1925 Principal organizer of the Second International Management Congress, Brussels.
1927 Secretary-General of CIOS.
1932 Vice-Chairman of CIOS.
1934 Died July aet. 51.
He was a Chevalier of the Order of Leopold and a Commander of the Order of the Crown of Roumania.

Personal Characteristics

Although Landauer could on occasion deliver a brilliant speech and captivate an audience, he usually preferred to remain in the background and even seemed unduly reserved in attitude towards the

243

people with whom he was in frequent contact. Yet he was endowed with much human sympathy. 'The well-being of his workers was a constant preoccupation. With what feeling did he speak to me on occasion of the day nurseries of one of his favourite factories. Himself a man without family, he was the protector of children and of the humblest of his employees.'[1]

Selected Publications

1935 *L'Organisation Scientifique*
Posthumous edition of Landauer's writings in various technical journals in Belgium and elsewhere. Published privately by the Comité National Belge de l'Organisation Scientifique (CNBOS) Brussels. The following are the articles reproduced in this book:—

1923 L'Organisation Industrielle et Commerciale dans l'Industrie Textile Belge.

1925 Les Prix de Revient Industriels.

1926 L'Organisation des Economies dans l'Administration de l'Etat.

1927 L'Avenir de l'Organisation Scientifique.

1927 Le Contrôle du Facteur 'Temps' dans la Fabrication.

1928 Formules d'Achat et de Vente dans l'Industrie Textile.

1928 L'Organisation scientifique dans l'Industrie Textile.

1928 Un Exemple Vécu de Rationalisation Industrielle: L'Oeuvre de Thomas Bata.

1928 Une Loi Générale de la Production Industrielle.

1929 La Direction à Distance.

1931 La Crise Economique et la Rationalisation.

1931-33 Les Crédits de Banque et le Contrôle Budgétaire.

1932 Comment j'embauche mon Personnel d'après ses Aptitudes.

1932 Entre l'Anarchie et la Dictature Economique: l'Issue; Questionnaire pour Servir à l'Examen Systématique de la Valeur Economique d'une Entreprise Industrielle.

1932 Les Principes de la Méthode Bedaux.

1933 Le Problème de la Distribution.

1933 Le Tissage à Métiers Multiples.

---

[1] Francesco Mauro, in *L'Organisation Scientifique,* the posthumously published collection of Landauer's writings.

Sam A. Lewisohn
(1884-1951)
United States

Sam A. Lewisohn was a leader in enlightened human relations in industry in the early 1920's, and one of the founders of the American Management Association.

His book *New Leadership in Industry* (1926) ushered in a new view-point in American business. It was a corrective to the previous burst of enthusiasm among managers for appointing specialized personnel officers responsible for maintaining good human relations

245

within their organizations. Lewisohn said: 'The manager cannot delegate this responsibility, even to a personnel officer; it remains his alone.' The book gathered together many of the different views on this, the most controversial industrial subject of the day, and exposed their fallacies. He asked: 'What does the worker want?' and answered: 'Justice, status, and opportunity.' Above all, Lewisohn stressed the need of the worker for the feeling of participation in a team and the need for managers to develop the intangible qualities of leadership capable of bringing this about. His outline of the basis, structure and functions of a personnel department was twenty years ahead of its time.

Sam A. Lewisohn's philosophy of management found perhaps its most enduring outlet in the part he played in founding the American Management Association. The change of name from 'National Personnel Association' which brought the AMA into existence in 1923 symbolized the new attitude to human relations in industry which he was himself advocating at the time. Twenty-five years later the AMA acknowledged its special debt to Lewisohn for the part he played in its foundation and development. He was the first elected president, and he gave to the AMA considerable material help at a time when its existence was financially threatened. His was one of the earliest visions of the potentialities of the AMA as an educative body or, as he termed it, 'an extension university for management groups'. To him therefore belongs part of the credit for the contributions to management of this great American organization.

Curriculum Vitae

1884	Born on 21st March, in New York City.
	Educated at Columbia Grammar School, Princeton University and Columbia Law School.
1907-10	With Law firm of Simpson, Thacher and Bartlett.
1910	Joined his father's business, Adolph Lewisohn & Sons, a Stock Exchange firm.
1921	Member of Economic Advisory Commission, President's Conference on Unemployment.
1923	Elected first President of the American Management Association (having been one of its founders). In 1926 he became Chairman of the Board until 1936.
1938	President, Miami Copper Co.: Chairman of the Board, Tennessee Corp.; President, South American Gold & Platinum Co.; President, General Development Co.; President, Kerr Lake Mines and Kerr Lake Mining Co.; and President, Adolph Lewisohn & Sons Inc.

1941	President, Castle Dome Copper Co., Inc.
1942	Consultant, Division of Industry Operations, US War Production Board.
1949	President, Copper Cities Mining Co.
1951	Died on 13th March aet. 67, in Santa Barbara, Cal.

He represented the American Management Association on the Council of the International Management Institute, and the employers of the United States at the International Labour Conference, Geneva, (1935).

Personal Characteristics

The name of Lewisohn in New York is indissolubly associated with the arts, for Sam A. Lewisohn followed in the tradition of his father as a renowned connoisseur and patron of music and painting. It was his conviction that life in this century was over-compartmentalized, and he sought in his own way of living what he believed to be a better ideal — the balance of interests between business activity, public work (he was a pioneer of prison reform) and enjoyment of the arts. That he achieved this ideal with integrity and generosity is the testimony of the many friends who remember him.

Selected Publications

BOOKS

1925 *Can Business Prevent Unemployment?* (co-author)
New York: Alfred A. Knopf.

1926 *The New Leadership in Industry*
234 pages. New York: E. P. Dutton & Co.

1945 *Human Leadership in Industry: The Challenge of Tomorrow*
112 pages. New York: Harper.

Francesco Mauro
(1887-1952)
Italy

Francesco Mauro was the pioneer of modern management in Italy, and one of the founders of the international management movement. Like many of the other pioneers, he was a man of wide activities: a distinguished engineer and refrigeration expert: a company director and a management consultant: a deputy of the Italian National Assembly and an international negotiator for his country.

He emerged as a personality in Italian industry soon after the First World War. He early became known for his advocacy of the new principles and techniques of management, and in particular, of the value of international exchange of information and experience as a means to progress. Through his work as a technician, executive and consultant, he was able significantly to influence the modernization of many Italian industrial concerns. In 1923 he founded the Italian Institute of Scientific Management (ENIOS), one of the earliest to be created, and became its first president (1923-7). In 1927 his international standing brought him the founder-presidency (1927-9) of the International Committee of Scientific Management (CIOS) and of the International Management Institute (1927-33) and thus associated Italy with him in the front rank of the international management movement. After 1929 he was vice-president of CIOS until 1938.

The Second World War brought a setback to the Italian Management Movement, but after its close Maura reconstituted the Institute as 'ENIOL' and worked hard to secure for it its former international recognition. His labours were rewarded in 1951 when he became president of the Italian Representative Committee for the Organization of Work (CIRIOL) and when in the same year he received the honorary presidency of CIOS. He was a pioneer of management education. The Business Management Course which he founded and directed at Milan Polytechnic was the first of its kind in Italy.

Finally, he was a significant contributor to the literature of management. Among his very many publications from 1910 onwards, some described applications of management techniques which he originated in organizations within his own control. Others stressed the advantages of plentiful exchange of information between firms, between industries, and between countries for the progress of management knowledge. Most important of all were his contributions to the philosophy of management. Mauro constantly stressed the fact that the science and techniques of management must be used as a tool for its social objectives, and for its ultimate goal, the satisfactions of the individual human being within the working group. His last book, *Organizzazione come Civilta* (Management as Civilization) (1952) was devoted to expounding this conviction.

Curriculum Vitae

1887   Born at Domodossola.
1909   Graduated as an electrotechnical engineer, Milan Polytechnic.
1911-12 Graduated as a refrigeration engineer, Ecole Superieure, Paris, and Milan Polytechnic.
1912-25 Secretary, Italian Refrigeration Association, and Assistant Lecturer in Refrigeration Technology, Milan Polytechnic.

1920-24 Founder-director Experimental Refrigeration Station, Milan University faculty of Agriculture.

1920-52 Vice-President, International Institute of Refrigeration.

1921 Deputy for Milan to the National Assembly.

1922-26 Delegate to the Financial Commission, League of Nations Disarmament Conference.

1924-27 Member of the Higher Council for National Economy.

1928-37 Professor of Mineralogy and Petrography, then of General Technology at Milan Polytechnic.

1938-43 President, National Commission of Refrigeration Studies at the National Research Council.

1952 Died aet 65.

He was a President of the Milan College of Engineers and Architects (1920-2) and of the National Association of Engineers and Architects (1922); Honorary President of the Italian Association of Management Consultants (AICO), Turin (1951); and a President or member of numerous economic and technical committees and commissions, both international and national.

In his capacity of planning engineer, Mauro in his earlier career superintended the construction of many important refrigerating and other mechanical engineering installations, and assisted in the reorganization or expansion of many others, including railway installations. He was also a director of several industrial and financial concerns.

Personal Characteristics

In addition to his innumerable offices, presidencies, platform speaking and other business and public activities, in addition to the many hours consecrated to the works of which he was the author, Mauro yet found time for fruitful leisure pursuits. He was a keen mountaineer, president of several clubs and author of a book on the subject; President of the Italian football Club of Milan; President of the Italian Olympic Committee; and took a keen interest in cinematography. It has been said that his outstanding personal quality, perhaps grounded on his firm religious faith, was a capacity for synthesis. He could be at the same time a technician, an executive, a teacher, an organizer and a statesman, and yet a simple and harmonious person.

Selected Publications

Mauro was a prolific writer of articles, studies and books, on many subjects. The following are the most important of his writings on management.

1927	*L'Organizzazione Scientifica nei suoi Aspetti Italiani ed Internazionali* (Scientific Management in its Italian and International Aspects) Rome: ENIOS.
1928	*L'Automatismo nell'Elettrotrazione* (Automatic control in Electric Traction) with Fiorentini Milan: Bertieri.
1928	*Le Osservazioni di un Ingegnere negli S.U.A.* (Impressions of an Engineer in the United States) Rome: ENIOS.
1930	*Esperienze di Organizzazione Giapponese* (Experience of Japanese Management) Rome: ENIOS.
1933	*L'Uomo e la Macchina* (Man and the Machine) Rome: ENIOS.
1934	*L'Ubicazione degli Impianti Industriali* (The Location of Industrial Factories) Rome: ENIOS.
1938	*La Programmazione degli Impianti Industriali* (Planning in Industrial Factories) Rome: ENIOS.
1941	*Il Capo nell'Azienda Industriale* (The Manager of an Industrial Firm) Milan: Hoepli.
1942	*Teratismi dell'Industria* (Anomalies in Industry) Milan: Hoepli.
1944-45	*Industrie ed Ubicazioni* (2 Vol.) (Industries and Locations) Milan: Hoepli.
1945	*Gli S.U.A. Visti da un Ingegnere* (The United States seen by an Engineer) Milan: Hoepli.
1948	*Impianti Industriali* (Industrial Factories) Milan: Hoepli.
1950	*F. W. Taylor: la Vita, Le Opere, Gli Epiloghi* (F. W. Taylor: Life, Works and Epilogues) Milan: La Cultura.
1950	*Scienza ed Industria* (Science and Industry) Milan: Barbier.
1952	*Organizzazione come Civilta* (Management as Civilization) Milan (ed Dott. A. Giuffre).

Bernard Muscio
(1887-1926)
Australia

Bernard Muscio provided an early contribution from Australia to the advancement of management. He came from Australia to be one of the first research workers in Great Britain to take up the study of 'the human factor' in industry.

In 1917 he had published in Australia a book entitled *Lectures in Industrial Psychology.* C. S. Myers, the pioneer of industrial psychology in Great Britain, recorded that he first perceived the possibilities of this field of work on reading Muscio's book in 1917.[1] The lectures achieved much popular success in Australia where they were delivered to working class audiences. In England, also, they gained acceptance as a text book when they were republished in 1920.

In 1919 Muscio was associated with Myers in organizing the Cambridge Summer School of Industrial Administration, where the curriculum was 'the study of certain industrial management problems, chiefly from the psychological point of view'. Muscio edited the book of lectures given during the School and published them as *Lectures in Industrial Administration* (1920). This was the first British book since Elbourne's of 1914 which could be described as a textbook on management. Its novelty was the importance given to the human factor.

In these early days of industrial psychology in Great Britain the work of the Health of Munition Workers Committee (formed 1915) and later the Industrial Fatigue (now Health) Research Board (formed 1919) was crucial in elaborating the new conceptions. Muscio was one of the latter organization's first investigators and contributed, from 1919-22, original research in the form of articles and reports on vocational guidance tests, fatigue measurement, motion study and other subjects.

The early industrial psychologists, of whom Muscio was one, were pioneers in pointing out that although time and motion study and other management techniques were improving the output of machines in industry, no comparable study was being made of the human being, whose contribution to output was obviously no less important. These psychologists were therefore first to ask the question: under what conditions will the human being in industry give of his best? We now know that the subjects of research they chose were not always those calculated to provide the right answer, for they concentrated on physical considerations which we have since learned are less significant than psychological considerations. But without the groundwork of original research which they contributed we should not have been able to develop the better understanding of human beings at work which we have today.

Curriculum Vitae

1887   Born at Purfleet, in New South Wales.

1912   MA, Sydney, in Philosophy. Woolley Travelling Scholarship.

---

[1] See Myers' autobiographical sketch in *History of Psychology in Autobiography,* Vol. III, p. 224 (details of publication in Appendix II).

1913   BA Gonville and Caius College, Cambridge, in Philosophy.
1914-16 Demonstrator in Experimental Psychology, Cambridge, assisting C. S. Myers, and in charge of the University Psychological Laboratory during the absence of Myers on war service in France.
1916-19 Lecturer in Psychology and Philosophy, Sydney. Gave his 'Lectures on Industrial Psychology' at Sydney University, first under the auspices of the Workers' Educational Association, and then in 1917 under the auspices of the University Extension Board.
1919-22 Senior Investigator for the Industrial Fatigue Research Board in Great Britain. This position entailed lectures at Cambridge.
1920   Lent by the Industrial Fatigue Research Board to the new National Institute of Industrial Psychology, as a special investigator.
1922-26 Challis Professor of Philosophy at Sydney.
1926   Died aet. 39, in Sydney.

Personal Characteristics

Bernard Muscio had a quality of extreme judiciousness which entailed perhaps a certain lack, or at least restraint, of enthusiasm. He possessed nevertheless a kindly and warm nature.

Selected Publications

BOOKS
1917 *Lectures on Industrial Psychology*
Sydney: Angus & Robertson. 2nd ed 1920, London: Routledge: New York: Button.
1920 *Lectures on Industrial Administration* (Editor)
276 pages. London: Pitman.

ARTICLES
1920 'Fluctuations in Mental Efficiency'
London: *British Journal of Psychology,* Vol. 10, No. 4.
1921 'Is a Fatigue Test Possible?'
'Feeling Tone in Industry'
London: *British Journal of Psychology,* Vol. 12, Nos. 1 & 2.
1921 'Vocational Guidance: a Review of the Literature'
London: Industrial Fatigue (Now Health) Research Board. *Report* No. 12.

1922 'Motor Capacity with special reference to Vocational Guidance'
London: *British Journal of Psychology*, Vol. 13, No. 2.
1922 'The Psycho-Physiological Capacities Required by the Hand Compositor'
'Three Studies in Vocational Selection' (with E. Farmer)
'The Measurement of Physical Strength with Reference to Vocational Guidance'
London: Industrial Fatigue (now Health) Research Board, *Report* No. 16.
1922 'On the Relations of Fatigue and Accuracy to Speed and Duration of Work'
'Two Contributions to the Study of Accident Causation' (with E. E. Osborne and H. M. Vernon)
London: Industrial Fatigue (Now Health) Research Board, *Report* No. 19.
1922 'Investigation into the Packing of Chocolates' (with R. St C. Brooke)
London: *Journal* of the National Institute of Industrial Psychology, Vol. 1.
1923 'Vocational Tests and Typewriting' (with S. M. Sowton)
London: *British Journal of Psychology*, Vol. 13, No. 4.

Armando Salles Oliveira
(1887-1945)
Brazil

Armando Salles Oliveira was a distinguished Brazilian statesman and the founder of the Brazilian management movement.

An engineer of wide industrial experience, he came into prominence during the world economic crisis of 1929. About this time he undertook in Sao Paulo, with the collaboration of others, the creation of the Institute for the Rational Organization of Work which in 1931 became 'IDORT', the national Brazilian Institute of Scientific Management recognized by CIOS. The economic crisis had given a profound shock to the Brazilian economy, helping to bring about the revolution of 1930. Oliveira participated in the movement to obtain a democratic constitution, and together with his colleagues in IDORT led a movement for the 'rational' and 'scientific' organization of the Government of Brazil.

In 1934 Oliveira was elected Governor of the State of Sao Paulo. From then until the Constitutionalist movement lost power in 1937 a development occurred which must surely be unique in the history of national management movements: IDORT became the official adviser of Oliveira's government, and scientific management became the platform on which the State's entire economic and social policy was based. The acts of Oliveira's government were characterized by their fidelity to the principles of good management. IDORT acted as official consultant for the reorganization of the public services, and led the Government through a turning point in the administrative history of Brazil. The administrative and fiscal structure of the public services was reorganized, technological research was provided for, social reforms introduced, the.University of Sao Paulo founded, technical education extended, and the management of the electric power system of the State overhauled. The State Transport System was provided with a Centre for Vocational Selection and Training.

1937 brought exile for Oliveira, from which his deliverance came only shortly before his death. His work in establishing IDORT was however a permanent achievement. The Institute prospered, and in 1954 it achieved a new international standing when it became the host, for the Tenth International Management Congress, to the management institutions of the free world.

Curriculum Vitae

1887   Born in the city of Sao Paulo.
        Studied engineering at the Polytechnic School of Sao Paulo. As a student, he was responsible for the construction of several parts of the railway line of the Mogiana Co., of which he later became the vice-chairman, and of the present electric power station of Marimbondo.

1923-28 Study tour of Europe, where he visited the great centres of engineers specializing in metallurgy, electricity, railways and chemical fertilizer production.

1932   Participated in the movement for obtaining a Brazilian constitution and in the following year was appointed by the President of the Republic as 'Federal Intervener' in Sao Paulo.

1934   Recognition given by the State Government of Sao Paulo of the Institute for the Rational Organization of Work as a body of public importance.
        Oliveira was at the same time charged with the administrative reorganization of the State Government.

1934   Elected governor of the State of Sao Paulo, and took up office in 1936.

1935   Honorary President of the Institute for the Rational Organization of Work.

257

1936	Gave the State Governor's patronage to the Scientific Management Day of the Public Administration, a conference organized by IDORT for the municipalities of Sao Paulo.
1936	Resigned the governorship of the State and took up leadership of the Constitutionalist Party, and later of the National Democratic Union, from which he was nominated as a candidate for the presidency of the Republic.
1937	Following on the coup d'état which abolished the democratic nature of the people's vote and in protest against the violation of the Constitution, he wrote a letter of appeal to the military chiefs of Brazil. He was arrested and exiled. He spent his exile in New York, Paris, and finally Buenos Aires.
1945	Freed from exile and returned to Brazil, he again entered politics in Sao Paulo but his health was impaired and he died at Sao Paulo this year, aet. 58.

He held the Grand Cross of the Order of Christ of Portugal and the Grand Cross of Reunited Poland, was a Grand Officer of the French Legion of Honour and Grand Officer of the Crown of Italy. He was a Doctor *honoris causa* of Sao Paulo University, and a member of Council of the Nationalist League.

Personal Characteristics

Oliveira became an idol of the people and in their eyes representative of the high ideals of the period of constitutionalist government. His release from exile was obtained by a petition of hundreds of Brazilian lawyers. His return to Sao Paulo, and his funeral not long after, were occasions for exceptional demonstrations of public esteem.

Selected Publications

1935 *Speeches*
Sao Paulo: Tipografia Siqueira.
1937 *Day of Democracy*
Rio de Janeiro: Livraria Jose Olimpio.
1937 *For the Future of Brazil*
Rio de Janeiro: Livraria Jose Olimpio.
1945 *Diagram of a Political Situation*
Sao Paulo: Editora Renascenca.
Messages of the State Governor of Sao Paulo to the Legislative Assembly. From 1914-1938 Oliveira was Director of the journal *State of Sao Paulo*.

By *courtesy of* The Courier & Advertiser, *Dundee*

James Alexander Bowie
(1888-1949)
Great Britain

James Bowie was an educationalist who did much to convert industry in Great Britain to the belief that management should be taught in educational institutions.

He was the first British writer of importance on education for management. His book *Education for Business Management* (1931) crystallized his own experience as perhaps the earliest full-time teacher of management in Britain, for he had been called to the Manchester College of Technology to teach in the Department of Industrial Administration (Britain's earliest management teaching establishment) in the year following its foundation in 1918. He also drew early attention in Britain to the work of the university business schools in America and urged in 1932, in his series of articles 'American Schools of Business' (later quoted in the Urwick Report, 1947) that British universities should take heed of the attitude to business adopted by their American counterparts. The books and articles which he published on other aspects of management also establish his right to be regarded as an author in advance of his time.

In his twelve years at Manchester, Bowie laid a sound basis for the present high prestige of the Manchester Diploma. The syllabus was imaginatively framed, Bowie being usually in advance of current thinking as to the subjects it should contain. At the same time it was kept practical. Bowie early drew attention to the possibilities of the

259

'case-study' method of teaching management in the form developed by the American business schools. His book *Education for Business Management* described the method in general terms, and the method was actually used in the Industrial Relations class at Manchester in the academic session 1930-31, the same year in which T. H. Burnham, the pioneer of British management teaching by case-study, began building up with G. A. Robinson the regular use of this method at the South-East London Technical College. Bowie was also watchful of the department's external relations: he maintained close contact with the business world and secured promotion for the department to university status.

After 1931, as Principal of the School of Economics, Dundee, Bowie again established a full-time post-graduate course in business administration. In Great Britain this was for some years one of the four leading courses in that subject — the other three being those at the Regent Street Polytechnic in London, the Manchester College of Technology, and the London School of Economics. In his later years his interests turned to the wider activities of his college as a whole and to the economic problems of his native Scotland. He continued nevertheless to give much time to management propaganda in speeches and writings, although it was not till after the Second World War that his activities bore much visible fruit. The branch of the Institute of Industrial Administration which he founded in Dundee is now active and flourishing, and some of the social and business movements which he sponsored there have, with the help of other and later supporters, finally justified his good judgement.

In 1954 the Institute of Industrial Administration established the Bowie Medal, to be awarded annually to a member of the Institute for a noteworthy contribution to management. Bowie's name was thus linked with the first award for services to management to be established by the British management movement.

Curriculum Vitae

1888   Born in Aberdeen.
       Took double honours in economics and philosophy at Aberdeen University (MA, later DLitt. in 1924), winning the Hutton prize.
       Concurrently with his university studies, he was partner and manager (1908-14) in the small family firm of Bowie and Son, builders and contractors.

1914-18 Saw service in the Royal Artillery in Egypt, Palestine, Greece and Bulgaria.

1919   Joined the Faculty of Technology in Manchester University, in the newly established Department of Industrial Administration. In 1926 he became head of the Department.

1931   Special Lecturer, Wharton Business School, the University of Pennsylvania, United States.

1931   Appointed Founder-Principal of the School of Economics and Commerce in Dundee.

1936-39 Served on the staff of the London County Council Management Summer Schools.

1940-43 Honorary Food Executive Officer and honorary Local Registration Officer for Dundee.

1943-46 On the staff of Personnel Administration Ltd., management consultants in London.

1946   Returned to the School of Economics, Dundee. The School has since his time gradually changed the emphasis of its teaching to concentrate on economics courses.

1947-48 Served on the staff of the Institute of Industrial Administration Management Summer Schools in Oxford.

1949   Died on 1st September in Dundee, aet. 61.

He was a Fellow of the Institute of Industrial Administration, and member of Council and of the Education Committee; Secretary of the Economics Section of the British Association for the Advancement of Science (1928-33); member of Council, British Association for Commercial and Industrial Education, and a founder-member of the British Institute of Management.

Personal Characteristics

Dr. Bowie was a 'gifted and versatile speaker, who made full use of that characteristic pawkiness which is the birthright of the Aberdonian. He had a wealth of experience and a great flair for translating that experience into an anecdote fitting to the occasion. He was always genial, and even when illness overtook him his spirit remained undaunted and he continued to show great fortitude.

'He was much in demand far and near to lecture on the wide field of economics and industrial topics and he had the rare ability of making the most obscure and profound subjects of interest to the ordinary man in the street.

'Dr. Bowie was a strong believer in descending from the purely academic and coming to grips with the practical side of life's problems and his contacts with everyday life greatly enriched his talks and discussions.

'The deep sincerity of the man, his happy friendliness, his ready desire always to help and his dynamic personality will be long remembered by all who came in contact with him.'[1]

Selected Publications

1922 *Sharing Profits with Employees*
230 pages. London: Pitman.
1930 *Education for Business Management*
200 pages. London: Oxford University Press.
1931 *Rationalization*
36 pages. London: Pitman. Reprinted from the *Times Trade and Engineering Supplement*, July-September 1930.
1939 *The Future of Scotland*
272 pages. London: W. & R. Chambers Ltd.

ARTICLES

1919 'The Need for a Science of Industrial Administration'
Chapter in *Lectures on Industrial Administration*, ed B. Muscio. London: Pitman.
1922 'Profit-Sharing—and Co-Partnership'
The Economic Journal, Vol. 32, pp. 466-476.
1927 'A New Method of Wage Adjustment in the Light of the Recent History of Wage Methods in the Coal Industry'
Economic Journal, Vol. 37, pp. 384-394.
1928 Articles on Co-partnership, Periodic Bonus Payments, etc., in Pitman's *Dictionary of Business Administration.*
1931 'Preparation for Management: The Manchester Experiment'
Business & Science (Papers read at the Centenary Meeting of the British Association for the Advancement of Science. London: Sylvan Press.
1932 'American Schools of Business'
Reprint of a series of articles in *The Manchester Guardian* from 8th September 1931 onwards.
1943 'Management—Today and Tomorrow'
London: *Journal* of the Institute of Industrial Administration, Vol. IV, No. 6. March.
1943 'American Developments in Education for Industrial Management'
Proceedings of the Conference on Training for Industrial Management, held by the Institute of Industrial Administration in London in March.
1945 'The Making of Scientific Management'
Book review in *Industry Illustrated*, London, June.

[1] Extract from an obituary in the *Courier & Advertiser*, Dundee, 3rd September, 1949.

Alfred Carrard
(1889-1948)
Switzerland

Alfred Carrard was the pioneer in Switzerland of vocational guidance and training in industry.

He came to this work not from the world of psychology, but from that of engineering. Ten years in a great Swiss engineering concern convinced him of the need, in the interests of industrial progress, to improve the human relationships among those who work in industry, to bridge the mental gap between managers and workers, and to find means by which the worker could better adapt himself to his job. In 1924 he abandoned his engineering career to take up the study of 'psychotechnics'[1] and to develop in Switzerland the facilities available for vocational selection, guidance and training in industry. He became the leader of a powerful movement and gained the collaboration both of the psychologists and of industry. He co-ordinated the different institutes of applied psychology. He published books and papers which were read in Switzerland and in many parts of Europe. He accomplished much original research, and from 1937 onwards engineering firms from many different countries sent representatives to him to learn his methods.

Because Carrard was not a psychologist but an engineer his methods were more empirical than those used by psychotechnical institutes in other countries. His particular contribution was to stress the moral, psychological and physical considerations which should prevail in vocational training. 'The man who is put on trust to complete a particular task,' he said, 'has an output and a vigour lacking in anyone who works mechanically, without responsibility and without feeling that he is enjoying the confidence of those for whom he works.' Thus his aim was, for example, to improve the training of apprentices by arousing their interest in the ultimate result of their work. Again because of his empirical approach, he was as ready to improve the practices of managers as those of workers, and his publications include several on the subject of industrial leadership.

Carrard has been called 'the founder of vocational guidance' in Switzerland and what his work lacked in psychological refinement it more than gained in practical effect. It is a tribute to his zeal and vision that other countries have also adopted the methods which bear his name, and have acknowledged him internationally as a pioneer.

Curriculum Vitae

1889   Born at Montreux on 26th January.
1899-1908 Montreux College and Berne Grammar School.
1908-12   Studied for engineering degree at the Federal Polytechnic School, Zurich.
1912-14   Doctor of Physics.
1914-24   Engineer with Brown Boveri & Co., Baden.
1924   Took up studies with Jules Suter and Hans Spreng at the Institute of Applied Psychology, Zurich.

[1] Psychotechnics may be defined as the application of psychological knowledge to practical problems, especially in industry and in economic activity.

1925	Director, Psychotechnical Institute of Zurich.
1927	Co-founder and First President, Psychotechnical Foundation of Switzerland, Zurich.
1936 onwards	Director, Institute of Applied Psychology, Lausanne.
1944	Special Professor, Federal Polytechnic School, Zurich, for Psychotechnics and Social and Applied Psychology.
1948	Died on 5th September aet. 59, in Lausanne.

Personal Characteristics

Carrard was undoubtedly a man with a sense of dedication. The distinguishing mark of his school has been described as respect for the individual human being. It was that which Carrard had found lacking in industry and which he made it his life-work to develop. He liked to say that every man had his own place in society, and that it was sufficient to show it to him and to train him how to hold it. His tests were devised, not to submit a man to an inquisitional examination in his job, but to enable the man to discover for himself his greatest natural aptitudes. He was kindly, sensitive, and modest.

Selected Publications

BOOKS

1932 *Le Chef: Sa Formation et sa Tache* (The Chief Executive: His Training and Task)
Neuchâtel: Editions Delachaux & Niestlé.

1935 *Die Erziehung zum Führer* (Formation for Leadership)
Zurich: Polygraphischer Verlag.

1941 *La Jeunesse de Demain. Reform Scolaire* (The Youth of Tomorrow. Educational reform)
Neuchâtel: Editions Delachaux & Niestlé. Translated into German in 1942 by Editions Emil Oesch, Thalwil-Zurich.

1942 *La Personne dans la Vie Economique et Sociale* (The Individual in Economic and Social Life)
In *La Suisse Forge son Destin,* Editions la Baconniere. Translated into German by Editions Emil Oesch, Thalwil-Zurich, 1944.

1944 *La Formation de la Personne* (Training of the Individual)
Thalwil-Zurich: Editions Emil Oesch. Translated into German 1944 by the same publisher.

1948 *Praktische Einführung in die Probleme det Arbeitspsychologie* (Practical Introduction to the Problems of Industrial Psychology) (part author with others)

Zurich: Rascher Verlag. Translated into French as *La Psychologie de l'Homme au Travail*. Neuchâtel: Editions Delachaux & Niestlé, 1953.

ARTICLES

1927 'Zur Psychologie des Anlernens und Einübens im Wirtschaftsleben' (The Psychology of Teaching and Practice in Economic and Industrial Life)
Schweizer Schriften für Rationelles Wirtschaften, No. 1.

1927 'Zur Psychologie der Arbeit Zur Psychologie der Führung' (The Psychology of Work—The Psychology of Leadership)
Schweizer Schriften für Rationelles Wirtschaften No. 3.

1928 'Le Developpement de la Psychotechnique en Suisse' (The Development of Psychotechnics in Switzerland)
Schweizer Schriften für Rationelles Wirtschaften No. 8.

Also various articles in the *Journal des Associations Patronales*, etc.

James Oscar McKinsey
(1889-1937)
United States

James O. McKinsey had a short life. But his influence on the art and science of management was of much importance. The key to that influence was the unusual degree to which he combined intellectual interest in the theory of business with practical capacity for applying and inducing others to apply theoretically valid criteria to actual situations.

Starting his business career as a certified public accountant, he was quick to appreciate a point which some professional accountants fail to realise, that accountancy can never be an end in itself. It is as a tool of good management that figures achieve importance and significance. Having grasped this unifying principle, he had one intellectual advantage over the majority of his contemporaries in management who had been trained as engineers: his basic education in law and accountancy had taught him to look at a business as a whole. From this appreciation of every business as a unity, coupled with his practical experience as a management consultant, flowed his special contributions to management thought and practice.

First, he focussed attention on the importance of budgeting as a major instrument of management. Budgeting and budgetary control are now accepted practice in all well-managed business enterprises. But McKinsey wrote the first standard book on the subject in 1922. He was unable to attend the International Conference on Budgetary Control held in Geneva in 1931 under the auspices of the International Management Institute. But his thought and his influence permeated almost every contribution to its proceedings.

He always insisted, however, that the structure of a budget must reflect not an arbitrary grouping of the figures designed to accord with accounting conventions or convenience, but the actual responsibilities resting on individuals. Thus his interest in budgeting led him directly to advocate sound organization planning as a basic element in the effectiveness of administration. He had a special facility for persuading top managements that the study of organization is not an academic amusement but a real factor in the economy of day to day operations. Thus he brought many leading corporations to appreciate that executives and supervisors can perform more effectively when they know what their responsibilities are, have authority commensurate with them and understand clearly their relationships with those discharging other functions.

He was also particularly sensitive to the interrelationship of business problems. He saw clearly that the solution to many difficulties had its roots not in the area in which the difficulty became manifest, but in some unexpected and apparently unrelated aspect of the business. A marketing defect might be cured through changes in manufacturing procedure and so on.

He was fruitful in making these new concepts of influence through many channels, in particular, through his teaching at the University of Chicago and through his considerable service to the American Management Association, of which he was chairman of the board at the time of his death.

Curriculum Vitae

1889	Born on a farm in Gamma, Missouri.
1912	PhB, State Teachers College, Warrensburg, Missouri.
1913	LlB, University of Arkansas.
1916	PhB, University of Chicago.
1917	Member of University of Chicago faculty, which led to professorship of accounting.
1917-19	Enlisted as a private in the Ordnance Department of the United States Army.
1919	MA, University of Chicago.
1919	Certified Public Accountant, Illinois.
1920-21	Lecturer on accounting, Columbia University, New York.
Ca. 1921-24	Chairman of the Board of Hamilton Bond and Mortgage Company, Member of firm of Frazer and Torbet, Certified Public Accountants.
1925-35	Senior Partner, McKinsey & Company.
1926-35	Professor of Business Policies, University of Chicago.
1935-37	Chairman of the Board, Marshall Field & Co.
1936-37	Chairman of the Board, American Management Association.
1937	Died in Chicago, aet. 48.

Selected Publications

BOOKS

1920 *Book-keeping and Accounting*
South Western Publishing Co., Revised 1939 by Edwin B. Piper, 2 volumes.

1920 *Principles of Accounting,* with A. C. Hodge
University of Chicago Press.

1922 *Budgetary Control*
New York: Ronald Press Co.

1922 *Budgeting*
New York: Ronald Press Co. } In the Business Administration series of which McKinsey was also general editor.

1922 *Organization*
New York: Ronald Press Co.

1922 *Organization and Methods of the Walworth Manufacturing Company—Cases and Problems No. 3*
University of Chicago Press.

1922 *Financial Management*
Chicago: American Technical Society.

1923 *Controlling the Finances of a Business* with Stuart P. Meech

New York: Ronald Press Co.

1924 *Business Administration*
South-Western Publishing Co.

1924 *Managerial Accounting*
University of Chicago Press.

1931 Chapters in *Handbook of Business Administration*, edited by W. J. Donald—Section II—Financial Management, Chapter IV. *Board of Directors, Board Committees, and Officers*, p. 391 and *The Finance Committee*, p. 412, McGraw-Hill Publishing Co. for the American Management Association.

1935 *Accounting Principles*, with Howard S. Noble
South-Western Publishing Co.

ARTICLES

McKinsey contributed many articles to management journals and publications, particularly those of the American Management Association.

Roberto Cochrane Simonsen
(1889-1948)
Brazil

Roberto Cochrane Simonsen, an outstanding Brazilian industrialist and public figure, was the earliest practitioner in his country of modern principles of management. In 1912 he founded and directed the Cia. Constructora de Santos, a construction company which expanded rapidly and became entrusted with many Government contracts in different Brazilian states. From 1916 onwards Simonsen was putting the ideas of Scientific Management into practice in this company, a decade before the beginning of the movement which led to the foundation of the Brazilian institute of management (IDORT) in 1931. His report to his shareholders in 1917 listed five principles on which the company's operation methods had been, and would continue to be based.

1 careful preliminary analysis of the task
2 preliminary planning of the best method, shortest time and lowest price
3 securing the best machinery, facilities, and the best men
4 establishing friendly co-operation between management and men in the effort towards low-cost production
5 control by observation of the cost of the work, with a breakdown permitting rapid calculation of detailed costs.

It was not surprising that with an approach to management so closely similar to that of F. W. Taylor, Simonsen built the Cia. Constructora de Santos into so uniquely successful a concern. Many years later (giving a lecture to IDORT in 1938) Simonsen said: 'I see with special pleasure the evolution of the various activities of IDORT because I have been, since the beginning of my professional life, a battler and a "doer" in this field. It was the Cia. Constructora de Santos which, for the first time in the country, openly preached the tenets of scientific management . . . We have also had the opportunity of applying these principles in a practical way in many engineering and industrial undertakings that have been entrusted to us. I can also observe, with great satisfaction, that several engineers who took their first professional steps in that company are today working for the advancement of IDORT and applying in IDORT the same principles instilled into them at the outset of their careers . . .'

By 1918 he was leading Brazilian industry to appreciate the central importance of the human factor in management. He expressed the situation thus:

'The greatest problem that we have before us, the engineers and administrators of the present day, is undoubtedly the economic utilization of work . . . The industrialists of today must abandon the old-fashioned patterns to consider, as a new force that indisputably exists, the discontent of the working man. We must give him without fear a just remuneration for his work if we do not wish to see production held up by our seeking to solve this problem wrongly, by political paths, when it could be solved rightly, by economic paths.'

and later:

'Only the scientific way of administering and rewarding work, in

272

which the two classes equally benefit, will avoid the impasse created by the inevitable reactions of the old systems, placing both parties on a footing of intimate co-operation, in favour of their legitimate interests.'

Influenced by the writings of H. L. Gantt, he gave much attention to methods of remunerating workers. He was convinced that the bad methods in operation were the greatest, if not the only cause of strikes, and as a means of mitigating industrial disputes and developing more scientific systems of payment he set up in Santos the first Board of Conciliation and Appeal in Brazil, a precursor of the Government-established Boards of Labour Relations. He planned and organized the National Workers' Training Service (Serviço Nacional de Aprendizagem Industrial, or SENAI) and the Social Service of Industry (Serviço Social da Industria, or SESI). SENAI ensures that youths in industry are vocationally trained at the employer's expense. It has brought a great improvement in the skill of Brazilian workers. SESI is sponsored and financed by employers to provide welfare services for workers, including care for balanced nutrition. Both these institutions are considered as models in Brazil today.

It was natural that Simonsen should be prominent in the founding of IDORT in 1931, and in the final phase of his career he was able to bring his national prestige as a statesman and a professor to the support of the movement. His pioneering work over many years was a great and original contribution to the development of management in Brazil.

Curriculum Vitae

1889   Born in Santos on 18th February. Trained as civil engineer in Sao Paulo Polytechnic.

1909-40 Founder and director of the Cia. Constructora de Santos.

1909-10 Engineer of the Southern Brazil Railway.

1911-12 Chief Director of the Prefecture of Santos, and Chief Engineer on the Committee of Santos Municipal Improvements.

1912-19 President, Cia. Frigorifica de Santos.

1919   Represented Sao Paulo in the Brazilian Commercial Committee's delegation visiting England, and was sole representative of Brazil at the International Congress of Cotton Industrialists, Paris, and responsible for the appointment of the Arno-Pearce Commission which helped Brazil to develop her cotton industry.

1919-24 Director, Cia. Frigorifica e Pastoril de Barretos.

1923-28 President, Sindicato Nacional de Combustiveis Liquidos.

273

1926-29 Director, Cia. Nacional de Artefactos de Cobre.
1926-27 President, Cia. Nacional de Borracha.
1934-37 Federal Deputy, during which time he served on several committees of the Federal Congress on social and economic matters.
1935-36 President, Confederacao Industrial do Brasil.
1938-41 Member of the Council for the Economic Expansion of Sao Paulo State.
1946   Federal Senator for the State of Sao Paulo.
1948   Died in Sao Paulo on 25th May, aet. 59.

At his death he was President of Cia. Constructora de Santos, Ceramica Sao Caetano S.A., Cia. Santista de Habitacoes Economicas, and Fabrica de Tecidos Santa Helena S.A.: Director of Cia. Brasileira de Credito Hipotecario: Partner of Murray, Simonsen & Co. Ltd. and Soc. Constructora Brasileira Ltda.

He was also Professor of Brazilian Economic History at Sao Paulo Free School of Sociology and Politics, and Technical Adviser of the Brazilian Institute of Geography and Statistics.

He served in the following public and professional bodies:

Sao Paulo Engineering Institute (President 1933-4)
Federation of Industries of Sao Paulo State (President)
Federation of Industries of Sao Paulo City (President)
Industrial Confederation of Brazil (Vice-President)
National Confederation of Industry (Vice-President)
Brazilian Economic Society (Member of Council)
Rio de Janeiro Engineers Club
American Society of Civil Engineers.

He was decorated as Commander of the Order of Orange-Nassau of the Netherlands.

Personal Characteristics

Dr. Simonsen was outstanding in the breadth and depth of his interests. There were few aspects of the social and economic life of Brazil in which he did not play a part, and it was for this reason that he was so often called upon to represent Brazil abroad. He nevertheless found time for important teaching work and for participation in the work of cultural institutes both at home and abroad. Finally, he achieved distinction in the world of literature when he was admitted in 1946 to membership of the Sao Paulo Academy of Letters.

Selected Publications

1911 *O Municipio de Santos* (The Municipality of Santos)

1912 *Os Melhores Aumentos Municipais de Santos* (Major Municipal Advances in Santos)

1919 *O Trabalho Moderno* (Modern Industry)

1923 *O Calcamento de Sao Paulo* (Highways of Sao Paulo)

1928 *A Orientacao Industrial Brasileira* (The Trend of Brazilian Industry)

1931 *A Construcao de Quarteis para a Exercito* (Building Barracks for the Army)

1931 *As Financas e a Industria* (The Finances of Industry)

1933 *A Margem da Profissao* (Approach to Professions)

1933 *Rumo e Verlade* (Trend and Truth)

1934 *Ordem Economica e Padrao de Vida* (Economic Order and the Standard of Living)

1935 *Aspectos da Economica Nacional* (Aspects of the National Economy)

1937 *Historia Economica do Brazil* (Economic History of Brazil) This book was the first important study of the economic aspects of Brazilian history.

1938 *Aspectos da Historia Economica do Cafe* (Aspects of the Economic History of Coffee)

1938 *A Industria em Face da Economica de Cafe Nacional* (The Coffee Industry and its Place in the National Economy)

1939 *Evolucao Industrial do Brazil* (Industrial Evolution of Brazil)

1939 *Objectivos da Engenharia Nacional* (Objectives of National Engineering)

1940 *Niveis de Vida e a Economia Nacional* (Living Standards and the National Economy)

1940 *Recursos Economicos e Movimentos de Populacao* (Economic Resources and Population Movements)

Clovis Ribeiro
(1891-1942)
Brazil

Clovis Ribeiro was the right-hand man of Salles Oliveira, and shares with Oliveira the credit for the achievements of IDORT.

Whereas Oliveira was an engineer, Ribeiro was by training a lawyer and an economist. In the years before the promulgation of the Constitution in 1932, Ribeiro was Secretary of the Commercial Association of Sao Paulo and from this influential position he worked actively, in collaboration with Oliveira, for political and economic reform. Ribeiro was also a founder of IDORT and became its first Secretary. Like Oliveira he realised the extent of the contribution which the work of IDORT could make towards State administrative reform. His opportunity came with the election of Oliveira to the Governorship of Sao Paulo State. Ribeiro became Secretary of Finance. His reforms were decisive and outstanding in the fiscal and financial system, in the administrative structure of the Civil Service, in Government economy of expenditure, and in several other economic fields. For the first time, the State administrative system took on characteristics based on the principles of good management. In this great progress Ribeiro's influence is recognized by the Paulistas to have been decisive.

In the later years of his career he continued to be a director of IDORT and Secretary of the Commercial Association. CIOS honours the name of Ribeiro with that of Oliveira as one who improved the business of government by applying the principles of the effective government of business.

Curriculum Vitae

1900 Student at preparatory school.
1910 Bachelor of Science and Letters.
1915 Bachelor of Juridical and Social Science (Doctor of Law) of the Faculty of Law of Sao Paulo.
1916 Agricultural work at Casa Branca and Paraibuna.
1920 Founder and director of a firm of publishers.
1925 One of the founders of the journal *Diàrio da Noite* of Sao Paulo and its director.
1926 One of the founders of the Nationalist League and of the Democratic League which played the leading part in the struggle for the secret ballot.
     As a legal adviser and Secretary of the Commercial Association, and economic and financial editor of the journal *State of Sao Paulo* he achieved a noteworthy orientation of opinion among the conservative classes, in all questions of agriculture, industry and commerce.
1931 Elected a director of IDORT at its foundation, and retained this post till his death.
1932 Participated in the Constitutionalist Movement.
1934 Drafted and promulgated the 'Great Letter' of 16th July. After the Constituent Assembly of Brazil was installed, he became economic advisor to the Deputies of Sao Paulo, particularly in studies of the distribution of income which had many repercussions in the tax organization of the State of the Brazilian Federation.
1935 Technical advisor to the Federal Council for External Trade, where he carried out noteworthy studies for the reorganization

277

of the merchant navy, among other projects.

1936 Under the government of Oliveira in the State of Sao Paulo, he headed the Secretariat of Finance, where he rendered great services to the State, such as: (a) regularized the collection of duties and taxes of the State; (b) reorganized the Secretariat for greater effectiveness; (c) created the Duties and Tax Tribunal which enabled those who paid taxes to have a voice in the fiscal matters which concerned them; (d) created an advanced course of study for Secretariat employees; (e) created the Customs Expedition Section; (f) created the Office for Economic and Financial Studies, and other services of a general nature concerned with State economy and with assistance to civil servants. All these measures gave a new impetus to the efficient collection of taxes with increased returns to the State, and this enabled the government to undertake a much more extensive administrative programme.

1940 Once the University College had been organized, he was appointed Professor of Political Economy while continuing to act as Legal Adviser and Secretary of the Commercial Association of Sao Paulo.

1942 Died aet. 51.

Personal Characteristics

Ribeiro was one of the most enthusiastic of the founders of IDORT and one of its most devoted supporters throughout his life. A man in whom any kind of ostentation was absent, he is remembered with affection by his colleagues in the Brazilian management movement.

Selected Publications

1924 'On the Non-Payment of Bills of Exchange'
1925 'The Crisis of the Port of Santos'
 Administrative studies
1927 'The Solution of the Crisis of the Port of Santos'—Conclusion
He published juridical, economic and financial studies on several national problems, such as: the collection of land duties and duties on commercial and industrial profits; the readjustment of the customs tariff; the collection of the 2% gold tax.

He was a director of the *Commercial and Industrial Review*.

Oliver Sheldon
(1894-1951)
Great Britain

Oliver Sheldon wrote a management 'classic': *The Philosophy of Management* (1923).

He spent all his working career in the service of Rowntree & Co., York, and was thus closely associated with the great advances in managerial practice being made there under B. S. Rowntree's direction. In 1921 Sheldon emerged as one of the founders of the Institute of Industrial Administration and a contributor to its *Journal*. In 1922 an article of his became the basis for a paper 'The Case for the Institute', which was an important document in the British management movement—one of the earliest cases made for the establishment of professional standards in management.

The Philosophy of Management at once became, and still remains, an authoritative textbook in both Britain and America. It was original in two ways. First, it put the arguments for the scientific method in management with a cogency not yet reached by any British writer on this subject. Secondly, it expounded the social responsibilities of management as a major partner in the community, alongside capital and labour. In the words of B. S. Rowntree's foreword, 'the author recognizes that business has a soul': there were not many articulate defenders of such a concept in industrial Britain in 1923. The scope and novelty of the book earned it great influence. In particular, it discussed the application of the functional principle to the higher organization of industrial enterprises. His distinction between administration and management has been widely quoted. Of special interest also is the unified code of management principles with which it concludes and which gave philosophical expression to the aims of the newly founded Institute of Industrial Administration. Written in a practical vein such as to appeal to practising managers, the book made also an imaginative appeal, drawing manifold activities of management into a single pattern around the two themes of scientific method and social responsibility.

Sheldon made further contributions to management literature in later years, notable for their clear analysis and precise definition of terms. Finally, he was prominent as B. S. Rowntree's colleague in organizing in the 1920's the Rowntree Lecture Conferences, the forerunners of the management conferences of today.

Curriculum Vitae

1894   Born on 13th July at Congleton, Cheshire. His father was the Town Clerk successively of Burnley and of Wimbledon. Educated at Burnley Grammar School, King's College School, Wimbledon, and Merton College, Oxford (BA).

1914-18 Commissioned in the East Surrey Regiment.

1919   Personal assistant to B. S. Rowntree at Rowntree & Co. Ltd., York. Became manager of the Associated Companies.

1931   Appointed to the general Board of Directors.

1951   Died on 7th August, aet. 57.

Outside his business interests, Sheldon was deeply concerned with the welfare of the City of York and held several important public offices in that city. He was a member and sometime Governor of the Merchant Adventurers, founder and Chairman of the York Georgian Society and one of the founders of the York Civic Trust of which he was Joint Secretary with the Dean of York.

Personal Characteristics

Oliver Sheldon was essentially a quiet thinker, a man who preferred to state a case and leave it to time and the gradual infiltration of truth to carry conviction to others. He hoarded his restricted capital of energy carefully, spending it as sparingly as he could on those things which came highest on his scale of values.

First on his list was his home. To sustain its deep personal satisfactions, for he had no private means, he had to win and retain his place in a large and competitive business undertaking. This he did quickly. And here again he selected a function which placed him a little apart from and outside the daily struggle of the parent organization. First as assistant to the director and subsequently as representative director with Rowntree's large circle of associated and subsidiary companies, he was the ideal personality to do all that could be done by gentle persuasion to integrate their activities and to lead them to assimilate what the parent company had to teach. It was an exacting task and one which would only be trusted to a man whose devotion to his duty was uninterrupted by too many outside interests.

Sheldon may have thought that he was unsuited for the role of propagandist. It is a strange fact that having written one of the most distinguished books in the field of management produced by an Englishman, he made little further public contribution. His daily work, however, was a constant if gentle sermon on management to a wide circle of directors. This and his home and some public service were the things that seemed to him of greatest importance.

Selected Publications

BOOKS

1923 *The Philosophy of Management*
296 pages. London: Pitman.
1928 *Factory Organization* part-author with Northcott, Wardropper and Urwick
London: Pitman. Reprinted 1937.

ARTICLES

1923 'The Elimination of Waste in Industry'
To 16th Rowntree Lecture Conference, Oxford.
1925 'Management as a Profession'
To 21st Rowntree Lecture Conference, Oxford.
1928 'Function of Administration and Organization'
'Industrial Organization'
'Distribution of Responsibility'
Articles contributed to the *Dictionary of Industrial Administration*. London: Pitman.

281

Henry (Hrant) Pasdermadjian
(1904-1954)
Switzerland

Dr. Henry Pasdermadjian was an author and speaker of international repute on the general subject of organization, and on the particular subject of retail management.

By birth Armenian, at the age of three a refugee in Western Europe, Pasdermadjian had a brilliant international career. His earliest writings on management were published when he was on the staff of the International Management Institute, Geneva. By the time of the Sixth CIOS Congress in 1935, to which he presented a paper, he had published articles in Swiss and French journals covering a wide range of management principles and practice. The list of his writings from then onwards, published in several languages and in several different countries, indicates the breadth of his contribution.

It was also a contribution in depth and his books are accepted as authoritative. In his writings on the philosophy of management, he stressed the impossibility of achieving results by using scientific techniques, unless they are adapted to the economic and social situation within which they must operate. He expounded the value of the scientific method and of long-term policy-thinking.

The world of large-scale retail management was fortunate in having the outlook of Pasdermadjian, engineer, economist and thinker on organization, brought to bear on its problems. As General Secretary for eighteen years of the International Association of Department Stores (founded in 1928 as a society for management research), he used to say 'My role consists in giving to department store management a new dimension. I am like the manager of an extra function—the function in charge of the future'. His contribution may best be judged by reading his internationally known books, *Management Research in Retailing* (1950) and *The Department Store* (1954). Of the first, Henry S. Dennison wrote in his foreword:

'This is much more than a lucid and eminently usable description of the adoption of the principle of Scientific Management by seven to ten European Stores . . . It is the most illuminating practical and readable description of the principles of Scientific Management and of their many varieties of application which I remember ever to have read.'

Because of the nature of this Association with its strictly limited membership much of his work has never been made available to a wider public. He was, for example, the author of the handbooks of the Association, seven in number, which remain probably the most comprehensive guides to various aspects of department store management ever compiled, and there is virtually no retailing problem on which he has not written for the benefit of the Association's members. His talent for synthesis enabled him to set out clearly and forcibly a large number of apparently contradictory ideas from various sources, particularly from the United States, and blend them into a whole in which certain fundamental principles became at once apparent. Much of the credit is his for the introduction and adaptation of American management ideas and techniques into European stores.

He was happiest and had most influence working at the level of top management and dealing with such questions as policy determination and control, or problems of organization structure. His paper on American department store organization, written in 1938, remains a model of its kind, and his work on the separation of buying and selling, the organization of the sales function, the job of the buyer, the position of the personnel function and so on, will not easily be superseded. The experience Pasdermadjian gained in retail management on the other hand, no doubt illuminated his thinking on the general issues of management and society. The book on which he was engaged at his death was to be called *The Second Industrial Revolution*, appraising the impact of the science of management on industrial development. It is a book of which the international management movement still stands in need.

Curriculum Vitae

1904   Born at Tiflis in Georgia on 17th April, son of an Armenian engineer. His parents led the Armenian resistance against invasion.

1907   Emigrated to Geneva, which remained his real home throughout his life. He was educated thenceforth in Switzerland, France and the United States: Civil Engineer's diploma at Zurich Polytechnic (1928); studies in commercial economics at Columbia University, New York; LID in economics at Grenoble University (1932).

1929-33 Assistant at the International Management Institute, Geneva.

1933-36 Engineer with Aluminium Ltd.

1936   General Secretary, International Association of Department Stores, in Paris, then Copenhagen, then (1950 onwards) Geneva.

1937   Member of the Distribution Commission of the International Chamber of Commerce.

1952   Special Professor at Geneva University in Industrial Organization and Industrial Accounting.

1954   Died in Geneva aet. 50 after a severe and protracted illness.

He gave support for many years to the Swiss National Management Council.

Personal Characteristics

'Although he passed the greater part of his life in Europe and was an enthusiastic visitor to the United States, Pasdermadjian remained essentially oriental. His intuition for foreign languages, his tact in negotiations, his liberal outlook in history and geography, his courage in the continuous sufferings of the last years, the careful management of his personal affairs, his patience and generosity towards others (to the chance visitor in particular), all indicated a man born and bred in the traditions of the East. At the same time, he owed much to France and French culture, which symbolized for him everything of the best that the western world possessed. He was at ease in all the cities of Europe, preferring especially Paris and Copenhagen, but he retained everywhere, towards men and things, the perspicacious and unbiassed outlook of the penetrating observer and the insatiable reader.'[1]

Selected Publications

1932 *L'Organisation Scientifique du Travail* (Scientific Management) 157 pages. Geneva: Georg.

[1] From the obituary by D. Knee circulated by the Secretary-General of CIOS.

1936 *Le Memento de l'Organisateur. 300 Suggestions pour Augmenter le Rendement d'une Entreprise* (The Organiser's Manual: 300 Suggestions for Increasing the Productivity of an Enterprise)
91 pages. Brussels: Comité National Belge de l'Organisation Scientifique.

1938 *Developments and Trends in Administrative Management*
Papers of the Seventh International Management Congress, Washington.

1947 *Le Gouvernement des Grandes Organisations* (The Government of Large Businesses)
225 pages. Paris: Presses Universitaires de France.

1947 *Principes de Comptabilité Industrielle* (Principles of Industrial Accounting)
76 pages. Neuchâtel: Delachaux et Niestlé.

1947 *Rationel Driftsorganisation* (Rational Business Organization)
179 pages. Danish translation by T. Bak-Jensen. Copenhagen: Schulz Forlag.

1949 *Le Grand Magasin—son Origine, son Evolution, son Avenir*
166 pages. Paris: Dunod.

1950 *Management Research in Retailing*
177 pages. London: Newman Books.

1951 *Les Frais Généraux, leur Traitement Comptable et leur Signification* (Overheads, Their Costing, and Their Economic Importance)
42 pages. Geneva: Librairie de l'Université.

1954 *The Department Store—Its Origins, Evolutions and Economics*
217 pages. London: Newman Books. In German, Köln Opladen, Westdeutscher Verlag, 1954, 216 pages.

1954 *Les Caractéristiques Economiques des Grandes Entreprises de Distribution* (The Economic Characteristics of Large-Scale Distributive Enterprises)
20 pages. Basle: *Revue Suisse d'Economie Politique et de Statistique.*

1955 *Quelques Aspects de l'Organisation des Entreprises* (Some Aspects of Business Organisation)
29 pages. Paris; *Revue d'Economie Politique* (published posthumously).

In addition, Pasdermadjian published from 1930 onwards a large number of articles, reports and studies in the journals of several countries. He was the historian of Armenia, his book having gained the Brémond Prize from the Paris School of Oriental Studies in 1954.

APPENDIX I

CHRONOLOGICAL LIST OF THE KEY MANAGEMENT BOOKS
AND PAPERS MENTIONED IN THE INTRODUCTORY SECTIONS
OF THE OUTLINES

DATE	TITLE	AUTHOR OR EDITOR
1826	Comparative View of the Various Institutions for the Assurance of Lives	Babbage
1832	On the Economy of Machinery and Manufactures	Babbage
1881	'The Nomenclature of Machine Details'	Smith
1885	The Cost of Manufactures and the Administration of Workshops, Public and Private	Metcalfe
1886	'The Engineer as Economist'	Towne
1889	'Gainsharing'	Towne
1891	'The Premium Plan of Paying for Labor'	Halsey
1895	'A Piece-Rate System'	Taylor
1896	The Commercial Organisation of Factories	Lewis
1901	'A Premium System of Remunerating Labour'	Rowan
1901	'A Premium System of Rewarding Labor'	Gantt
1901	'The Proper Distribution of Establishment Charges'	Church
1903	'Principles of Collective Work'	Adamiecki
1903	Shop Management	Taylor
1905	Concrete Plain and Reinforced	Thompson
1910	Factory Organization and Administration	Diemer
1911	Principles of Scientific Management	Taylor
1912	Construction Costs	Thompson
1913	'Engineering Workshop Organisation'	Renold
1913	Principles of Industrial Organization	Kimball
1913	Psychology and Industrial Efficiency	Münsterberg
1914	The Science and Practice of Management	Church
1914	Factory Organization and Accounts	Elbourne
1915	'The Progressive Relationship of Efficiency and Consent'	Valentine
1915	Scientific Management and Labor	Hoxie
1916	Administration Industrielle et Generale	Fayol
1916	Industrial Leadership	Gantt
1917	In Days to Come	Rathenau
1917	Lectures in Industrial Psychology	Muscio
1917	Scientific Office Management	Leffingwell
1917	Taylor System in Franklin Management	Babcock
1918	The New Economy	Rathenau
1918	'Present-Day Applications of Psychology'	Myers
1920	Advice to Students of the National Colleges wishing to Familiarize Themselves with the Methods of Scientific Management in Industry	Le Chatelier
1920	Graphic Production Control	Knoeppel
1920	Lectures in Industrial Administration	Muscio
1921	The Human Factor in Business: Experiments in Industrial Democracy	Rowntree
1922	Budgetary Control	McKinsey
1922	'Ten Years' Progress in Management'	Alford
1923	The Philosophy of Management	Sheldon
1924	Management's Handbook	Alford
1924	A Manual of Standard Processing Time	Hegner

287

Year	Title	Author
1925	*Office Management Principles and Practice*	Leffingwell
1926	*New Leadership in Industry*	Lewisohn
1926	*Profit Sharing and Stock Ownership for Employees*	Dennison
1927	'Ten Years of Standardisation in Germany'	Hellmich
1928	*Dictionary of Industrial Administration*	Lee
1928 onwards	*Prosperité*	Michelin Brothers
1929	*The Art of Management*	Gérard
1930	*The Model Stock Plan*	Filene
1931	*Education for Business Management*	Bowie
1931	*Organization Engineering*	Dennison
1931	*Rationalization and the World Economic System*	Streeruwitz
1932	'American Schools of Business'	Bowie
1932	*The Chief Executive: His Training and Task*	Carrard
1933	*The Human Problems of an Industrial Civilisation*	Mayo
1933	*Profit Engineering*	Knoeppel
1933	*Psychotechnics*	Sollier
1933	*The Second REFA Book*	Meyenberg
1934	*Cost and Production Handbook*	Alford
1934	*The Flexible Budget*	Williams
1935	'Management and the Optimum'	Hopf
1935	*Scientific Management*	Landauer
1937	*Economic History of Brazil*	Simonsen
1937	*A Man's Profession*	Dautry
1942	'Twenty-Five years of Standardisation in Germany'	Hellmich
1943-45	'New Perspectives in Management'	Hopf
1944	*Production Handbook*	Alford & Clark
1945	*The Social Problem of an Industrial Civilisation*	Mayo
1946	'Adapting the Industrial Organization to Changing Conditions'	Hopf
1947	'Evolution in Organization during the Past Decade'	Hopf
1949	'The Cultural Mission of the Engineer'	Hellmich
1950	*Management Research in Retailing*	Pasdermadjian
1952	*Organization as Civilisation*	Mauro
1954	*The Department Store*	Pasdermadjian

APPENDIX II

SELECT BIBLIOGRAPHY OF PUBLICATIONS DEALING WHOLLY OR IN PART WITH THE HISTORY OF MANAGEMENT

In addition to the publications listed, the Editor has had access to a number of obituary notices and other lesser papers. He will be glad to supply details of these supplementary sources upon request

Description of publication	Name of pioneer or subject, about which information is given or references are made.
ALFORD, Leon P. *Henry Laurence Gantt, Leader In Industry* 310 pages. Memorial Volume published by The American Society of Mechanical Engineers. New York: Harper, 1934	*Gantt*
AMERICAN MANAGEMENT ASSOCIATION *25 Years of Management Progress* 16 pages. New York: 1948	*Dodd* *Lewisohn* *McKinsey*
AMERICAN SOCIETY OF MECHANICAL ENGINEERS *History of Scientific Management in America* 10 pages. Prepared for the 1938 International Management Congress by H. S. Dennison, H. P. Dutton, H. P. Kendall, H. S. Person and S. E. Thompson. New York: *Mechanical Engineering,* September 1939	*History of management in the United States*
BABBAGE, Charles *Passages from the Life of a Philosopher* 496 pages. London: Longmans Green, 1864.	*Babbage*
CANNONS, H. G. T. *Bibliography of Industrial Efficiency and Factory Management* 167 pages. London: Routledge, 1920	*Bibliography of management publications in the English language*
CHEVALIER, J. and PEHUET, Louis *L'Organisation du Travail en France depuis Cent Ans* 58 pages. Paris: Comité National de l'Organisation Française, 1949	*History of management in France*
CIOS (Comité International de l'Organisation Scientifique) *Manual* 2nd edition 1952-53. 80 pages. Historical chapter, pp 23-30. Geneva: office of CIOS	*History of the international management movement*

289

CITE UNIVERSITAIRE
Hommage à Raoul Dautry
35 pages. Paris: 1952   *Dautry*

CLARK, Pearl Franklin (Mrs Wallace)
The Challenge of American Know-How
172 pages. New York : Harper, 1948   *Clark*

COLE, Margaret
Robert Owen of New Lanark
231 pages. London: Batchworth Press, 1953   *Owen*

COMITE NATIONAL DE L'ORGANISATION
FRANCAISE
Promotion les Frères Michelin
26 pages. Paris: 1950-51   *Michelin brothers*

COPLEY, Frank Barkley
Frederick W. Taylor   *Taylor, and history*
2 vols, 472 and 467 pages. Published by the Taylor   *of management in*
Society. New York and London: Harper, 1923.   *the United States*
                                                                with mention of
                                                                many other
                                                                pioneers

DENNISON Manufacturing Co.
Memorial Booklet, Henry S. Dennison
Framingham, Mass.: 1952   *Dennison*

DICTIONARY OF AMERICAN BIOGRAPHY
20 vols. New York: Scribner Co, 1928-37.   *Follett, Gantt,*
                                                                Halsey, Hoxie,
                                                                Münsterberg,
                                                                Taylor, Towne,
                                                                Valentine

DICTIONARY OF NATIONAL BIOGRAPHY
22 vols and supplement. London: Oxford Univer-   *Babbage, Lee,*
sity Press, 1908-9   *Owen*

DRURY, Horace Bookwalter
Scientific Management: A History and Criticism   *History of*
249 pages. New York: Columbia University (Long-   *management in the*
mans Green), 1915. 2nd edition, 1918   *United States*

DUPONT, J. B.
'Outline of the Present Position of Applied Psychology in Switzerland'
10 pages. *Bulletin* of the Association Internationale
de Psychotechnique (Psychologie Apliquée). Paris:
Vol 3, No 2, July-December 1954   *Carrard*

DUTTON, Henry P.
'A History of Scientific Management in the United
States of America'
6 pages. *Advanced Management.* New York: *History of*
Society for the Advancement of Management,   *management in the*
October 1953   *United States*

FORTUNE MAGAZINE
The Fruitful Errors of Elton Mayo ... Who Pro-
poses to Management and Labour a Social Basis
for Industrial Peace
New York: November 1946   *Mayo*

290

FRÉMINVILLE, Charles de
Evolution de l'Organisation Scientifique du Travail
Paris: *Revue de Métallurgie*, April-May 1926

History of management in France

GILBRETH, Frank B. and CAREY, Ernestine
Cheaper by the Dozen
247 pages. London, Melbourne, Toronto: Heinemann, 1949. Also *Belles on Their Toes,* Heinemann, 1950

Gilbreth

GILBRETH, Lillian Moller
The Quest of the One Best Way
64 pages. Chicago: Society of Industrial Engineers, 1924 (published privately)

Gilbreth

HAYES, E. P. and HEATH, Charlotte
History of The Dennison Manufacturing Company
202 pages. Published for the Business Historical Society and the Harvard Graduate School of Business Administration by the Harvard University Press, Cambridge, Mass, 1930

Dennison

HOPF, Harry Arthur
'Historical Perspectives in Management'
38 pages. Ossining, New York, Hopf Institute of Management, 1947

International history of management

HOPF, Harry Arthur
'Soundings in the Literature of Management—Fifty Books the Educated Practitioner Should Know'
28 pages. Publication No 6. Ossining, New York: Hopf Institute of Management, 1949

Bibliography of management publications in the English language

HOPF, Harry Arthur
'The Management Movement at the Crossroads'
28 pages. Ossining, New York: Hopf Institute of Management, 1933

History of the international management movement

HOPF INSTITUTE OF MANAGEMENT
Net Results
Periodical published by the Hopf Institute of Management, Ossining, New York. Nos 9 and 10, Vol 23, September-October 1948, and No 5, Vol 24, October 1949; biographical and obituary issues

Hopf

HUNT, Edward Eyre (ed)
Scientific Management since Taylor
263 pages. New York: McGraw Hill, 1924.

History of management in the United States

INSTITUT DES HAUTES ETUDES DE BELGIQUE
Discours Prononcés à la Mémoire du Docteur Paul Sollier
Brussels: 8th February 1934

Sollier

INDUSTRIFORBUNDETS RATIONALISERINGS-KONTOR A.S.
Rationalisation in Denmark, Finland, Norway and Sweden
30 pages. Oslo: 1954

History of management in Denmark, Finland, Norway and Sweden

JOHNSON, Gerald W.
Liberal's Progress
268 pages. New York: Coward-McCann Inc, 1948   *Filene*

KESSLER, Harry Graf
Walther Rathenau, sein Leben und sein Werk
London: Gerald Howe Ltd, 1929   *Rathenau*

KIMBALL, Dexter S.
I Remember
259 pages. New York: McGraw Hill, 1950   *Kimball*

LaDAME, Mary
The Filene Store
541 pages. New York: Russell Sage Foundation,
1930   *Filene*

LEENER, de
Un Grand Belge—Ernest Solvay
Brussels: Office de Publicité, 1942   *Solvay*

LEWISOHN, Sam A.
Memorial Booklet
50 pages. Published by his family and friends.
Stamford, Conn: Overbrook Press, September
1951   *Lewisohn*

MASON, Alpheus Thomas
Brandeis: A Free Man's Life
714 pages. New York: Viking Press, 1946   *Brandeis*

METCALF, H. C. and URWICK, L. (ed)
Dynamic Administration, by Mary Parker Follett   *Introductory*
320 pages. London: Pitman, 1949.   *chapter summariz-*
ing the life and
work of Mary
Parker Follett

MICHELIN & CIE
Edouard Michelin
20 pages. Memorial Booklet, privately printed,
1940   *Michelin*

MUNSTERBERG, Margaret
Hugo Münsterberg, His Life and Work
462 pages. New York: Appleton & Co, 1922   *Münsterberg*

MURCHISON, Carl (ed)
A History of Psychology in Autobiography
Autobiographical sketch by C. S. Myers.
15 pages. Worcester, Mass.: Clark University Press,
Vol III, 1936. London: Oxford University Press,
1936   *Myers*

NATIONAL CYCLOPAEDIA OF AMERICAN
BIOGRAPHY   *Alford, Brandeis,*
35 vols. New York: James T. White & Co, 1932   *Clark, Dodge,*
Filene, Kimball,
Münsterberg,
Smith, Taylor,
Towne

292

NATIONAL MANAGEMENT COUNCIL OF THE
USA
  Harry Arthur Hopf, Fifth CIOS Gold Medallist
  48 pages. New York: 1940   *Hopf*

OWEN, Robert
  The Life of Robert Owen (autobiography)
  London: Effingham & Wilson, 1857-8, 2 vols   *Owen*

PEHUET, Louis
  Un Chef qui Etait un Homme—M. Raoul Dautry
  Paris: Journal of the Comité National de l'Organi-
  sation Française, November 1951   *Dautry*

PODMORE, Frank
  Robert Owen
  667 pages. London: Allen & Unwin, 1924   *Owen*

REICHSKURATORIUM FUR
WIRTSCHAFTLICHKEIT   *International*
  Handbuch der Rationalisierung   *history of*
  Berlin: 1930   *management*

REVUE DE METALLURGIE
  Vol 35. Memorial issue devoted to Henry Le
  Chatelier, January 1937   *Le Chatelier*

ROBACK, A. A.
  History of American Psychology
  425 pages. New York: Library Publishers Inc,
  1952   *Münsterberg*

ROLL, Erich
  An Early Experiment in Industrial Organisation   *Boulton Jr. and*
  320 pages. London: Longmans Green, 1930   *Watt Jr.*

ROSE, T. G.
  A History of the Institute of Industrial   *Bowie, Elbourne,*
  Administration   *and the history of*
  204 pages. London: Pitman, 1954   *the management*
                                                                    movement in
                                                                    Britain since 1920

ROWNTREE & CO. LTD.
  B. Seebohm Rowntree, 1871-1954. In Memoriam
  36 pages. York: 1954   *Rowntree*

SALES APPEAL
  London: November-December 1953   *Michelin*

SHAW, Anne G.
  The Purpose and Practice of Motion Study
  311 pages. Manchester: Harlequin Press Co Ltd,
  1952   *Gilbreth*

SIMPSON, Robert G.
  Case Studies in Management Development
  140 pages (chapter IX, The Dennison Manufacturing Company)
  New York: American Management Association,
  1954   *Dennison*

SOCIETE AMICALE DES ANCIENS ELEVES DE
L'ECOLE NATIONALE DES MINES DE ST.
ETIENNE
  Un Grand Ingenieur—Henry Fayol
  by Henry Verney
  51 pages. And Circular No 188, recording the
  speeches at the Dinner of Honour, 1925   *Fayol*

SOLOMONS, David
  Studies in Costing
  643 pages. London: Sweet & Maxwell Ltd, 1952   *Church, Emerson*

STEVENS INSTITUTE OF TECHNOLOGY
  Classified Guide to the Taylor Collection
  New York: American Society of Mechanical
  Engineers, 1951   *Taylor*

TAYLOR SOCIETY
(now Society for the Advancement of Management)
  Frederick Winslow Taylor: A Memorial Volume
  108 pages. New York: 1920   *Taylor*

THOMPSON, C. Bertrand
  Scientific Management   *Early history of*
  878 pages. Harvard University Press, 1914.   *scientific manage-*
  London: Oxford University Press, 1914   *ment in the United*
                                                   States, and selected
                                                   articles by early
                                                   pioneers

TORRENCE, George P.
  James Mapes Dodge: Mechanical Engineer,
  Pioneer in Industry
  24 pages. New York, San Francisco, Montreal:
  Newcomen Society in North America, 1950   *Dodge*

URWICK, L.
  Management's Debt to the Engineer
  7 pages. Calvin W. Rice Lecture, September 1952.
  New York: American Society of Mechanical   *History of*
  Engineers, reprinted from *Mechanical Engineering*, *management in the*
  May 1953   *United States*

URWICK, L.
  The Development of Scientific Management in
  Great Britain
  85 pages. A report distributed to members of the   *British pioneers,*
  Seventh International Management Congress, 1938.   *including appendix*
  London: *British Management Review*, Vol III,   *devoted to Hans*
  No 4 (Reprinted as a separate booklet)   *Renold*

URWICK, L. and BRECH, E. F. L.
  The Making of Scientific Management   *International*
  Vol I: *Thirteen Pioneers* 196 pages. Latest ed 1951   *history of manage-*
  Vol II: *Management in British Industry* 242 pages.   *ment; mention of:*
  Latest ed 1953   *Babbage, Denni-*
  Vol III: *The Hawthorn Investigations* 226 pages.   *son, Elbourne,*
  Latest ed 1949: London: Pitman   *Fayol, Follett, de*

Fréminville, Gantt,
Gilbreth, Le
Chatelier, Rathe-
nau, Rowntree,
Taylor (Vol I);
Boulton & Watt,
Owen, Lewis,
Renold (Vol II);
and Mayo (Vol
III)

VITELES, Morris S.
Industrial Psychology
652 pages. New York: W. W. Norton & Co, 1932   *Münsterberg*

WHO WAS WHO IN AMERICA
Vol I: 1897-1942   *Alford, Barth,*
Vol II: 1943-1950   *Clark, Diemer,*
Chicago: A. N. Marquis & Co Ltd, 1942 and 1950   *Emerson, Filene,*
Gilbreth, Halsey,
Hathaway, Hopf,
Hoxie, Leffingwell,
McKinsey,
Münsterberg,
Smith, Taylor,
Thompson, Towne,
Valentine,
Williams

WHO'S WHO IN ENGINEERING
6 vols. New York: Lewis Hist. Publishing Co,   *Barth, Clark,*
1942-8   *Diemer, Hatha-*
way, Hopf, Kim-
ball, Thompson

YOST, Edna
Frank and Lillian Gilbreth; Partners for Life
372 pages. New York: The American Society of
Mechanical Engineers, 1949. New Brunswick:
Rutgers University Press, 1949.   *Gilbreth*

295

INDEX

Names of pioneers are printed in bold type, eg **Adamiecki, K.**, and the page numbers printed in italics refer to the main outlines dealing with each pioneer.

Lewis, J. S. *44 et seq;* 37, 48, 112, 113
Lewisohn, A. 246, 247
Lewisohn, S. A. *245 et seq*
Lloyd George, Rt Hon David 158

Macdonald, Rt Hon James Ramsay 158
Mauro, F. *248 et seq*
Mayo, G. E. *220 et seq;* 175
McKinsey, J. O. *267 et seq*
Metcalfe, Capt H. *29 et seq*
Meyenberg, F.-L. *184 et seq*
Meyer, E. 185
Michelin, A. *55 et seq*
Michelin, E. *55 et seq*
Michelin, E. (son of Edouard Michelin) 57
Michelin, P. (son of Edouard Michelin) 57
Münsterberg, H. *97 et seq;* 165
Muscio, B. *252 et seq*
Myers, C. S. *164 et seq;* 252, 253 254

Newton, I. 11

Oliveira, A. S. *256 et seq;* 276, 277, 278
Owen, R. *5 et seq;* 37

Pasdermadjian, H. *282 et seq*
Person, H. S. 82

Rankin, R. 210
Rathenau, W. *121 et seq*
Renold, Sir Charles 50
Renold, H. *48 et seq*
Ribeiro, C. *276 et seq*
Richmond, J. R. 38
Rivers, W. H. R. 166, 222
Robinson, G. A. 260
Roosevelt, F. D. R. 88
Roosevelt, T. 60

Rowan, D. 38
Rowan, J. *36 et seq;* 69
Rowntree, B. S. *155 et seq;* 134, 197, 279, 280
Rowntree, J. 158

Sheldon, O. *279 et seq;* 47
Siemens, C. F. von 153
Simonsen, R. C. *271 et seq*
Slaby, Professor 153
Smith, Dean 103
Smith, Oberlin *18 et seq;* 30
Smith, Mrs Oberlin 20
Sollier, P. *94 et seq*
Solvay, E. *14 et seq*
Spreng, H. 264
Streeruwitz, E. S. (R. von) *172 et seq*
Stretch, Rev M. 3
Suter, J. 264

Taylor, F. W. *72 et seq;* 1, 3, 10, 15, 18, 19, 22, 26, 29, 30, 32, 33, 37, 41, 46, 49, 55, 56, 60, 61, 64, 65, 69, 70, 71, 80, 81, 82, 83, 89, 90, 91, 92, 98, 103, 107, 108, 112, 126, 127, 128, 130, 138, 139, 141, 145, 148, 161, 162, 166, 184, 189, 201, 202, 203, 225, 229, 243, 272
Thompson, C. B. 19
Thompson, S. E. *126 et seq*
Thomson, W. 38
Towne, H. R. *25 et seq;* 18, 37, 41, 60, 68, 71

Valentine, R. G. *161 et seq*

Watt, J. (Jr) *1 et seq;* 37
Watt, J. (Sr) 2, 3
Weir, W. 38
Welch, H. J. 165
White 77
Williams, J. H. *169 et seq*
Wilson, T. W. 198

Yale, L. (Jr) 27

298

HISTORY OF MANAGEMENT THOUGHT

An Arno Press Collection

Arnold, Horace Lucian. **The Complete Cost-Keeper.** 1901

Austin, Bertram and W. Francis Lloyd. **The Secret of High Wages.** 1926

Berriman, A. E., et al. **Industrial Administration.** 1920

Cadbury, Edward. **Experiments In Industrial Organization.** 1912

Carlson, Sune. **Executive Behaviour.** 1951

Carney, Edward M. et al. **The American Business Manual.** 1914

Casson, Herbert N. **Factory Efficiency.** 1917

Chandler, Alfred D., editor. **The Application of Modern Systematic Management.** 1979

Chandler, Alfred D., editor. **Management Thought in Great Britain.** 1979

Chandler, Alfred D., editor. **Managerial Innovation at General Motors.** 1979

Chandler, Alfred D., editor. **Pioneers in Modern Factory Management.** 1979

Chandler, Alfred D., editor. **Precursors of Modern Management.** 1979

Chandler, Alfred D., editor. **The Railroads.** 1979

Church, A. Hamilton. **The Proper Distribution Of Expense Burden.** 1908

Davis, Ralph Currier. **The Fundamentals Of Top Management.** 1951

Devinat, Paul. **Scientific Management In Europe.** 1927

Diemer, Hugo. **Factory Organization and Administration.** 1910 and 1935

Elbourne, Edward T. **Factory Administration and Accounts.** 1919

Elbourne, Edward T. **Fundamentals of Industrial Administration.** 1934

Emerson, Harrington. **Efficiency as a Basis for Operation and Wages.** 1909

Kirkman, Marshall M[onroe]. **Railway Revenue.** 1879

Kirkman, Marshall M[onroe]. **Railway Expenditures.** 1880

Laurence, Edward. **The Duty and Office of a Land Steward.** 1731

Lee, John. **Management.** 1921

Lee, John, editor. **Pitman's Dictionary of Industrial Administration.** 1928

McKinsey, James O. **Managerial Accounting.** 1924

Rowntree, B. Seebohm. **The Human Factor in Business.** 1921

Schell, Erwin Haskell. **The Technique of Executive Control.** 1924

Sheldon, Oliver. **The Philosophy of Management.** 1923

Tead, Ordway and Henry C. Metcalfe. **Personnel Administration.** 1926

Urwick, L[yndall]. **The Golden Book of Management.** 1956

Urwick, L[yndall]. **Management of Tomorrow.** 1933